American Conversations

In the ***Puerto Rican Studies*** series, edited by

Luz del Alba Acevedo, Juan Flores,

and Emilio Pantojas-García

ELLEN BIGLER

American Conversations

Puerto Ricans, White Ethnics, and Multicultural Education

Temple University Press

Philadelphia

Temple University Press, Philadelphia 19122

Published 1999
Printed in the United States of America

♾The paper used in this publication meets the requirements of the American National Standard for Information Sciences—Permanence of Paper for Printed Library Materials, ANSI Z39.48-1984

Library of Congress Cataloging-in-Publication Data

Bigler, Ellen
American conversations : Puerto Ricans, white ethnics, and multicultural education / Ellen Bigler.
p. cm. — (Puerto Rican studies)
Includes bibliographical references and index.
ISBN 1-56639-687-5 (alk. paper). —ISBN 1-56639-688-3 (paper : alk. paper)
1. Multicultural education—United States. 2. Multiculturalism—United States. 3. Puerto Rican children—Education (Middle school)—New York (State)—Case studies. 4. Education, Bilingual—New York (State)—Case studies. 5. Puerto Ricans—New York (State)—Social conditions—Case studies. 6. New York (State)—Race relations—Case studies. 7. Educational change—New York (State)—Case studies. I. Title. II. Series.
LC1099.3.B477 1999
370.117'0973—dc21

98-42317

Our public schools have, by any reasonable standard, enjoyed great success. . . . Masses of immigrants, the poor, the illiterate have been educated and, through education, have achieved unprecedented upward mobility.
Albert Shanker (1971), president of the United Federation of Teachers

What if the narrative of other ethnic group progress through the schools is a legend and the institutions of economic and political advancement have never served more than a favored few, compelling large numbers to live in poverty and social discrimination?
Colin Greer (1972:25), educational historian

Contents

Acknowledgments

So many people deserve mention for the part they played in bringing this book to fruition. I want to first thank the people of Arnhem who gave so freely of their time, but who necessarily have been given pseudonyms and will remain nameless. The willingness of community members to share their time with an outsider, and the cooperation of school administrators and Arnhem teachers in opening their school and classroom doors to me, made this book possible. I hope that I have done justice to them in representing their thoughts and concerns on the many issues addressed here.

I had the good fortune of working with an excellent dissertation committee and supportive faculty at the University at Albany, State University of New York, during the early phases of this project. James Collins deserves special recognition for his invaluable intellectual guidance and support, and his dedication to mentoring his students so well. Among other things, he taught me to think more critically about the educational institutions I have been immersed in for virtually my entire life. Emilio Pantojas-García and Virginia Sánchez Korrol (at City University of New York) guided me toward a fuller understanding of the Puerto Rican experience in the United States. Gail Landsman provided unflagging encouragement and constructive guidance, as did Walter Zenner.

A SUNY Albany anthropology department fellowship helped fund the initial stages of my academic research. A

U.S. Department of Education grant through the National Research Center on Literature Teaching and Learning at SUNY Albany provided funding for my field research and very useful reviews of early drafts of my findings; suggestions from Center reviews by Alan Purves, John Calagione, Pedro Pedraza, Celia Denishi, Roseann Duenas Gonzalez, and Caroline Heller ultimately made their way into Chapters 4, 5, and 6. Funding provided by the president of the University of Puerto Rico allowed me to present my work at the 1996 annual Puerto Rican Studies Association meeting in Puerto Rico and to discuss my findings with leading scholars in Puerto Rican studies; Emilio Pantojas-García deserves special thanks for, among other things, working on my behalf to secure that opportunity. José Macias and Kathryn Anderson-Levitt helped me to further refine the community analysis found in Chapter 4 for publication in *Anthroplogy & Education Quarterly*. Pedro Pedraza and Blanca Vázquez at Centro de Estudios Puertorriqueños similarly provided valuable feedback on my analysis of language issues in school and community, for publication in the *CENTRO Bulletin*. Additional funding support from the Rhode Island College Faculty Research Fund and faculty release time from the School of Education and Human Development at Rhode Island College secured much-needed opportunities to complete this book. I am also grateful to Sharon Kayes for all her help, and to Myra Blank at Rhode Island College for diligently tracking down untold numbers of books on my behalf.

The many constructive suggestions, the patience, and the good humor of senior editor Doris Braendel at Temple University Press have been invaluable in moving my manuscript forward. Everyone should have the good fortune to have an editor like her. Bonnie Urciuoli's excellent and very thorough review of my manuscript helped me to better frame events in Arnhem within the context of a national ongoing dialogue on race and the place of the Puerto Rican community in American society. Héctor Cordero Guzmán encouraged me to see the Puerto Rican experience within a larger global context. Finally, many friends over the years have sustained me and contributed in so many ways to the end product through their ongoing conversations about the issues I raise, their feedback, and their emotional support, including Katherine Bigler, João Botelho, Sue Dauria, Lelia Giuttari, John Kramb, Michael LeBeau, Pat McEvoy, Willis Poole, Phyllis Ryan, Martha Sánchez, Milburn Stone, David Thomas, Fiona Thompson, Esther Thorpe, and Greg Wilsey. This book is dedicated to Henry and Jeanneatta Bigler, who taught me to believe in the value of education, and to Thomas Bigler (1965–1980), whose warmth and generosity left their mark on all who knew him.

Portions of Chapter 4 were published in *Anthropology & Education Quarterly* (Theme Issue "Racial and Ethnic Exclusion in Education and Society") in the article "Telling Stories: On Ethnicity, Exclusion, and Education in Upstate New York" (June 1996, volume 27, no. 2), pages 186–203.

Portions of the text were published in *CENTRO* in "Dangerous Discourses: Language Politics and Classroom Practices in Upstate New York" (Centro de Estudios Puertorriqueños, Hunter College, City University of New York, Winter 1996–1997, volume IX, no. 9), pages 26–42.

Portions of Chapters 4, 5, and 6 were published as technical reports through the National Research Center on Literature Teaching and Learning at the State University of New York, University at Albany (Bigler 1994b; Bigler 1996a; Bigler and Collins 1995).

American Conversations

Introduction

Talking "American"

Debra Moskowitz (Euro-American Spanish language teacher, age thirty): Why are these [Puerto Rican] kids doing this? Why are they not speaking English when they can? Why aren't they trying to fit into the mainstream? . . . There's never going to be an American identification if we all have our own areas. They're no different than earlier waves. They worked, they learned the language, and that was your key to success.

Sonia Cruz (Puerto Rican junior high school student): I think it [the book *Felita,* by Nuyorican author Nicholasa Mohr] was *so* good. She talks in Spanish and English. Like in true life.

Carmen Morales (Puerto Rican junior high school student): It [*Felita*] was good. 'Cause it told about prejudism and we learned a lot out of it, like not to pick on people because of their color.

The views of the world expressed in these quotations are not randomly held and idiosyncratic. They reflect two distinct maps of society and two distinct discourses concerning social reality that divide Latinos and particularly Puerto Ricans from older, now largely English-speaking Americans. At the same time, the speakers and the communities their views represent are closer than one might suspect at first glance. Debra Moskowitz, Sonia Cruz, and Carmen Morales are, respectively, a teacher and two students in an upstate New York junior high school. They reside in the same city and are citizens of the same nation. In short, they occupy common space, even if they do not share common ground, which makes understanding their differences and resolving those differences vital. This book is about the conflict between these points of view, and about a specific conflict over school curricula and the places of English and Spanish in the public schools in their community, Arnhem, New York.

Debra Moskowitz understands the situation of her students and the other Puerto Ricans in the community according to a belief system about what is required for mobility and success in American society, one which also identifies the elements that guarantee continued failure and stagnation among her students. On her map of the world public use of the Spanish language among native speakers is dysfunctional and rooted in indolence. Debra's beliefs underscore the theme of historical justice: that each group must follow paths to success laid out by earlier groups. Debra passes over significant consideration of issues of prejudice, racism, and the special circumstances of the Puerto Rican experience in the late twentieth-century American economy. She does not necessarily ignore these obstacles, but sees them as surmountable challenges that confront all new groups in American society.

For Sonia Cruz, Debra's student, "true life" is a world understood through the rhythms of both Spanish and English, as it is for the Nuyorican characters in Nicholasa Mohr's (1979) book, *Felita*. For Sonia, *Felita* seems real precisely because it refutes the artificially maintained monolingualism and monoculturalism that dominate the classrooms of Arnhem and similar upstate New York communities. Her classmate Carmen Morales agrees, coining a new word—"prejudism"—to link the prejudice and racism that figure so prominently in both Carmen's experiences and those of the main character, Felita, when she moves to a new neighborhood that doesn't want "her kind."

I came to know Debra, Sonia, Carmen, and other Arnhem residents in the process of examining the struggle in their school and community over the need for bilingual and multicultural education, one that ultimately brought in a state education department investigative team. Their community was not one well equipped to deal with conflicts requiring a broad understanding of the forces behind the thrust for multiculturalism in recent years, nor was it was a town with the surplus resources to lubricate consensus.

In the early 1990s, when the conflict erupted, Arnhem was well into its third decade of economic decline. This city that once drew thousands of early twentieth century southern and eastern European immigrants to work in its then-modern mills and factories today offers few such opportunities to newcomers. Abandoned mills dot the skyline, serving only to refresh the memories of older residents as they talk about hard work and upward mobility. Many of the offspring of these citizens, meanwhile, have left the area in search of better employment opportunities. In its white neighborhoods Arnhem is clearly becoming a town of senior citizens; 30 percent of the Euro-American residents of Arnhem are over fifty-five years old. Made insecure by a shrinking job base and living on fixed retirement incomes, these citizens feel rightfully besieged by taxes, especially the property tax that provides the principal support for the city's schools. A 1980s surge in Arnhem's property taxes thus spawned a political culture that by the early 1990s was devoted to the ethic of holding the line on property taxes and viewing every spending initiative as the granting of "special favors" to the undeserving. The schools, with their growing Puerto Rican enrollments, were caught in the vise of this anti-tax, anti–special favor movement.

The predominantly Puerto Rican Latino community of Arnhem is even more afflicted by the city's long economic downturn than are the older Euro-American residents. There is visible poverty in the East End neighborhoods where most Latinos live. These are the same neighborhoods where many of the senior citizens grew up during Arnhem's boom days, when jobs and hopes were plentiful. For Sonia and Carmen, however, this is a community of shrinking opportunities and decaying services, where the Euro-Americans who dominate political and economic life feel besieged and set upon by the city's structural problems. Moreover, Sonia and Carmen have a relationship to their homeland that is unlike anything experienced by earlier generations of European immigrants. Puerto Rico has never been an independent nation, and changes in transportation and communication today make it readily accessible to the Puerto Ricans who migrated to the mainland in large numbers beginning in the 1940s. Puerto Ricans move freely back and forth between island and mainland.

In recent years ethnic, generational, and class conflicts have surfaced repeatedly in Arnhem. Politically active and well-organized Euro-American senior citizens have emerged as the most powerful faction in local politics. Most significantly, this faction has gained the majority vote on the local school board. The emerging political power of these senior citizens, in turn, has given a significant voice to the generalized complaints of the white population. Whites believe, with often expressed bitterness, that the "minority"[1] or "Hispanic"[2] (terms synonymous to them with "Puerto Rican") population of their city is growing too rapidly. The white population has focused with special vehemence on the common use of Spanish in public places. To them that is an offensive sign of Latinos' unwillingness to follow the mythic path to individual success and upward mobility that is such an important landmark on the map of social reality as maintained by the Euro-American community.

Local events in the fall of 1991 further increased the open expression of anti–Latino and anti-Puerto Rican sentiments. In New York State, proposed "multicultural" curriculum changes were making headlines and touching off a national debate about their necessity and wisdom (e.g., Henry 1990; Ravitch 1990; Reinhold 1991). In Arnhem the local expression of this debate led to a public uproar. Asked to comment on the state's proposed curriculum changes, school board member John Marris responded with a disparaging comment about Latinos. The Latino community demanded an apology; Marris refused. The confrontation escalated to demands for Marris's resignation and finally to the real questions troubling the community: Was there discrimination toward Latinos in the schools and the community at large? What changes should be made in the schools to meet the needs of Latino children and students? The debate highlighted the contrasting discourse of the two communities. Minority spokespersons (Latinos and one African-American woman) complained about prejudice and discrimination, and asked that the schools be altered to better meet their needs. The majority Euro-Americans—led by senior citizens—criticized Latinos' "laziness," their failure to take advantage of opportunities, and their inability to surmount the challenges mastered by earlier immigrants. They defended the traditional educational system that they controlled and supported as a cornerstone in creating productive and loyal Americans.

Social analyst Henry Louis Gates proposes that we think of American culture as "a conversation among different voices . . . that some of us weren't able to join until recently" (1995:7). In that vein, I propose the phrase "talking 'American'" to characterize this ongoing negotiation of what it is to be "American" and what characterizes the "American" experience. In Arnhem the most important arena for this discourse was the contentious debate about the meaning, content, and implications of public education. In the following pages I tracked the roots of these discourses as shaped by differing class locations, racial and ethnic experiences, and historical trajectories in an effort to better understand them. I also explored the educational implications for the city's growing Latino population of the sorts of policies and practices that are supported by such discourses.

Legacies of the Civil Rights Movements

The events that transpired in Arnhem are part of a larger ongoing national "conversation" about multiculturalism. Talk of "multiculturalism" and "diversity" is suddenly everywhere, from programs on how to manage a diverse work force effectively to heated debates about history and literary canons (see, for example, Gordon and Newfield 1996). Statistical data confirm its ubiquity. References to multiculturalism in the Nexis database of major newspapers climbed from zero in 1988 to fifteen hundred in 1994 (Glazer 1997:7), and advocacy of multicultural education extends back to the 1960s and 1970s. It is therefore tempting to assume that the education that culturally diverse students like Sonia and Carmen receive today differs significantly from what their parents experienced in the New York City schools in the early 1960s.

Indeed, Sonia's and Carmen's education *has* been different to some extent. Today's students, for instance, in all likelihood will never encounter books containing passages such as the following, taken from a text published by the state of California and used in its public schools in the

1950s: "Back of the big house stands rows of small cabins. In these cabins live the families of Negro slaves. . . . The small black boys and girls are pleased to have the white children come to play with them. . . . In time many people came to think that it was wrong to own slaves. Some of the people who owned slaves became angry at this. They said that the black people were better off as slaves in America than they would have been as wild savages in Africa. Perhaps this was true. Most of the slaves seemed happy and contented" (cited in Hughes 1993:129).

Today's U.S. history and literature texts in schools *are* more "multicultural" and sensitive to cultural stereotyping than texts in the 1960s (Reinhold 1991). Students speaking languages other than English on school grounds will also no longer be punished for their "transgressions," as they were in that era (Crawford 1995). U.S. schools are now legally required to provide all students with assistance learning English, if needed.

Such changes are a legacy of the social movements of the 1960s and 1970s, which marked a turning point in our nation's history. People of color and women successfully raised public levels of awareness of racism and sexism in educational institutions and the media. African Americans first, then Chicanos, Puerto Ricans, Native Americans, and women attacked the structures of inequality that limited their opportunities for upward mobility. The very existence of an American "melting pot" was challenged, and longstanding institutional barriers to opportunity in the United States were brought down. Ethnic studies and women's studies programs found homes at the university level, affirmative action programs opened doors that had been closed throughout the nation's history, and a growing number of people of color entered the ranks of the middle class.

Among Euro-Americans the belief that changes since the 1960s have leveled the playing field for people of color, leaving them well-positioned to achieve the upward mobility that so many in their parents' generation experienced, is now widely accepted. Increasing numbers of Americans from non-European backgrounds *have* achieved greater economic and educational success as a result of the civil rights movements, lending support to such views. The reality, however, is that dreams of upward mobility have failed to materialize in the years since for historically oppressed groups as a whole, in particular African Americans, Chicanos, Puerto Ricans, and Native Americans.

This fact is not lost on Americans from historically oppressed groups. While Euro-Americans may be convinced that the so-called "American dream" now includes all Americans, African Americans, for instance, have become increasingly skeptical about whether it applies to them at all (Hochschild 1995). Blocked upward mobility and continuing inequitable educational outcomes for students of color—at a time when the nation itself is becoming more racially diverse—have in turn fueled demands for multicultural reform in the nation's public schools. People of color who have achieved greater representation in sites of influence, including educational arenas, are joined by their Euro-American allies in an ongoing quest to find out why a more equitable society across racial, gender, and class lines continues to elude the United States.

Schooling and Opportunity

An enduring American myth holds that U.S. public schools have historically functioned as meritocratic institutions. Mainstream Americans typically perceive schools as the vehicle through which earlier immigrant groups achieved upward mobility and were incorporated into the mainstream. They also believe that those now on the lower rungs of the social class ladder—whether recent immigrants or racial minorities now "free" to achieve upward mobility thanks to the civil rights legislation of the 1960s—can follow in the footsteps of other ethnic groups by taking advantage of equal educational opportunities.

There is an unfortunate consequence of this myth. If schools in the popular imagination provide opportunities for upward mobility, and if the barriers minorities have historically faced in the United States have been removed, then equality of opportunity for all Americans is now considered a given. If minority members fail to succeed, they have no one but themselves to blame. Certainly it can't be the opportunity structure of the larger society, or the school practices themselves, that may be implicated in inequitable educational outcomes.

Since the 1960s educational anthropologists have challenged and undermined this myth. They have looked in particular at how and why children from minority racial and linguistic backgrounds and the working class leave school without the educational credentials of their mainstream peers. Their works, and those of other educational researchers and reformers concerned about enduring educational and societal inequalities, have mutually enriched one another, contributing to a body of scholarship that today falls under the rubric of multicultural education.[3]

Advocates argue that multicultural education benefits all students and can help redress societal and academic inequalities.[4] Curricula and texts in English and social studies classrooms that more accurately depict the experiences, perspectives, and contributions of diverse groups are seen as integral to a solid multicultural education foundation. Students of color are believed to benefit by having their lives and members of their ethnic groups included and represented in the classroom in positive ways, Euro-American students by developing a greater respect and appreciation for diversity and having negative societal stereotypes undermined. In the process, all students become more aware of both injustice and its roots and their potential as citizens in a democracy to effect change.

Multicultural education reform challenges not only the curriculum but also classroom pedagogy and school practices. "Culturally responsive pedagogy" requires sensitivity to the differing linguistic and cultural resources and identities of students. Significantly, social, political, and cultural issues beyond the classroom doors can enter into the educational process, whether in the dialect a student brings to class, divergent communication patterns of home and school, or students' perceptions of the likelihood of education enhancing opportunities for upward mobility. Classroom practices that affirm student diversity, draw on students' home knowledge, and provide students opportunities for academic engagement while minimizing student resistance to learning become an important objective (e.g., Davidson 1996; Edelsky 1991; Jacob and Jordan 1993). Institutional practices such as tracking (e.g., Oakes 1985) and parental outreach programs (see Nieto 1996) are meanwhile examined closely for the ways in which they contribute to unequal educational outcomes along racial and class lines. In short, multiculturalism in the schools, with its goal of more equitable educational outcomes, seeks equal recognition of the histories, perspectives, and cultural expressions of nonmainstream groups in school curricula, policies, and classrooms as part of a larger struggle for social change.

Such projects for change are disruptive. Multicultural reformers seek to incorporate the cultural expressions of groups that reflect their experiences in a society with enduring racial and economic divisions. Those divisions shape their narratives of identity and linguistic and cultural practices in ways that differ significantly from those of dominant social groups. Altering the school to accommodate, rather than ignore or repress, the collective identities of socially and economically marginalized racial minorities invites into the classroom cultural traditions, values, and modes of expression that differ from those of the social mainstream. As anthropologists long have argued, schools are not autonomous, but rather are part of larger social and cultural formations; multiculturalism in the schools consequently confronts tremendous barriers.

Not surprisingly, resistance to multicultural and bilingual education projects intended to address racial inequities, alongside resistance to initiatives such as affirmative action, has been sustained in many quarters of mainstream America. Serious multicultural school reform presents a profound challenge to the ideology of equality of opportunity in the United States. The American dream, which rests on an assumption that all U.S. citizens have the opportunity to succeed through their own efforts, has long been a central ideology of Americans. When we incorporate the historical experiences and perspectives of oppressed social groups, we challenge popular assumptions about the openness of American society in general. Multicultural educators' arguments also implicate schools in the reproduction of the social order, when schools have long been viewed as the major vehicle for upward mobility.

It is essential that we address the glaring educational disparities that persist across ethnic and racial groups. Classrooms today are more likely to include students of color, the foreign born, or those who speak another language than the classrooms of a generation ago. If current projections are accurate, by the year 2020 students of color will make up almost half (46 percent) of the nation's total school-age population, and one out of every five children will be from a poor home (Banks and McGee Banks 1997:193).

Meanwhile, the nation's teacher education graduates have grown more homogeneous in the past two decades; in 1996 Euro-Americans represented more than 90 percent of all teacher education graduates (Sengupta 1997). Creating opportunities for teacher education students—most of whom have grown up in homogeneous white neighborhoods—to fully understand the perspectives and experiences of racialized and impoverished groups of Americans remains an ongoing challenge. Most teacher education programs now include a course on multicultural education (albeit oftentimes as an add-on, rather than infusing perspectives throughout their program requirements). The presence of such courses, however, does not mean that multicultural education perspectives are being successfully addressed in teacher education programs (e.g., Larkin and Sleeter 1995; Macedo 1993). Teacher educators (e.g., Cochran-Smith 1995; Sleeter 1995) document their ongoing and only partially successful struggles to encourage white students to question the powerful ideologies of equal opportunity.

Background to the Study

Understanding how educational change is supported or resisted, implemented or subverted, requires careful attention to the responses of social actors "on the ground," so to speak, and ethnographic research provides the means to do so. Struggles over multiculturalism surfaced in Arnhem in 1991, sparked by disparaging remarks made by a Euro-American school board member about Latinos. The subsequent uproar brought to the fore the barely submerged ethnic, generational, and class conflicts in the community.

I had the good fortune of having already done fieldwork in the school and the community, and was well situated to examine how the various social actors—including minority community leaders, white ethnics, teachers, and minority students—participated in the ensuing conflict.[5] To better understand various perspectives I attended and observed public events (including school board meetings, pickets, a public forum to air grievances, ethnic festivals, openings of museum exhibits on community immigration, and a school graduation), and collected materials in the media (television, radio, and local papers) relating to the debate over education. I conducted open-ended interviews with teachers, students, community members, administrators, and key participants in the debate and "hung out" in both the junior high school faculty room and several classrooms over the course of the 1991–1992 school year, with later follow-up interviews. Classroom observations in the district's junior high school the year before the community debate, meanwhile, provided me with important baseline observations of the schooling experiences of the district's growing Latino student population.

Although pressure for multicultural reforms may originate outside the schools (e.g., in the minority community), or from above (e.g., the district's response to later New York State Education Department [NYSED] recommendations), it is at the level of the classroom teacher that changes are accommodated or resisted, thus requiring close attention to school and classroom on my part. In my own quest to better understand the dynamics of educational resistance and change I began by observing a range of classrooms, subsequently narrowing my focus to one social studies and three English classrooms. I then observed in these classrooms two to three times per week over the course of the 1991–1992 school year. While teachers are often uncomfortable with researchers entering their classrooms, I had the advantage of having taught for several years in another upstate New York community and knowing some of the district's teachers; I believe this enhanced their acceptance of my presence in the building. I also attended English department meetings and regional meetings for English teachers at which multicultural literature was a topic of discussion. I periodically conducted more formal interviews with school personnel and students during the 1991–1992 school year, and followed up these interviews in the autumn of 1992 and of 1993. The school and classroom analyses of teacher and student treatment and responses to diversity that are described and analyzed in Chapters 4, 5, and 6 draw on these many observations and conversations.

Contextualizing the Conflicts in Arnhem

Understanding local struggles around multicultural education requires attention to both the local and the larger social, economic, and historical contexts in which these events are embedded. Arnhem's history in many important respects parallels the histories of other similarly situated communities in the deindustrializing Northeast, and provides important insights into the origins of the worldviews of its longtime Euro-American residents. The experiences of Arnhem's Euro-American residents, however, are not shared by the city's more recently arrived Puerto Rican population. The white ethnic population of southern and eastern European heritage ultimately escaped racialization in the United States, whereas the Puerto Rican community did not. Understanding the differing historical and educational experiences of Puerto Ricans and white ethnics in the United States provides insights into the conflicts over multiculturalism in Arnhem. Analysis of the experiences of white ethnics sheds light on why resistance to multicultural initiatives that draw on "race cognizance" is sustained in these quarters; attention to the general experiences of Puerto Ricans points to reasons for their participation in struggles for educational reform.

The American dream became a reality for significant numbers of white ethnics in the post–World War II years as the expanding economy and the successes of the union movement provided opportunities for upward mobility for large numbers of Americans. Economic mobility in turn fostered educational success and a positive orientation toward schools. Access to the American dream, however, eluded many Puerto Ricans and other people of color. Racial minorities in general were poorly positioned to take advantage of the postwar era of economic expansion. Puerto Ricans entering the mainland in large numbers encountered both the realities of life in a racially divided nation and a deindustrializing economy that profoundly limited their opportunities for upward mobility.

Anthropologist John Ogbu (1987) has argued that for nonwhite groups, one consequence of a history of sustained racial and economic oppression has been a different set of relationships between school and community. In Ogbu's framework, African Americans, Chicanos, Puerto Ricans, and Native Americans are "involuntary minorities." They may see little connection between educational success and occupational mobility as a consequence of their experiences with job ceilings and unequal school provisioning, and they may be distrustful of educational institutions. This different relationship of "involuntary" minorities to the schools, as expressed in their lack of support for the status quo in schools, is visible in the demands of Arnhem's minority leaders for school change.

Euro-American members of the community did not argue for the need for educational change; community and school discourses on multiculturalism in Arnhem differed appreciably across groups. In their influential *Racial Formation in the United States,* Michael Omi and Howard Winant (1986) identify three competing discourses or paradigms for thinking and talking about race in U.S. history that are useful in considering such different orientations. Ruth Frankenberg (1993), using their model, proposes terms to characterize the three competing/coexisting/overlapping discourses[6] on race that Americans draw from: "essentialist racism," "color-evasiveness," and "race cognizance." Elements of all three discourses were visible in Arnhem, and I borrow her terminology as a useful shorthand for describing and analyzing the community and school discourses around multiculturalism that I encountered.

"Essentialist racism" presupposes the existence of biologically distinct races that can be hierarchically arranged, with whites on top. This discourse dominated in the West well into the twentieth century. Essentialist racism profoundly shaped U.S. history, and its effects continue to haunt the country today. Such discourses reemerge on occasion (e.g., Herrnstein and Murray 1994); more typically they reappear in new forms, where they constitute a sort of "neoracism," or "racism without races," a phenomenon noted in recent years across pluralistic Western societies (cf. Balibar and

Wallerstein 1991; Macias 1996; Wetherell and Potter 1992). These new racializing discourses move away from physical features and focus instead on other essentialized characteristics that are claimed to make groups unassimilable, such as cultural or linguistic differences.

Essentialist racism also provides the backdrop against which newer discourses around race are constructed and continue to be played out. As Frankenberg notes, "Essentialist racism has left a legacy that continues to mark discourses on race difference in a range of ways. First, precisely because it proposed race as a significant axis of difference, essentialist racism remains the benchmark against which other discourses on race are articulated. . . . It is in ongoing response to that moment that movements and individuals—for or against the empowerment of people of color—continue to articulate analyses of difference and sameness with respect to race" (1993:139).

The second paradigm, one of "color evasiveness" or "color blindness,"[7] emerged in large measure in response to racial essentialism. It incorporates less problematically the dominant cultural ideology of equality of opportunity embedded in the American dream. It also provides an appealing alternative for Americans disturbed by the blatant racial inequities that have persisted throughout most of the nation's history. Sociologist Robert Park and his followers (see Park 1950) drew on and helped popularize a discourse of color-blindness when they posited a universal process through which all groups would be incorporated into the national community, ignoring the significance of race in the American experience (Omi and Winant 1994). The views of Arnhem teacher Debra Moskowitz that opened this chapter draw from just such a discourse when she says of the Puerto Rican community, "They're no different than earlier waves."

Total assimilation is no longer envisioned as necessary or even desirable. In the current post–"new ethnicity" age, where claims that "we are all multiculturalists now" resonate with the general public (Glazer 1997), *some* "differences" among groups are safe and permissible (for instance, using a language other than English at cultural events or performing ethnic dances). Other differences, however—using a language other than English in public spaces when involved in daily activities or failing to achieve upward mobility—invoke moral evaluations and "racializing" discourses (e.g., Chock 1995; Urciuoli 1996) that draw from the paradigm of racial essentialism, albeit in new forms.

"Race cognizance" constitutes a third discursive repertoire. The civil rights movement (initially organized within the framework of ethnicity theory) and the subsequent black pride and black nationalism movements provided the template for other racialized groups to organize.[8] "Difference" once again reappears as in the first paradigm, but this time is defined by the oppressed groups themselves rather than imposed on them from outside. People of color organized around race, asserting and valorizing their own group identities. Attention to the significance of race in shaping people's histories and contemporary social locations in turn helped counter the limited explanatory power of the prevailing ethnicity paradigm. Multicultural education projects embracing "critical multiculturalism" and appearing under various rubrics including "education that is social reconstructionist," transformative education, critical pedagogy, or antiracist education (e.g., Banks 1997; Lee 1995; Nieto 1996; Sleeter and Grant 1988) today provide a "race-cognizant" voice that attends to the sociopolitical context of education and challenges dominant discourses.

It is against this third discursive repertoire, and drawing on earlier ones, that opposition to programs that attempt to address the consequences of racial inequality are often articulated. Many whites remain uncomfortable with any valorization of race. They may also see "color blindness" as preferable to "race cognizance" because this most recent discursive repertoire returns the focus to race, which carries negative connotations from an earlier era. Such views were visible in Arnhem as community members debated the educational needs of the city's minority youth. Spokespersons for each side laid out conflicting visions of what counts as "American" and disagreed as to whether schools organized along traditional lines served the needs of all students equally well. Many of the city's junior high school teachers[9] drew from this discursive repertoire, and were reluctant to address potentially controversial issues in the classroom that acknowledged or addressed racial inequality. Such responses were not universal however; teachers' treatment of nonmainstream linguistic practices and multicultural literature and their responses to students' ethnic and racial backgrounds varied considerably. These variations, I argue, can have an effect on students' involvement in the classroom.

The events that transpired in Arnhem and the responses of variously positioned social actors as examined in the upcoming pages emerged within a particular local context. It is, however, a context that reflects many of the general demographic, political, social, and economic trends that have shaped the United States. Arnhem's story may be uniquely its own, but Arnhem is in many respects a microcosm of the larger society, and to listen in on Arnhemites "talking 'American'" can illuminate both the challenges and the possibilities that exist for social change.

1 The Making of Arnhem, the "Friendly City"

> It was the best of times—period. When Stan Bronowski [age sixty-seven] talks about life in Arnhem before World War II, he tells no *Tale of Two Cities*. . . . "My father never stopped working in the mills. . . . He never got a pension . . . . Needs were simple. . . . Everybody was equal. No one was really better than anyone else . . . ." With the war came the changes. Stan's voice changed when he talked about the war. The smile left his face . . . . After the war, the mills started leaving along with the people. . . . "The big difference today is [our] kids are all moving away. Before everyone wanted to stay here. . . . [Now] there's nothing here."
> —"Outlook '85: Our Past, Present, Future," supplement to *Arnhem Record*[1]

Arnhem[2] traces its beginnings to the late 1700s, when it first emerged as a small, somewhat remote upstate New York village. Native Americans living in the region at that time were rapidly displaced by European immigrants and their descendants, eventually including English, Dutch, German, Irish, and Jewish settlers. In the decades following the Civil War regional industries began to prosper; Arnhem, with its seemingly inexhaustible supply of water power and access to a major river, was on its way to becoming the proverbial boom town. The industrialization then transforming the nation likewise transformed Arnhem. An 1870 business directory sang the city's praises, pointing to the production of more than $500,000 worth of coffins annually, four thousand pounds of soap per week, and twenty thousand clothes wringers per year, plus the use of forty thousand bushels of grain by the local malt house. Large numbers of southern and eastern Europeans, particularly Italians, Poles, and Lithuanians, had been drawn to the city to work in its carpet, garment, button, and broom factories. The 1870 population of ninety-five hundred climbed to thirty-two thousand by 1910. Representatives of one trade organization optimistically opened in 1905 that "the natural advantages for manufacturing purposes are practically inexhaustible. Arnhem possesses all the elements for the growth of a great and prosperous city. Within 20 years it ought to have a population of 50,000."

While Arnhem's population never hit that projected peak (topping out at 35,000 in the 1930s), projections of the city's economic future did appear to be accurate. In its heyday, local lore maintains, Arnhem was home to more than thirty millionaires, allegedly the highest per capita rate in the country. A local clergyman, now aged ninety-seven, recalls the era:

> The '20s and '30s were a time of hectic prosperity. We were drunk with prosperity. The mills in the city and in Harman were flourishing. There were a lot of millionaires and there was bathroom gin. Money was plentiful. We were just getting over World War I and everyone went on a spree. (*Arnhem Record,* "Outlook '85")

Local annals, however, also recount the day-to-day struggles that immigrants faced, laboring for one dollar a day and only gradually pushing their pay average to nine dollars a week with a twelve-hour work day. Attempts by the Knights of Labor to unionize the mill hands in 1896 following a pay cut failed when mill owners united and closed their plants, refusing to negotiate for eight months. Silk mill workers struck for ten months in 1920, and carpet company weavers struck for an equivalent period in 1921. Not until the late 1930s were the city's textile workers unionized, under the auspices of the National Labor Relations Act passed by Congress in 1935.

Older community members today can reel off the names of the ethnic neighborhoods that dominated the city landscape in their youth: Little Italy, "Polack" Hill, Kearney Hill, Money Hill (the wealthy area, home to long-settled, successful residents), Pancake Hill, and Dutch Hill among them. These citizens remember their parents and grandparents continuing to speak their native languages at home and in the ethnic clubs and churches that proliferated throughout the city. They also recall the days when ethnic group boundaries were more rigidly maintained—when marrying outside one's ethnic group, and particularly one's religion, was frowned on; youth hung out in ethnic cliques that had their bases in the ethnic neighborhoods and local elementary schools; and parents admonished children of marrying age to "stick with your own kind." Not until after World War II did interethnic and interreligious marriages become more acceptable for these descendants of southern and eastern European immigrants. Despite significant intermarriage, today almost two-thirds of Arnhem's Euro-American population still identifies ethnically as all or part Italian, Polish, or Lithuanian.

It was also after World War II that the beginnings of industrial flight and evidence of its long-term impact first appeared. As in other northeastern cities built around manufacturing, Arnhem's industrial base began eroding. Employers were moving to the South, where, without strong unions, labor costs were significantly lower. Arnhem's largest mill closed its doors in 1955, and a media story soon characterized the city as "New York's latest distress area." By 1968 carpet looms across Arnhem had been shut down and sold off; knitting mills stood abandoned; and the broom-making industry, with the advent of vacuum cleaners, had become little more than a relic. The vacant shells of the factories that once employed thousands of workers today stand as silent reminders to residents of those earlier, more prosperous times, and a profound sense of a lost golden era is apparent in the reminiscences of older community members. One local journalist captured their sentiments well in a feature story on the town's history that included the story of Stan Bronowski, a prominent Arnhem senior citizen and long-time restaurateur:

> Like stories heard from most natives of Arnhem his age, the story starts on a boat across an ocean in a place where life just wasn't good enough. . . . His tale is about one city: A place filled with good people, plenty of action, and work for anyone who wanted it. He talks about a homogeneous place—most had the same, did the same, lived the same and wanted the same. The thread that tied the "good place" together was the mills.

When the owners of those mills packed up and headed south, employers offering lower wages, uncertain employment, and few benefits moved in to fill the void. Some initially recruited workers for this burgeoning secondary labor market; in other cases people migrated to the area on their own in search of work. Arnhem's present-day Puerto Rican and Costa Rican populations gained a foothold during this era. Puerto Ricans began making their way north as early as the late 1940s and the 1950s in the wake of Operation Bootstrap, the U.S. government program that industrialized the island and, in the process, displaced agricultural workers. Costa Rican men, according to local lore, were drawn to the community in the early 1960s for factory work and to play for the city's soccer team,[3] recruited by a priest who had worked in Costa Rica. These earliest migrants in turn established the family networks that helped pave the way for later (im)migrants.[4]

Media coverage and discussions with community members suggest that this emerging Latino community, residentially concentrated in the city's East End, was merely "tolerated" during the early decades of its existence. It also appears that community members were largely excluded from many traditional avenues for upward mobility, including access to better jobs.[5] With the construction in the 1970s of the Arnhem Mall—what one Latino leader refers to as the "Arnhem Wall"—the Latino population was further isolated from the Euro-American population. Once, the town's parades, community events, and shopping district had run the entire length of the main street, incorporating the East End, and people had moved freely across ethnic neighborhood borders. Now the mall blocked the free flow of traffic from one neighborhood to another.

Arnhem's relatively small Latino community increased rapidly in the 1980s, echoing the national trend, and today a growing number of Latinos live scattered throughout the city. Between 1980 and 1990 the city's Latino population grew by 70 percent, and by 1990 school records counted Latinos as 17 percent of the total student population. The 1990 census report put Latinos at 12 percent of the city's population, but many community members estimate their numbers to be much greater.[6] Puerto Ricans today make up 75 percent of the city's Latino population and Costa Ricans, the second-largest group, 12 percent. Dominicans represent 6 percent; Peruvians 3 percent; and Mexicans, Cubans, Argentinians, and Colombians the remaining 4 percent. Peruvians, Colombians, and Argentinians, unlike the overwhelming majority of working-class and poverty-class Puerto Ricans concentrated in the city projects and the East End, live scattered across the city in middle-class neighborhoods. These differing housing patterns suggest that Peruvians, Colombians, and Argentinians in Arnhem are representative of the more middle-class nature of South American immigration to the United States.

There are hierarchies within hierarchies in Arnhem. The city's Costa Ricans are often contrasted favorably with Puerto Ricans: the former are typically portrayed as hardworking, family-oriented, law-abiding citizens who keep up their homes and are concerned about their children's education. Latinos who are not Puerto Rican often resent being taken for Puerto Ricans because the latter have such low status in the community.[7]

The perception that Puerto Ricans are looked down on not only by whites but also by other Latinos was one voiced by many I spoke with. A conversation I had with two young women and their friends and family who wandered through their kitchen while we were talking one afternoon points to their awareness of the stigmatization of Puerto Ricans in the community. Lidia Perez, who moved from New York City twelve years ago, rents the downstairs half of a house on the East End; her cousin Doris lives upstairs. Their two-family wooden-sided house, separated from its neighbors by driveways on each side, looks much like all the other houses that line the streets of the older neighborhoods in Arnhem, popular now, as when they were built, for their potential to easily accommodate extended families.

What started out as a formal interview soon evolved into an invitation to spend the afternoon with Lidia and her friends and family. Adults and children, smiling shyly at me when introduced by their mothers, wandered in and out of the kitchen where several women were putting together the makings of a stew for dinner. The conversation ranged from how Lidia's family came to settle in Arnhem and their frustrations with the schools to what aspects of their Puerto Rican heritage their children were likely to retain as second-generation "mainlanders." Lidia worries that her children don't speak Spanish to her anymore; she wants them to be proud of their Puerto Rican heritage. She is acutely aware that Puerto Ricans are often disparaged not only by whites but also by other Latinos, as is her close friend Marta Gomez:

> *Lidia Perez:* That Costa Rican lady [married to a Puerto Rican] told me when her kids go to school [and] people ask them what they are, they [should] say, "I'm Costa Rican," because the Puerto Ricans are troublemakers.
>
> *Marta Gomez:* Like I said, Costa Ricans and the Dominicans think that they're better than anybody else. I'm not saying all of them, but I think that a majority of them.

Like Lidia, an increasing number of the city's growing Puerto Rican population are transplants from metropolitan areas in the northeast seeking escape from the crime and violence of inner-city neighborhoods. Today more than 50 percent of Puerto Ricans in the mainland United States live outside New York City (Glasser 1995). They represent a growing trend among transplanted Puerto Ricans of fleeing big-city problems for the relative security of smaller cities (Glasser 1995; Stains 1994), and the reception they receive from "old-timers" in Arnhem is strikingly similar to the responses they encounter in other northeastern cities such as "Steel Town" (Soto 1997) and Allentown, Pennsylvania (Stains 1994).

Other Puerto Rican parents I interviewed had also moved upstate from the New York City area in the 1980s after hearing about Arnhem from relatives and friends already living there. Luz Ortiz, a young mother in her early thirties who works the night shift in a local factory, is typical of these migrants. Her parents came from the island to New York City in the 1950s and raised her and her five siblings in neighborhoods that were growing increasingly dangerous. Luz and her sister, Ana Flores, traced for me the story of their family's migration upstate, a resettlement that eventually came to include their parents and all of their siblings' families.

Ellen: And did everybody come basically for the same kinds of reasons?

Luz: Yes.

Ana: For better education for our children, better atmosphere.

Luz: Better atmosphere, more or less.

Ana: We feel that here they have a better chance of progressing.

Luz: They have better values here, not so much drugs. Where I lived in a building [in New York City], I lived in a good place and the rent was going up too high and I had to leave. Then I went to this building. . . . They put the door there every two weeks, metal doors, and they come and they steal the doors. They steal the lightbulbs.

Ana: We had junkies outside . . . people running up and down, and people on crack . . . and my kids were coming out of school, they had to be walking through people that were sitting on the stoops and shooting up. And there were shootings in the hallway during the night. You had to be careful before you walked out your door, make sure you didn't get shot. So it was horrible. There was no heat, no hot water sometimes in the winter.

While senior citizens in Arnhem may complain about the deteriorating quality of life in the city, for Puerto Ricans like Luz and Ana Arnhem is a reprieve from the struggles that confronted them in larger metropolitan areas. Luz chuckles when telling of her first encounter with Arnhem's "notorious" East End:

> Oh yes, when I came here, people said, "Oh, the East End is so bad." I drove on the East End a million times, and I told my sister, "where is this East End that people talk about?" It didn't occur to me to look at signs. I knew how to go from my sister's house to my father's store, and to the mall, that's all I needed. Never looking at where was East Broad. [My sister] said, "You *are* [living] on East Broad!" Where's all these—I expected junkies and fights and bums and drugs, and it was so quiet. I mean, these people got to go to New York City to see what bad is.

While such migrations from troubled urban areas have fueled a growing Latino population in Arnhem, the city's overall numbers continue to decline. Arnhem's population, peaking at almost 35,000 residents in 1930 and still at over 32,000 as late as 1950, today stands at 21,000. Many younger members of the Euro-American workforce have left the community in search of better employment opportunities. Senior citizens, ages fifty-five and older, now represent more than over 30 percent of the population; 47 percent of all households in Arnhem include at least one person over age sixty.

The 1990 census statistics suggest important differences between the Euro-American and the Latino communities.[8] One third of Arnhem's Latinos were born in Puerto Rico. Almost 80 percent of the Latino population speaks Spanish in the home; 81 percent of the Spanish speakers also report that they speak English "very well" or "well." Twenty-five percent of Latino respondents did not go beyond grade eight in school; another 27 percent did not finish high school. Only 4 percent hold a college degree.

The percentage of whites who did not complete high school is also high (34 percent versus 52 percent for Latinos). Given the large numbers of senior citizens and the fact that the majority of the pre–World War II generation did not graduate (Meier 1992), however, it is likely many of those whites who did not complete school are members of the senior citizen population. Twelve percent of whites, meanwhile, have completed a college education.

Economically the Latino population also lags far behind its Euro-American counterparts. The unemployment rate for Latino adults during the time of the community debate in 1991 and 1992 was estimated at 22 percent; 40 percent live in substandard housing and only 2 percent own their own homes.[9] Twelve percent of whites were living below the poverty level, compared to 34 percent of Latinos. Per capita income for whites was $12,228; for Latinos it was $7,427.[10] Taken as a group, Latinos are "newer," poorer, and have less formal education than local whites.

Today there is considerable friction between the Arnhem's elderly Euro-Americans and the more recently arrived Latino population, and it is these seniors who are most vocal in their criticism of the Latino community and the costs of educating a new generation of Americans. It is not uncommon, particularly among senior citizens, to hear complaints about the city being "overrun" and "destroyed" by Latinos. Talk of "all the violence in the schools" and how "those people" don't take care of their homes and children is common. Letters to the editor and calls to local talk show hosts frequently claim that Latinos expect handouts and flock to the city because it allegedly has the most generous welfare payments in the state. John Roche, a city resident in his late fifties who teaches in the junior high school, summarized the grievances in an interview:

> They resent them. . . . You can't blame them. You pick up the paper every day, and these people are constantly in trouble with the law. . . . They are also, when you look at the budget, the county budget is gonna show you that they use up the vast majority of the welfare budgeting, they get welfare in this county, a great deal of it is paid out to the Puerto Ricans, and, see people, they resent that. I've often felt myself, why do they hate them so much, but it doesn't take you too long. . . . They don't try to better themselves, they go on welfare, it's costing us a fortune to keep them here, they are always in some kind of trouble, and that's all they do is cause a problem, even in our educational system, you know, even in school.

Local Latinos are well aware of such sentiments, and many privately discuss how they bitterly resent being looked down on and stereotyped by whites:

> *Luz Ortiz:* [Mario] came home and he was mad. He says "Mom, I went in there and I was just looking around. I wasn't doing anything," [and] she followed him all over the store. And this happens in a lot of places. . . . It still frustrates Mario when he goes into places and he says, "Well, they watch me." "Well, honey, that's a fact of life and we have to learn to live with it, because that's the way people are."
>
> *Blanca del Valle:* You know by the way they talk to you, and the way they talk down to you, that they are prejudiced.

Many local Euro-Americans also bitterly complain about Latinos using Spanish in public. Spanish speakers in public places may encounter overt hostility, and are frequently accused of being too lazy to learn English or of being unwilling to become "American." Hostility toward accommodating Spanish speakers surfaces in the newspaper, in public meetings, and in informal conversations. For instance, when the local newspaper printed a public notice in both English and Spanish of the danger of drinking polluted tap water, many angry calls and letters to the editor bristled with resentment:

> The next time you feel the need to "serve the community" by printing an article in another language, be sure to serve all of Arnhem's residents, and print your story in Polish and Italian—two nationalities that are the cornerstones of this city. (Letter to the editor, *Arnhem Record,* April 29, 1993)

This, then, is the local context in which the fierce struggles around multiculturalism and bilingualism arose in Arnhem. Understanding how those "two nationalities," Poles and Italians, became the "cornerstones" of cities like Arnhem while Puerto Ricans as a group remain relegated to the lower rungs of the social class ladder is essential to making sense of such conflicts. It is to this matter that we now turn.

2 Marginality, Mobility, and the Melting Pot

America is God's Crucible, the great Melting-Pot where all the races of Europe are melting and re-forming! A fig for your feuds and vendettas. . . . into the Crucible with you all!
—Israel Zangwill, *The Melting Pot* (1909:37)

Contemporary struggles over "multiculturalism" in the United States cannot be understood without also considering the sociohistorical context in which these struggles have evolved. From the very conception of the nation people of color were excluded from the imagined national community; it is this marginalization and exclusion,[1] all but invisible in the public arena until the 1960s, that have fueled the current multicultural thrust.

From the outset the nation's founders sought to limit eligibility for citizenship. In 1790 Congress passed a bill limiting naturalization to "free white citizens." African-American, Native American, Puerto Rican, and Mexican populations, meanwhile, were forcibly incorporated into the nation without being extended the rights and protections granted to Euro-Americans. People of African descent, most of them enslaved through 1865, were granted citizenship and their men given the right to vote under the Fourteenth and Fifteenth amendments after the Civil War. Despite Constitutional changes, though, they remained legally segregated and essentially denied the vote–through the use of literacy tests, poll taxes, violence–throughout the South and much of the Southwest.[2] Through the 1960s African Americans would remain without the legal protections and rights accorded Euro-Americans, and it has been little more than a quarter century since those barriers to equality fell.

Other people of color also have fared poorly. Puerto Rico became a colony of the United States in 1898, without any say on the part of its people. Puerto Ricans were granted U.S. citizenship in 1917, making possible their participation in World War I. Mexicans too were granted citizenship, with the signing of the Treaty of Guadalupe Hidalgo following the Mexican American War of 1846–1848, but for both groups the reality[3] has been less than ideal: "In spite of legal rights, Puerto Ricans and Mexicans have remained largely unacknowledged as 'fellow' citizens of Americans throughout much of the twentieth century. Denied full citizenship and human rights by the customary practices of exclusion, they could be routinely bounced in and out of the 'national community' according to the ever-changing political and economic needs of the nation" (Oboler 1995:38).

Native Americans, decimated in the wake of war and the genocidal policies of the 1800s, were not granted citizenship until 1924. Chinese and Japanese workers, meanwhile, encountered violent racial hostility in the United States. Indeed, Asian immigration was essentially halted with passage of the 1882 Chinese Exclusion Act and the 1908 Gentlemen's Agreement. Not until the 1952 McCarran-Walter Act were all Asians granted naturalization eligibility. Mexican Americans were deported during the Great Depression and Japanese Americans were forced into innternment camps during World War II. Not until 1967 did the Supreme Court rule antimiscegenation laws unconstitutional, compelling the sixteen states that still had them to repeal the ban on interracial marriages.

The long-term historical perspective in the United States has often been woefully shortsighted. It is easy to lose sight of the fact that "for most of American history, women of any race and men who were Native American, Asian, black, or poor were barred from all but a narrow range of 'electable futures.'[4]. . . . Until recently no more than about a third of the population was able to take seriously the first premise of the American dream" (Hochschild 1995:26).

What the excluded groups (except white women) shared was a perception by Euro-Americans of being racially "other." It was a designation also applied, albeit for a far briefer period of time, to Irish Catholics in the mid- to late 1800s, and to southern and eastern European immigrants in the late 1800s and early 1900s. These groups, too, were conceptualized as inferior racial stock capable of damaging the national well-being (Gould 1981; Ignatiev 1995; Roediger 1991). Racist sentiments, in tandem with post–World War I isolationism, ultimately culminated in the passage of the 1920s National Origins Acts, putting into place for almost half a century a quota system that favored those judged to be more "acceptable" as future Americans. These various acts severely curtailed immigration from southern and eastern Europe while favoring northern and western Europeans' entry into the United States. Not until the mid-1960s, with the civil rights movement focusing attention on the nation's racial biases, were these national ("racial") origins biases eliminated.[5]

Being "American" had come to be construed as being "white," a category of belonging that slowly came to embrace the religious and cultural "otherness" of the Irish and southern and eastern Europeans. "Americanness" and "whiteness" continue to be seen in many quarters as synonymous. Thus the phrase "Americans are still prejudiced against blacks" is immediately comprehensible to many (Lieberson 1985, in Williams 1989); a third-generation Japanese-American historian may easily be asked by a taxi driver where he learned English so well (Takaki 1989); a white woman from New Jersey can sing the praises of a new Vietnamese restaurant to a journalist, reporting, "We were there the other night and we were the only Americans there" (Takaki 1989:6).

This racialized framework within which the nation evolved has its roots in the age of European expansion and conquest of the Americas, when Europeans encountered a far greater degree of physical and cultural diversity than they had previously known. While awareness of physical differences—a sort of proto–racial awareness—certainly existed before the European encounter of the Americas, the modern conception of race and "the distinctions and categorizations fundamental to a racialized social structure, and to a discourse of race" (Omi and Winant 1994:61) took shape only after 1492. "Given the dimensions and the ineluctability of the European onslaught, given the conquerors' determination to appropriate both labor and goods, and given the presence of an axiomatic and unquestioned Christianity among them, the ferocious division of society into Europeans and 'others' soon coalesced" (1994:62).

Today's seemingly self-evident racial categories of "black" and "white" as understood in the United States have roots in the early decades of the country's colonial period. "Black" came to represent a conflation of peoples with multiple identities—Yoruba, Ibo and so on—"rendered 'black' by an ideology of exploitation based on racial logic—the establishment and maintenance of a 'color line'" (Omi and Winant 1986:64). "White" emerged as a form of self-identification after 1680, where earlier self-descriptive terms had been first

"Christian" and then "English" and "free" (Jordan 1977, cited in Omi and Winant 1986:64). Similarly, "Indian" was a creation of the European settlers, a construction born of conquest and enslavement that denied a diversity of cultures (Mohawk 1992). Processes of *racialization,* whereby racial meaning is extended "to a previously racially unclassified relationship, social practice or group" (Omi and Winant 1986:64), were thus well underway by the time later waves of European immigrants reached the nation's shores.

Seeing "race" is so commonsensical in the contemporary world that it typically goes unrecognized as a social construct that varies across time and space, and is instead experienced as "an *essence,* as something fixed, concrete, and objective" (Omi and Winant 1994:54). A tale of three umpires said to have been told by social psychologist Hadley Cantril aptly illustrates the differences between essentialist and constructionist orientations: "The first umpire said, 'Some are balls and some are strikes, and I call them as they are.' The second replied, 'Some's balls and some's strikes, and I call 'em as I sees 'em.' The third thought about it and said, 'Some's balls and some's strikes, but they ain't nothing till I calls 'em'" (Henshel and Silverman, 1975:26, cited in Rosenblum and Travis 1996:2).

Like the first umpire's take on balls and strikes, essentialists perceive race to be "out there," a biological given equally apparent to all. From the constructionist perspective of the third umpire, where balls and strikes only exist when he names them as such, "*social* processes determine that one set of differences is more important than another, just as social processes shape our understandings of what those differences *mean*" (Rosenblum and Travis 1996:3).

But if "race" is a social construct and not a biological reality,[6] as most anthropologists now argue, it is nonetheless very real in that it profoundly affects people's life chances and commonsense ways of situating the self and others. The "one-drop rule" in the United States that makes anyone with a single black ancestor "black" is an American racial construction. Thus a blue-eyed blond who is 1/32 of African ancestry could be classified as "black" by the state of Louisiana, as Susie Phipps discovered in the mid-1980s when she challenged the "colored" designation on her birth certificate through the court system (Omi and Winant 1994) and lost.[7]

Because they *are* social constructions, notions of "race" vary cross-culturally, as the range of intermediary Latin American racial terms and the fluidity of racial categories in Latin America so clearly illustrate (Rodríguez 1994). And because they are social constructions, racial constructions are also continuously being challenged and transformed. Today many Americans with multiracial backgrounds are contesting the rigid boundaries of racial categorization in the United States that force them to choose one racial identity over another. Racially mixed Americans are calling for a revision of the census categories (see Sanjek 1994:119). Students of mixed European and Asian ancestry are claiming dual identities and forming "Hapa" (a Hawaiian word meaning half and half) organizations (Takaki 1997). Latinos are contesting the efficacy of the "racial" category "Hispanic" as used by the U.S. government (e.g., Melville 1988; Oboler 1995).

Throughout U.S. history these conceptions of race, grounded in religion and later in "science," have been used to legitimate existing societal and global inequities. Nineteenth-century European and Euro-American monogenists may have held that all humanity descended from a single source, but they also claimed that the races had declined to different degrees from Eden's perfection. The polygenists flatly rejected common descent; to them the various races represented separate biological species and could be hierarchically organized, with whites on top (Gould 1981).

By the mid-1800s these theories began to give way to more "scientific" explanations that alleged to prove objectively the superiority of the northern and western European peoples. Craniometry, based on an assumption that skull size reflects intellectual ability, was one popular means. The American physician Samuel Morton measured skulls from various so-called racial groups and claimed to have the very "facts" that would lend credibility worldwide to the American school of polygeny. "Needless to say, they [the results] matched every good Yankee's prejudice—whites on top, Indians in the middle, and blacks on the bottom; and among whites, Teutons and Anglo-Saxons on top, Jews in the middle, and Hindus on the bottom" (Gould 1981:53–4).[8]

Faith in the ability of scientific techniques to measure innate intelligence gained further credibility with the advent of intelligence quotient (I.Q.) testing in the early 1900s (Gould 1981). Adherents[9] claimed that score differences among groups were evidence that southern and eastern Europeans, African Americans, Mexicans, and Native Americans were intellectually inferior. It was genetic endowment, the reasoning went, that produced such vastly different intergroup scores. Even European peoples could be ranked: "Moral character, intelligence, and social worth were inextricably connected and biologically rooted. . . . Study after study exhibited the 'low intelligence' of 'wards of the state' and social deviants. . . . Immigrants, tests showed, were particularly prone to low intelligence. Professor Henry Goddard's 1912 study, sponsored by the U.S. Immigration Service, found that 83 percent of Jews, 80 percent of Hungarians, 79 percent of

Italians, and 87 percent of Russians were feeble-minded, based on 'culture-free' tests. "(Bowles and Gintis 1976:196).

Test results were used to justify societal inequalities. For instance, Lewis Terman, an influential Stanford psychologist, argued that class boundaries merely reflected these innate differences. "Scientific" findings were used to argue for restriction of immigration, continuance of Jim Crow laws, and an Americanization program for Native Americans (Gould 1981).

Not surprisingly from today's vantage point, the Poles, Jews, and Italians who were among those scoring in the 80s on I.Q. tests in the 1920s would see their scores rise by 20 to 25 points by the 1970s, in tandem with their upward social mobility (Sowell 1977). The belief in innate intelligence differences among biologically distinct races dies hard, however. Despite repeated attempts by much of the scientific community to counter the notion of discrete biological races that can be hierarchically arranged (e.g., Gould 1981; Smedley 1993), such notions live on in recent claims to the intellectual inferiority of African Americans (e.g., Herrnstein and Murray 1994; Jensen 1969).

Irish and Southern and Eastern European Immigrants in the Racial Order

It was not obvious from the outset that the Irish (Ignatiev 1995; Roediger 1991) or the later southern and eastern European immigrants (Gould 1981; Sacks 1994) would join the ranks of American "whites." The Irish Catholic "race" was variously characterized by native-born Euro-Americans as low brow, savage, groveling, bestial, lazy, wild, simian, and sensual in the pre–Civil War years (see Roediger 1991). The U.S. Census Bureau, which already differentiated between

Americans of native-born and foreign-born parentage, maintained yet another category for the Irish.

But while the Irish may have shared much with African Americans, situated as they were at the bottom of the social class ladder and similarly despised by the British in their homeland, their shared experiences were not conducive to the development of identification with, or compassion for, black Americans. Irish immigrants and Irish American workers were among those most violently opposed to any measures to better the plight of blacks. The desperate state of affairs they found themselves in, as historian David Roediger (1991) notes, fed their desire to embrace "whiteness" and set themselves apart from blacks. Their numbers made that politically possible. Courted by the Democratic Party for their votes and laying claim as whites to their rights to jobs, the Irish soon found Blacks easy targets with little political muscle or opportunity to resist attacks.

Turn-of-the-century southern and eastern European immigrants were also initially considered racially "other" (Gould 1981). Part of the poorest strata of society in their homelands, these newcomers lived and worked in deplorable conditions and for minimal wages in the nation's burgeoning urban industries. By 1900, with one third of the U.S. population first- or second-generation American, the nation's eastern cities had taken on a decidedly ethnic flavor; in the first decade alone of the new century the U.S. population of 75 million grew another 8.8 million through immigration (Parrillo 1997). These newcomers, overwhelmingly Catholic or Jewish and speaking languages other than English, were soon perceived by many Americans as a threat to national well-being and unity. Their linguistic, cultural, and "racial" differences were disparaged by those who had come before, many of whom equated the newcomers' impoverishment and wretched living conditions with their alleged cultural or genetic inferiority, or both.

> The notes of a new, or at least hitherto unemphasized chord from the nativist lyre began to sound—the ugly chord, or discord, of racism. Previously vague and romantic notions of Anglo-Saxon peoplehood, combined with general ethnocentrism, rudimentary wisps of genetics, selected tidbits of evolutionary theory, and naive assumptions from an early and crude imported anthropology produced the doctrine that the English, Germans, and others of the "old immigration" constituted a superior race of tall, blonde, blue-eyed "Nordics" or "Aryans," whereas the peoples of eastern and southern Europe made up the darker Alpines or Mediterraneans—both "inferior" breeds whose presence threatened, either by intermixture or supplementation, the traditional American stock and culture. (Gordon 1991:251)

Theories of cultural inferiority went hand in hand with these notions of racial inferority: "They [Poles] were [seen as] ignorant, illiterate, and dirty; they spoke little English if any at all; their families, the sociologists of the time assured us, were chronically 'disorganized.' They had no tradition of freedom and responsibility; they lacked political maturity. They were a bad bet to assimilate into American society" (Greeley 1991:276). Sociologist Richard Alba traces the existence of similar views of Italian Americans: "The Italians were perceived as prone to crime, both organized and that spurred by passion and vengeance, the latter symbolized for Americans by the stiletto (in Higham 1970:66–67). The Italian distinctiveness was perceived in physical terms as well: the immigrants were 'swarthy' and seemed to bear other signs of physical degradation, such as low foreheads" (1988:139).

Nor did the growing population of eastern European Jews, who would later come to be characterized as a "model minority," escape public sanction. In 1882 the *New York Tribune*, in language that as Micaela di Leonardo (1995:170–1) notes parallels contemporary mainstream characterizations of minority poor, had this to say about the newcomers: "Numerous complaints have been made in regard to the Hebrew immigrants who lounge about Battery Park, obstructing the walks and sitting on the chains. Their filthy condition has caused many of the people who are accustomed to go to the park to seek a little recreation and fresh air to give up this practice. . . . The police have had many battles with these newcomers, who seem determined to have their own way" (quoted in Higham 1981:67).

If the United States held out the hope of a better life, it was clearly not because a warm welcome was extended to the newcomers. The "melting pot" metaphor that would be employed to describe their incorporation into American society and would profoundly shape American discourse on immigration and ethnicity for the next half century (Glazer 1997) suggested that the various populations would all contribute to the forging of a new people. The hard reality, however, was that immigrants were subjected to intense pressures to "Americanize," to give up their foreign ways, languages, and names. A crushing "Anglo-conformity" (see Gordon 1991) more accurately characterized the expectations held for them. An excerpt from *Ford Times* describing the Ford Motor Company English School Melting Pot rituals of 1916 suggests the popular pressures that immigrants and their children encountered:

> The feature of the graduation exercises was a unique pageant. . . . Across the back of the stage was shown the hull and deck of an ocean steamship docked at Ellis Island. In the center . . . was an immense caldron across which was painted the sign "Ford English School Melting Pot.". . . Dressed in a foreign costume

> and carrying his cherished possessions wrapped in a bundle suspended from a cane . . . [the immigrant] descended the ladder into the "Melting Pot," holding aloft a sign . . . "Syria," "Greece," "Italy.". . . From it they emerged dressed in American clothes, faces eager with the stimulus of the new opportunities and responsibilities opening out before them. Every man carried a small American flag in his hand. (cited in Sollors 1986:89–90)

Today's arguments for "multiculturalism" have their origins in this era.[10] Early twentieth-century arguments for cultural pluralism, first put forward by philosopher Howard Kallen, coexisted alongside the melting pot ideology (see Gordon 1991). This cultural pluralist movement, however, could not successfully repel the nativism and xenophobic sentiments that flourished in the World War I and Depression era. Nor would these cultural pluralists embrace the nation's largest minority population; not only were African Americans rendered literally invisible in discussions on assimilation of "the races," they were also ignored by these early critics of Americanization and assimilation (Glazer 1997; Hollinger 1995).

Schooling and the Social Order

Public schooling came to be seen as the means for molding the children of immigrants into good citizens, much as it had been conceptualized in an earlier era. The first major expansion of public schooling in the United States had taken place in the mid–nineteenth century. This initial expansion had not been about meeting demands for a more literate workforce; literacy preceded rather than arose from the spread of mass schooling (see Cook-Gumperz 1986a).[11] Rather, common school education, as an excerpt from a school committee memorandum of the times illustrates, was intended to have a significant moral and political educational component: "The object of education is by no means accomplished by mere intellectual instruction. It has other aims of equal if not higher importance. The character and habits are to be formed for life . . . the habit of attention, self-reliance, habits of order and neatness, politeness and courtesy. . . habits of punctuality" (Springfield, Massachusetts, School Committee 1854:11–13, quoted, in Bowles and Gintis 1976:169).

Here children from poor and immigrant homes could learn the proper values and respect for hard work and independence. In these common schools rich and poor alike could come together so that the poor could learn from their betters, ultimately benefitting national well-being by reducing the potential for social strife. Students were to learn the benefits of republicanism not directly from their teachers, who were not to be trusted with the political education of young children, but rather from their texts, which taught respect for the sanctity of private property, acceptance of the status quo, and the inherent authority of those in power (Mosier 1947, in Nasaw 1979). Schooling was sold as advantageous for society: "the best police for our cities, the lowest insurance of our houses, the firmest security for our banks, the most effective means of preventing pauperism, vice and crime" (Messerli 1972, in Nasaw 1979:81). Yet the hard reality that went unaddressed by school reformers was that most children were unable to benefit from such schools because of their families' poverty and dependence on the children's labor at home and in factories. Common school reformers, dependent on the factory owners and businessmen to support their drive for educational change, failed to call for legislation that would have promoted greater equality: a redistribution of wealth, child labor regulation, and a living wage that would permit parents to support their families and send their children to school.

Events at the end of the nineteenth century propelled a second major set of changes in the organization of public schools. Massive numbers of working-class and immigrant children were entering the secondary schools once dominated by Anglo-Saxon middle-class youth; enrollment grew more than 700 percent between 1880 and 1918. Mass immigration, enforcement of compulsory education laws, and the passage of child labor laws during this era brought growing numbers of American youth into the public schools (Oakes 1985). If these newcomers were to become productive Americans, popular sentiment held, they would have to abandon their potentially subversive foreign cultures and languages and become Americanized. This school population growth and the push for Americanization through schools converged with other trends between 1880 and 1930, including the spread of the ethnocentric ideas of the social Darwinists and a movement to promote the model of the school as an efficient factory system designed to mass produce an educated citizenry capable of meeting the needs of industry (Nasaw 1979; Oakes 1985). Public schooling as we know it today thus evolved as a product of the competing forces of democratic impulses and the needs of the capitalist economic order (Bowles and Gintis 1976; Nasaw 1979; Oakes 1985).

The form that public schools took during this era largely reproduced rather than undermined the social divisions of the larger society. By the early twentieth century overt curriculum tracking had emerged, one track promoting vocational education as the appropriate curriculum for non–college-bound students, the other continuing a tradition of elite academically directed education. Children were initially sorted into these programs based on ethnic, racial, and class backgrounds, a practice that conflicted with the ideology of the United States as an open society.

By the end of World War I tracking assignments were based on ostensibly more scientific measures: the I.Q. test (and later, other forms of standardized testing). I.Q. tests became the sine qua non of educational decision making. A survey of 150 city school systems in 1932 revealed that three quarters of them were assigning students to curriculum tracks based on such test scores (Bowles and Gintis 1976: 196). The alleged objectivity of these early tests, today recognized as culturally biased (Gould 1981), made it possible for many to believe that the schools really *were* meritocracies, efficiently sorting children into programs that best served their individual abilities and needs. School counseling programs further legitimated the process by making tracking appear voluntary, with students and parents counseled as to what choices might best fit each student's needs. The possibility that tracking practices might put working-class and minority students at a disadvantage went unacknowledged.

U.S. schools today remain little changed from the shape they assumed during the turbulent era of the 1890s through the 1920s. In that period their mandate was not to equalize opportunity or address questions of how the larger social and economic inequalities of society played into student outcomes, but to maintain the social order and meet the needs of industry and business for workers with diverse sets of skills. This was also a period of overt racial and ethnic hierarchy, and opportunities for schooling reflected such societal assumptions. Although schools may have been conceptualized as the vehicles through which immigrants and migrants to urban areas were to learn proper values and be assimilated into the American cultural mainstream, people of color were largely excluded from consideration for incorporation into the imagined community. An ideology of Anglo-Saxon racial superiority supported their schooling—if they were to receive any—in separate and inferior educational facilities and programs (Menchaca and Valencia 1990). For Native American children schooling also meant attending off-reservation boarding schools where (like many Spanish-speaking children) they were subjected to the additional insult of being punished for using their native languages (Leap 1981). While minorities could point to the obvious inequalities in their being forced to attend such segregated and inferior schools, it was not until the 1960s, when legal barriers fell, that the vision of public schools as meritocracies was seriously challenged on the academic front.

The Expanding Middle: Economic Mobility as the Prelude to Educational Success

The children and grandchildren of southern and eastern European immigrants did not acquire the educational credentials that would foster their upward mobility. This was the school system that the first generations of white ethnics encountered and from which they turned away (e.g., Covello 1972). The overwhelming majority of the second and third generations were bound for blue-collar jobs. Social scientists, meanwhile, sought explanations for the lack of upward mobility in the cultures of such groups—citing "fatalism" and "familism,"[12] for example—often contrasting them with the more upwardly mobile eastern European Jews who had entered the country during the same years. Jews, however, had arrived in the United States with the skills and experiences to give them a head start over southern and eastern European peasants, making early economic ascent possible (Steinberg 1989). It was this more secure economic niche that in turn allowed the Jews to take advantage of expanding educational opportunities. For them, economic mobility thus largely preceded educational mobility. Without an economic head start and expanded opportunities, the high value Jews placed on education would not have been activated (Steinberg 1989).

The class position from which children entered schools significantly affected the likelihood of their remaining in school and the educational programs they were offered (Greer 1972; Oakes 1985). Immigrant and working-class children were expected to leave school early to enter the workforce, and those who remained in school longer were guided toward vocational programs. In Arnhem, for instance, the school district's first ESL (English as a Second Language) teacher, now retired and in his 70s, recalled being taught in school how to operate the looms used in local textile mills. In an era when large numbers of unskilled and semiskilled workers were essential to the economic order, there was no public outcry for school reform to alleviate the economic inequalities that persisted along racial and ethnic lines. Unequal outcomes were accepted by school personnel, who viewed them as the inevitable consequence of the genetic or cultural deficiencies of those on the bottom rungs of the social class ladder. The existence of the schools and the continuing expansion of public education appeared to be proof enough that schools were providing opportunities for all to participate to the fullest of their capacities.

Yet if the descendants of southern and eastern European immigrants were not using the schools as a vehicle for upward mobility, how, then, did they come to achieve middle-class status and join the ranks of the mainstream? At the end of the 1930s the possibility that the children of this wave of immigrants would experience large-scale upward mobility would have seemed unlikely (Alba 1988; di Leonardo 1992).

The children and grandchildren of southern and eastern European Catholic immigrants were not staying in school at rates even comparable to the general population. White ethnics lagged behind their more economically advantaged white counterparts in years of schooling completed; in 1930, for instance, only 11 percent of Italian children who attended New York City high schools finished, at a time when more than 40 percent of the total school population was graduating (Covello 1972, in Alba 1988). The relative lack of educational credentials, however, did not translate at that time into the disadvantage that it does in today's economy. Opportunities for employment that secured a living beyond what the immigrant generation had experienced in their homelands were available for their children who left school without graduating.

What changed for these white ethnics was not their educational credentials, but rather the expansion of economic opportunities. Upward mobility was significantly advanced by the favorable conditions that existed in the World War II era and its aftermath. In answer to the question "How did Jews become white folks?" Karen Sacks underlines the significance of this era for both Jews and other white ethnics:

> Did Jews and other Euroethnics become white because they became middle class? That is, did money whiten? Or did being incorporated in an expanded version of whiteness open up the economic doors to a middle-class status? Clearly both tendencies were at work. Some of the changes set in motion during the war against fascism led to a more inclusive version of whiteness. Anti-Semitism and anti-European racism lost respectability. The 1940 census no longer distinguished native whites of native parentage from those, like my parents, of immigrant parentage. . . . Economic prosperity played a very powerful role in the whitening process. . . . The postwar

period was a historic moment for real class mobility and for the affluence we have erroneously come to believe was the U.S. norm. (1994:86–8)

For white ethnics, a fortuitous set of circumstances came together beginning in the 1940s that raised the standards of living of that generation and catapulted their children squarely into the mainstream. The entry of the United States into World War II spurred industrial production, removing the last vestiges of the Great Depression. Prolabor legislation of the 1930s and worker struggles led to industrial CIO union success in organizing many semiskilled workers and tying wages to the cost of living by the end of the 1940s. White ethnic semiskilled workers and their families in particular benefited; in the 1950s upwards of a quarter of the American population was raised to a level at which they were able to join both members of the middle class and skilled blue-collar workers in purchasing homes and cars in the 1950s (Davis 1986; see also Candeloro 1992).

Structural occupational shifts beginning in the 1940s and 1950s, with a significant expansion in white-collar jobs, also opened up new opportunities for white ethnics without their having to displace others to attain middle-class status. The GI Bill, intended in part to reduce the potential for class conflict that was beginning to emerge with the massive demobilization of troops following the war (Sacks 1994), provided virtually free college education and vocational training for former GIs. With a rapidly expanding economy and the promise of upward mobility, many took advantage of the offer (Candeloro 1992; Davis 1986). Almost half of those who served in the military received a free college education at government expense, and college attendance doubled from 15 percent of the college-age population in 1940 to 30 percent by 1954. The National Defense Education Act of 1958 continued to keep college costs accessible to working-class students throughout the 1960s.

Greater economic prosperity in the postwar years contributed to the erosion of white ethnic neighborhoods and ethnic segregation in the workforce. Massive postwar federal investment in highway construction and low-cost interest rates on mortgages for former GIs enabled urban workers to purchase homes outside the city (also contributing to the loss of tax revenues for city centers).[13] Urban ethnic enclaves, which had never been particularly homogeneous neighborhoods despite their public association with distinct national origin groups (Massey and Denton 1993), were thus further eroded as white second- and third-generation ethnics joined the postwar exodus to the suburbs. The proportion of metropolitan residents living in suburbs rose from one-third to more than one-half the population between 1940 and 1970 (Massey and Denton 1993:44). High rates of intermarriage among all European ethnic groups provide still further evidence of the erosion of white ethnic boundaries (e.g., Glazer 1993, Lieberson and Waters 1988); one researcher (Alba 1985), for instance, found that half of all Italian-American Catholics born since World War II had married Protestants.

For the descendants of southern and eastern European Catholic immigrants, upward mobility was not the product of educational success (Canderloro 1992; Covello 1972; Greeley 1991; Kantowicz 1992), popular myths notwithstanding; on the contrary, educational success was in large measure an outcome of upward mobility. Whereas social scientists may have once despaired of their educational progress, today Italian Americans attend college at rates comparable to their percentage of the general population (McKenney, Levin, and Tella 1985 in Candeloro 1992).[14]

The Paradox of the "New Ethnicity" among White Ethnics

Ethnicity, at least for the younger generations, has become unmoored from its social structural foundations (e.g., Alba 1985; Candeloro 1992; Kantowicz 1992). White ethnics once considered to be extremely unlikely candidates for assimilation into the mainstream have achieved near parity with older European ethnic groups, and intermarriage, which further blurs ethnic distinctions, has proceeded apace. European ethnic boundaries have eroded to the point analysts speak of the "twilight of ethnicity" for southern and eastern European Catholics (Alba 1988; Waters 1990). For today's descendants of turn-of-the-century immigrants, fully integrated into the mainstream, ethnic identity has become largely a voluntary phenomenon. White ethnic identity today is more aptly characterized as what Herbert Gans (1979) labels "symbolic ethnicity," in which people may attempt to maintain some psychological connection to their ethnic origins, but not so as to prevent them from participating in the mainstream.

Given this history, the emergence of white ethnic movements in the 1970s at first glance appears contradictory: white ethnics and the media celebrating their ethnic communities and their cultural distinctiveness when trends for the past generation pointed to the approaching "twilight of ethnicity." The white ethnic communities that journalists and scholars wrote of were also based on the largely unexamined assumption "that there *were* in fact such discrete phenomena: long-term, self-reproducing, ethnically homogeneous inner-city neighborhoods. In reality, American white ethnic populations throughout the nineteenth and twentieth centuries, no matter how abused or discriminated against by majority society, lived in ethnically heterogeneous and shifting urban and suburban neighborhoods—and moved often" (di Leonardo 1994:173).

The emergence of claims to white ethnic identities in the 1970s was not a forgone conclusion. Rather, such claims arose from a particular constellation and conjuncture of events (di Leonardo 1994). In the 1950s and 1960s civil rights and black cultural nationalist movements, African Americans laid claim to themselves as an identifiable group that had suffered discrimination and was entitled to redress. The white ethnic community construct borrowed these basic ideological tropes to stake out its own claim to entitlements. White ethnics also borrowed the language of black assertions of pride in their historical struggles, culture, and heritage.

By the 1970s several trends had emerged that would fuel struggles over multiculturalism and its related manifestations including bilingual education, immigration policies, and curriculum debates. A small but growing percentage of people of color assumed positions of power, both within academia and in the larger society, with enhanced opportunities to push for educational and social reforms. At the same time, people of color as a whole continued to confront barriers to upward mobility, making it apparent that the earlier civil rights movement had failed in accomplishing many of its intended objectives. Meanwhile, inflation, economic dislocation, and challenges to Americans' views of themselves as the major world power threatened the faith of growing numbers of Americans in the American dream. For many white Americans downward mobility for their children became a distinct possibility. Those in the working class saw their economic futures and those of their children threatened by the loss of many high-paying blue collar jobs and the collapse of the union movement.

By the 1980s a powerful conservative reaction to the Great Society federal programs and civil rights gains was firmly entrenched, and the new social movements were being blamed for the difficulties facing American society. As Michael Omi and Howard Winant noted, however, in the wake of the "great transformation" that had occurred in the 1960s it became impossible to argue for an explicitly racist ideology, and new arguments arose: "Any 'legitimate' politics must claim to favor racial equality *in the abstract,* even if specific egalitarian measures are condemned. . . . The right had been able to rearticulate racial meanings once again. This time, though, it was not the justice but the very *meaning* of racial equality which was at stake. The right, especially the neoconservatives, had institutionalized their interpretation—focused on 'equality of opportunity' and explicitly oblivious to 'equality of result' as the national 'common sense'" (1994:140–1).

Recent scholarship suggests that among whites (of southern and eastern European ancestry in particular) a new European-American identity is emerging, one that is particularly visible in times of ethnic and racial conflict over resources. This shared identity draws its strength from perceptions of a common past: "From every group, one hears essentially the same story of people who came poor, suffered from discrimination and other early burdens, but worked hard and eventually made their way in the new land. . . . The thrust of European-American identity is to defend the individualistic view of the American system, because it portrays the system as open to those who are willing to work hard and pull themselves over barriers of poverty and discrimination" (Alba 1990:313–17).

The Power of the "Great School Legend"

The profoundly racialized social order that existed in the United States until little more than a quarter-century ago, and that in many important respects continues to exist, is easily obscured by an ideology of equality and equal opportunity. Within that framework schools are conceptualized as the primary vehicle for achieving upward mobility. The myth of schools as the means by which earlier impoverished immigrant groups have achieved upward mobility and assimilation, what Colin Greer (1972) terms the "Great School Legend," endures. White ethnics in Arnhem, as we shall see in Chapter 4, attribute their group's economic success and assimilation to hard work and the insistence that their children do well in schools. They blame Puerto Ricans for their lack of upward mobility as a group, even though, as previously noted, the economic mobility of white ethnics largely preceded their educational mobility.

We can never know whether schools organized along different lines might have fostered more equitable educational outcomes for these older generations of Americans. We also cannot know what would have been the economic consequences of more equitable educational outcomes. It was to be the successes of the union movement and the expanding U.S. economy beginning in the 1940s that would provide white ethnics the opportunities for accumulating economic capital. This economic capital, in turn, enhanced both the likelihood that their children could postpone their entry into the workforce and their acquisition of "cultural capital" that (unrecognized by participants in the educational process) privileges mainstream children in schools and fosters educational success (Bourdieu and Passeron 1977). Without enhanced opportunities for mobility, white ethnics as a group would likely have remained in working-class communities in which differing linguistic and cultural practices, and orientations to schooling, would have significantly affected opportunities for academic success.

For the older generation of white ethnics in Arnhem, their parents' and grandparents' experiences, and the success they or their children attained, figure prominently in their construction of "being American." Success in schools and society is attributed solely to individual effort. Many of the teachers as well were among the white ethnics able to take advantage of the expansion of higher education in the 1950s and 1960s, the first generation to achieve a college education and move into the middle class. The assumptions they bring to their educational endeavors are the product of a particular set of experiences. Those experiences, in interaction with institutional forces, exert a strong influence on their classroom practices, as we shall see in Chapters 5 and 6.

The experiences of white ethnics, however, have not been equally shared by people of color. Puerto Ricans on the mainland were evaluated early on according to the ethnicity paradigm as the "newest" immigrant group poised to make its way up the social class ladder. As Chapter 3 underlines, however, this "immigrant analogy" fails in important ways to capture Puerto Ricans' experiences. Those, in turn, have profoundly shaped their relations to schools and to American society.

3 Puerto Ricans Enter a Racialized Social Order

I am two parts /a person
boricua[1] /spic
past and present
alive and oppressed
given a cultural beauty
. . . and robbed of a cultural identity
—from "Here," by Sandra María Esteves (1974)

Puerto Ricans' participation in multicultural debates in the United States cannot be fully understood without first looking closely at the island's mode of entrance into the United States and the subsequent experiences of Puerto Ricans as racialized "others." The "immigrant analogy" would situate Puerto Ricans as only the most recent in a long line of immigrant groups, each one equally positioned for upward mobility and assimilation into the American mainstream. In this case, however, the analogy is inherently flawed. It ignores critical differences: a long history of racial discrimination and stigmatization, a colonial relationship that shaped Puerto Ricans' entry into mainland society, and the global transformations and changed economic context that today confront groups situated at the bottom of the social class ladder. Without attention to such vitally important matters, groups that "fail" in achieving the sought-after upward mobility risk being constructed as pathologic, a "problem" to be explained by reference to the members' cultural and linguistic practices or individual orientations.

The racialized social order that had developed in the United States by the late 1800s also helped shape the United States' relationship with its newly acquired colony of Puerto Rico after 1898. Assumptions of cultural superiority on the part of white American business and government representatives who flooded into Puerto Rico went hand in hand with assumptions of racial superiority: "It soon became evident that most American policymakers did not feel that Puerto Rico and the other islands could be self-governing states in the ordinary process of statehood. Not only were their inhabitants tropical people and, therefore, decadent, but they were culturally alien and racially 'mongrelized.'" (Moore and Pachon 1985:7).

Thus began what was to become a long and troubled relationship between the United States and Puerto Rico, in which U.S. dominance and the imposition of English and "Americanization" in schools emerged as the dominant official policy for the first half of the century (Morris 1995; Negron de Montilla 1970). The United States government set out "to Americanize Puerto Rico with a vengeance" (Zentella 1981:219), even to the point of anglicizing the name to "Porto Rico." Protestant missionaries were invited to the island, and the Catholic schools were largely replaced by a secular public school system in which students were taught in English. Here, too, as on the mainland, schools were envisioned as the vehicle through which the "newcomers" could be molded into loyal and cooperative Americans. Victor Clark, the "architect" of this new educational system, articulated the dominant sentiments of United States government policymakers in 1899: "The great mass of Puerto Ricans are as yet passive and plastic. . . . Their ideals are in our hands to create and mold. If the schools are made American and the teachers and pupils are inspired with the American [spirit] . . . the island will become in its sympathies, views, and attitude . . . essentially American" (cited in Negrón de Montilla 1975:13).

School practices were deliberately designed to further the goals of American government and business interests. American teachers were recruited; new teacher certification regulations required a mastery of English; students and teachers were encouraged to take trips to the United States; textbooks and curricula from the mainland were imported; high priority was given to the teaching of English, with a dominant policy of "English only" remaining in effect until 1948; and American holidays, symbols, and heroes were promoted in the schools (Negrón de Montilla 1970). Such practices reached their most extreme under Puerto Rican Commissioner of Education Juan B. Huyke (a pro-U.S. political party leader appointed to his post by E. Montgomery Reily, the U.S.-appointed governor), who held his position from 1921 to 1930:

> All High School seniors were obliged to pass an oral English examination before they were given their diplomas. The printing of school newspapers written only in Spanish was prohibited. A School Society for the Promotion and Study of English Language was organized in all schools in the 8th, 9th, and 10th grades. Among the duties of the members of this society there were first, to wear a small American flag in the buttonhole and, second, to speak English everywhere to one another. Regulations issued by the Department made English the required language at teachers' meetings and suggested that conversations between pupils and teachers should be in English. . . . Ranking among schools was given in terms of performance in English tests. All official documents addressed to the teachers were required to be in English and all supervisors were required to use English in their visits to the schoolrooms. (Negrón de Montilla 1970:291–2)

Not only were Puerto Ricans given the message that English was superior to Spanish, their own Spanish was evaluated as inferior. "One of the most damaging legacies of US colonialism in Puerto Rico," Ana Celia Zentella (1997:268) notes in citing from a 1901 "Report to the Governor" that disparaged Puerto Rican Spanish, "is the linguistic insecurity implanted by notions like 'pure Spanish,' 'unintelligible,' 'patois,' and 'little value as an intellectual medium.'" This troubling history cannot be ignored in making sense of Puerto Ricans' sentiments once on the mainland: "The dominant themes of the US practices and policies on the island, i.e., that Puerto Rican Spanish is inferior to that of Spain, that English is corrupting Puerto Rican Spanish, and that progress means becoming American by adopting the English language and North American cultural values, are the legacy that is part of the baggage that Puerto Ricans take with them to the mainland" (Zentella 1985:44).

Imposition of English on the island and in the schools came to symbolize U.S. attempts to deliberately weaken Puerto Rican culture and identity.[2] That Puerto Ricans today continue to speak Spanish after a century of American rule suggests that Puerto Ricans living on the island have resisted cultural and linguistic assimilation (Zentella 1981). Lending weight to that theory, Nancy Morris (1995) in examining Puerto Rican identity among island elites found that her informants unequivocally articulated a distinct Puerto Rican identity. According to Morris, "the Spanish language" was the most consistently cited response to the question of what "Puerto Ricanness" entails.

United States rule has also engendered ongoing debates about "the national question"—whether Puerto Rico should retain its current status as a United States commonwealth, become a state, or become independent. These debates have waxed and waned for decades and provide a forum in which resistance to the American presence on the island is given voice. Colonialism inevitably begets opposition from some members of the dominated group (Fanon 1968); while politically marginalized in Puerto Rico, the existence of an "articulation of resistance, defiance, and struggle against oppression" has provided a different context from which Puerto Ricans may interpret their relationship to the dominant society in the United States (Rodríguez 1989:14).

The economic consequences of Puerto Ricans' colonial legacy and their experiences on the mainland further foster conditions promoting the persistence of distinctive (albeit transformed) cultural characteristics and a strong sense of group identity. The Puerto Rican "diaspora" after World War II (though Puerto Ricans on the mainland can trace their presence back to the turn of the century [Sanchéz Korrol 1983]) brought hundreds of thousands of them to New York City within a short period of time. This massive emigration was driven by the displacement of traditional modes of subsistence on the island, an outcome of the decision to transform the plantation economy into an industrial one through Operation Bootstrap (Nelson and Tienda 1988). Economic displacement coincided with rapid population expansion, creating a ready pool of surplus labor that U.S. employers were eager to recruit. When agreements between the Truman administration and the colonial government resulted in lower airfare from the island to New York City (Grosfoguel and Georas 1996), mass migration to New York City to fill the lower-level jobs being vacated by the upwardly mobile became a real possibility.

And a mass migration it was. Between 1940 and 1960, the number of Puerto Ricans living on the mainland jumped from seventy thousand to nearly nine hundred thousand, with most settling in the New York metropolitan area. By 1990 the mainland Puerto Rican population had reached 2.5 million. Despite significant return migration beginning in the 1960s, more than 40 percent of all Puerto Ricans now live off the island. Fifty-eight percent of the population still in Puerto Rico, meanwhile, live below the poverty line (see Cordero Guzmán 1993).

Puerto Ricans themselves, arriving at a time when many urban experts felt the city was near collapse, were often blamed for their poverty and the changing urban environment.[3] As early as 1947 the *World-Telegram*, a New York paper, was inflaming racist public sentiment in language that sounds eerily familiar in the current anti-immigrant climate: "The Puerto Ricans are destroying the economy and suffocating the culture of their adopted community. . . . [Puerto Ricans] are the cause of the incredibly bad housing situation. . . . The police have followed groups of them arriving at the airport . . . heading straight for the welfare offices in East Harlem" (cited in Vega 1984:230).

Migrants to the mainland, eager to find work, soon faced diminishing job prospects. Despite the postwar economic growth of the late 1940s that drew Puerto Ricans and African Americans to the metropolis, economic changes with far-reaching consequences for the newcomers were already underway (Torres 1995). Rapid expansion of the New York Puerto Rican community had coincided with the beginning of a massive shift in the United States economy, from manufacturing—the sector in which Puerto Rican workers were overwhelmingly concentrated—to a service-based economy. In 1960, 60 percent of New York Puerto Ricans were employed in manufacturing jobs; in the subsequent decade New York City lost 173,000 jobs, and in the

1970s it lost another 268,000 jobs (see Rodríguez 1989). Simultaneously, Puerto Ricans' labor struggles contributed to making them "too expensive" for manufacturing jobs in the informal sector, which relied heavily on the cheapest possible labor; employers instead turned to new Latino immigrants willing to work for substandard wages (Grosfoguel and Georas 1996). Plant relocation to the suburbs, alongside the difficulties of negotiating transportation, high housing costs, and exclusionary practices designed to keep nonwhites out, put inner-city minorities at a further disadvantage. White flight to the suburbs in turn eroded the tax base of the city. Restrictive union policies and practices (including nepotistic father–son clauses, exclusionary racial practices, and seniority rules) meant that Puerto Ricans' access to economically secure jobs was further reduced (Rodríguez 1989). The result, for many Puerto Ricans, has been their heavy concentration in the secondary labor market and the deteriorating inner cities. These are conditions that favor ethnic solidarity and the maintenance of ethnic practices: "These two factors—residential and occupational concentration—are especially crucial to the formation of ethnic group solidarity in that they produce common class interests, lifestyles and friendships. When the ethnic experience includes rejection, discrimination and oppression, the elaboration of ethnic ties provides a ready system of support for groups distinguishable by race, national origin or language" (Nelson and Tienda 1988:51).

To complicate the economic struggle, Puerto Ricans also confront a biracial order in moving to the mainland that seeks to divide the Puerto Rican community into "black" and "white": "Puerto Ricans entered a heterogeneous society that articulated an assimilationist, melting-pot ideology, but that, in fact, had evolved a racial order of dual ethnic queues, one White and one not-White. . . . The irony was that Puerto Ricans represented the ideal of the American melting-pot ideology—a culturally unified, racially integrated people" (Rodríguez 1989:49). Different shades of color among Puerto Ricans have translated into profoundly different experiences (Klor de Alva 1991; Rodríguez 1989). The issue of identity on the mainland has been particularly salient for dark-skinned Puerto Ricans (e.g., Thomas 1967), who must deal with a society that regards them above all else as black.

The connections between African American and Puerto Rican communities—in terms of shared experiences of prejudice and discrimination, but also the cultural and linguistic fusion that grows out of shared neighborhoods, schools, and workplaces and the Afro-Caribbean elements brought to the island–are reflected in much of the "Nuyorican"[4] literature and the community's artistic productions, including the "Latino rap" that has emerged recently (see for example analyses in Cortes, Falcón, and Flores 1976; Flores 1993; Flores, Attinasi, and Pedraza 1981; Mohr 1982). Puerto Rican organizations such as the Young Lords Party also saw important connections with the black community, and sought to challenge the racism within the Puerto Rican community. "Puerto Ricans like myself [Pablo Guzmán], who are darker-skinned, who look like Afro-Americans, couldn't do that [avoid seeing connections between the black and the Puerto Rican experiences in the United States], 'cause to do that would be to escape into a kind of fantasy. Because before people called me a spic, they called me a nigger" (Young Lords Party 1971:74).

The racialization of Puerto Ricans on the mainland, however, does not depend solely on skin color:

> No matter how "blonde or blue-eyed" a person may be, and no matter how successfully he can "pass" as white, the moment that person self-identifies as Puerto Rican, he enters the labyrinth of racial Otherness. Puerto Ricans of all colors have become a racialized group in the imaginary of white Americans, whose racist stereotypes cause them to see Puerto Ricans as lazy, violent, stupid, and dirty. Although Puerto Ricans form a phenotypically variable group, they have become a new "race" in the United States. . . . The demeaning classification as "spiks" in New York designates the negative symbolic capital attached to being Puerto Rican. (Grosfoguel and Georgas 1996:193)

Racial prejudice, of course, is not unknown in Puerto Rico (e.g., Jimenez Román 1996; Rodríguez-Morazzani 1996; Seda Bonilla 1983; Zenón Cruz 1975), despite frequent disavowal of its existence there. It is generally conceded to be less virulent, however, than on the mainland. Racial classification in Puerto Rico is based more on phenotype and class than on genotype. A spectrum of racial types exists, with categories delineated by color, class, facial features, and hair texture. Intermarriage across "racial" lines is fairly frequent, and access to housing, voting, institutions, and government policies has never been conferred to people based on racial group membership (Rodríguez 1989).

The differing responses of island and mainland communities to Mattel's 1997 release of "Puerto Rican Barbie" (see Navarro 1997) suggest the greater racial awareness of mainland Puerto Ricans. The doll was well received in Puerto Rico as a welcome recognition of the island's culture. Many mainland Puerto Ricans, however, took offense at her light skin, Anglicized features, and colonial-tiered dress–as well as the accompanying historical information that ignores the presence of the island's original inhabitants, the Tainos, on the island that Columbus "discovered."

The differentiation that exists between mainland and island, cultures can be brought home all too forcefully to those who return to the island and find themselves regarded as "Americanized" (Martinez 1988). Puerto Ricans looking to find their roots and true home on the "lost tropical paradise" so often invoked in the nostalgic discourse of their parents (Klor de Alva 1989) may be particularly stunned by the rejection; the main character in Pedro Juan Soto's "Hot Land, Cold Season" asks, "If I am an American, a gringo, a Yankee down here, and up north I am a Puerto Rican, a spik; what in hell am I really? Who am I? Where do I belong?" (in Seda Bonilla 1977:115). But at the same time that mainland cultural patterns have evolved in directions that differentiate mainlanders in important ways from those on the island, a pattern of circular migration between the island and mainland—the *va y ven* (back-and-forth) phenomenon that emerged so prominently in the late 1960s—also fosters the cultural and linguistic revitalization of mainland communities and ongoing connections to the island. "Puerto Rican culture today," notes Nuyorican ethnographer Juan Flores, "is a culture of commuting, of a constant back-and-forth transfer between two intertwining zones" (1991:18).

The circular migration in which so many Puerto Ricans participate appears initially to be solely a matter of individual choice, and driven by people's perceptions of where chances for employment appear relatively better.[5] When unemployment on the mainland rises, fewer migrate and "return migration" rates climb; when conditions worsen on the island, the reverse occurs (Maldonado 1976). Macro-level analyses, however (e.g., Bonilla and Campos 1981; Morales 1986), shift the focus to the forces underlying such decisions, the economic and political dependence of Puerto

Rico and its position in the global economy, and to the consequences for Puerto Rican migrants:

> Direct colonial relations, as an uninterrupted legacy and ever-present reality, govern the motives and outcomes of the whole migratory and settlement process, and fix a consistently low ceiling on the group's expectations and opportunities. For Puerto Ricans, the "blessings" of American citizenship have been even worse than mixed. Under the constant sway of colonial machinations, citizenship has been a set-up for stigmatization and pathological treatment, more than outweighing, over the long haul, any advantageous exemption from the most pressing of immigrant woes. (Flores 1996:183)

Analysts of the Puerto Rican experience argue that in many respects the migrants closely resemble "colonial emigrants," such as Jamaicans in London or Martinicans in Paris, and that the legacy of colonialism has much in common with the legacy of slavery experienced by African Americans (Grosfoguel 1995; Grosfoguel and Georas 1996).

The first post–World War II mainland-born or -raised Puerto Rican generation also came of age during the anticolonial and civil rights movements of the 1960s. Puerto Rican leaders joined other cultural nationalists, organizing politically to improve their communities and asserting their entitlement to a distinct identity and pride in their ethnic heritage. Like other racial minorities, by the late 1960s and early 1970s mainland Puerto Ricans were actively challenging assimilationist models of incorporation into the American mainstream for failing to factor in the significance of racial and political oppression and for devaluing cultural pluralism.

A significant effect of this self-examination and empowerment has been to launch a challenge to the binary system operating in the United States that permits no middle ground: one should speak either Spanish (to be dropped as soon as possible) or English; identify as either black or white; be either Puerto Rican or American (see Bruce-Noboa 1987; Flores 1985; Flores, Attinasi, and Pedraza 1981; Klor de Alva 1988). The rejection of those assumptions by a highly visible and vocal segment among both the Puerto Rican and Mexican American populations, and their rechristening of themselves as "Nuyoricans" (or other versions of the term) and "Chicanos," respectively, attests to similar processes taking place within both communities.

> We are bilingual and bicultural, and for both Chicanos and Nuyoricans those terms signal a complex duality of transcendence and denial, harmony and imposition, solidarity and disadvantage. (Flores 1985:1)

> These groups claim legitimate residence in the space between the poles, and from there they demand and exercise the right to self-determination. They have pondered their situation, decided that it is their real state . . . (and) blatantly assert a new hybrid identity, which in turn redefines the nationalistic binary opposition into a preliminary dialectic form which has begun to spring the logical, irrepressible international synthesis. . . . The names are signs of new identity, perhaps still in the making, but nonetheless real. (Bruce-Noboa 1987:232–4)

For Chicanos, notes Juan Flores, the borderlands they inhabit should be perceived "not as kind of a no-man's-land, but as a well-spring of cultural innovation and identification" (Flores 1991:18). Similarly, the Nuyorican experience "is showing how it is possible to struggle through the quandary of biculturalism and affirm the straddling position. Not with the claim to be both but, as the title of a poem by Sandra María Esteves words it, with a pride in being 'not neither'" (Flores 1991:18).

Much of these general experiences of Puerto Ricans are

visible in their specific situation in Arnhem. There the Puerto Rican population is "racially" mixed and aware of the racial prejudices surrounding them. Puerto Ricans in Arnhem remain heavily concentrated in the secondary labor market,[6] and, for the most part, residentially segregated from the white community. While many in the community are second- and third-generation "mainlanders," there is a segment of the population that moves back and forth between the mainland and the island, and one routinely hears Spanish, intermingled with English, spoken in the stores, in the schools, and on the streets. In the East End, storefront churches and the local Catholic church conduct services in Spanish. At the Latin music store, run by a local disc jockey who broadcasts live on Saturday afternoons, a visitor can hear everything from traditional plenas and boleros to salsa music and "Latino rap." Pictures of Tito Puente, Celia Cruz, Lisa M, Queen Latifah, and KT of Latin Empire cover the walls, and one shelf houses devotional candles painted with an image of the Virgin Mary alongside ingredients needed for Santería rituals. In any bodega scattered throughout the neighborhood one can pick up a Spanish-language newspaper, purchase just about every Goya product imaginable, and catch up on the latest local gossip with the proprietor. Cable television offers viewers access to the Spanish-speaking world on Univision. Ads for travel to the island hang in the store windows, tangible evidence of the enduring connections to Puerto Rico.

Puerto Ricans and Relations to Schools

Minority community leaders in Arnhem raised concerns about the educational status of Puerto Rican youth that echo those voiced throughout the twentieth century. Difficulties encountered by Puerto Rican students on the island were replicated in their schooling experiences on the mainland. A 1935 report issued by the New York Chamber of Commerce placed the "problem" for mainland students in the community and among the students themselves, based on conclusions made after testing Spanish-dominant students in English. The report's authors concluded that many of the students were "retarded in school according to age . . .[and] so low in intelligence that they require education of a simplified, manual sort, preferably industrial, for they cannot adjust in a school system emphasizing the three R's. . . . [They] betray a family mentality which should not be permitted admission here, further to deteriorate standards already so seriously impaired by mass immigration of the lowest levels of populations of many nations" (cited in Rodriguez-Morazzani 1997:61).

In the 1960s the Puerto Rican community on the mainland, joining in struggles for bilingual education and community control, organized to actively challenge such depictions and the educational systems in place for their children (Pedraza 1997; Rodriguez-Morazzani 1997). Their concerns were not unfounded: in 1964 the Puerto Rican Community Development Project released statistics on educational outcomes in 1964 that were appalling. Only 13 percent of Puerto Ricans over the age of twenty-five had graduated from high school the previous year, compared to 40 percent of whites, and only 1.6 percent of the academic (regents) diplomas had gone to Puerto Ricans (Rodriguez-Morazzani 1997:62).

Today, more than thirty years later, Puerto Ricans, along with other Latinos,[7] African Americans, and Native Americans, continue to lag behind the mainstream in school performance and remain concentrated on the lower rungs of the socioeconomic ladder. As a whole Puerto Ricans fare significantly worse than their white counterparts on conventional measures of educational achievement that are linked to the likelihood of continuing education and ultimately to economic well-being. Only three of every five Puerto Ricans over age twenty-five have finished high school, and 50 percent more whites than Puerto Ricans between the ages of eighteen and twenty-one attend college. Whites are also more than twice as likely as Puerto Ricans to graduate from college.[8]

The connections between educational success and future earnings go far to illuminate the problem of poverty in the Puerto Rican community. In 1995 male college graduates averaged $61,717 and females $37,924, whereas high school graduates fared much worse: $32,708 for males and $21,961 for females. The average income for dropouts is even more alarming: males earn $23,338 and females $16,319. Significantly, average earnings of male dropouts have actually *declined* by more than $6,000 in 1995 dollars since 1979 and earnings of male high school graduates by almost $5,000 (McCormick and Press 1997).

Even when students of color do graduate from high school, in retrospect the quality of education they receive is not necessarily equivalent to that enjoyed by white students. Minority students in deteriorating inner cities across the nation attend schools segregated by poverty and race, where per pupil spending may be half the amount spent in wealthier suburban districts (Kozol 1991). School spending per pupil in Manhasset, New York (on Long Island), for instance, was $15,084 in 1989–1990 while New York City per pupil spending was $7,299; in Niles Township High School (a Chicago suburb) spending per pupil was $9,371 while in Chicago (all grades) spending was $5,265. In 1990, spending per pupil in the Arnhem school district was $5,630; the four other school districts in the county spent from $900 to $2,300 more per pupil.[9]

When educational attainment is held constant, minorities will still earn less than whites (see Rodríguez 1989; Sue and Padilla 1986). The extent to which discrimination in the labor market persists is not easily documented, but findings in a 1990 Urban Institute Report are informative. Young Anglo and Latino men were paired and given identical resumes and then sent out to apply for jobs. Sixty-four percent of the Anglos were invited for an interview, compared to 48 percent of the Latinos; 43 percent of the Anglos received job offers, compared to 28 percent of the Latinos (Cross et al. 1990, cited in Cordero Guzmán 1993).

The cumulative result of all this is that Latinos, like people of color in general, are much more likely than whites to live in poverty and experience unemployment. In the United States in 1995, 16 percent of white children lived in households below poverty level; a shocking 39 percent of Latino children and 42 percent of African-American children were similarly situated (Smith et al. 1997). Per capita income in 1993 was $16,800 for whites, $9,863 for blacks, and $8,830 for Hispanics (*American Almanac 1995–1996*:479).

These statistics, grim as they may be, fail to capture the situation of Puerto Ricans who, when disaggregated from all Latinos, fare even worse. Statistics published by the Children's Defense Fund (1989 data) better capture their reality: while 37.1 percent of all Latino children lived below the poverty level, 48.4 percent of Puerto Rican children were below poverty level (Miranda 1991, cited in Cordero Guzmán 1993). Puerto Ricans remain among the poorest racial/ethnic groups in the United States; in 1993, 36.5 percent lived below the poverty level, surpassing African Americans (33.1 percent) and other Latino groups.[10] Labor market statistics likewise highlight the dramatic differences across groups in the labor market. In 1994 unemployment as reported the U.S. Bureau of Labor Statistics (not taking into consideration those who had given up looking for work or the extent to which people were underemployed) was 9.9 percent for Hispanics (11.6 percent for Puerto Ricans), compared to 5.3 percent for whites and 11.5 percent for African Americans (*American Almanac 1995–1996*:400).

Government policies have provided little relief from such grim figures. A recent international study (Smith et al. 1997) documented, based on data available, that the United States was the only wealthy industrialized country in 1986 to have double-digit child poverty rates *after* adjusting for taxes and government transfers. The U.S. child poverty rate was 20.4 percent after transfers; rates in other similarly situated countries were far lower: Canada 9.3 percent, the United Kingdom 7.4 percent, France 4.6 percent, and the former West Germany 2.8 percent.

Nor have U.S. courts provided assistance toward ameliorating the inequities that persist for students attending schools in impoverished communities. Government support for changing the status quo, which characterized much of the 1960s, had eroded by the 1970s, undermining the potential for change that came about with the Supreme Court decision in *Brown v. Board of Education*. In 1973, for instance, in *San Antonio Independent School District v. Rodriguez* the Supreme Court overturned by a five-to-four margin a federal district court decision that found Texas in violation of the equal protection clause of the U.S. Constitution for providing children in an impoverished, mostly Latino school district less than half as much funding per pupil as a nearby wealthy district. As a consequence, in Texas, as in many states, dramatically unequal funding for wealthy Anglo versus impoverished Latino communities persists. A similar attempt to foster greater educational equity was narrowly overturned in 1974, when in *Milliken v. Bradley* the Supreme Court overruled (again by a five-to-four margin) a district court order that sought to integrate the children of Detroit with those in wealthier suburbs. The outcome, as Kozol noted, has been to "lock black and Latino children into the isolation and abandonment we see today" (1994:704). Minority youth today are far more likely to attend schools with high poverty rates, where differences in the learning environment and the level of financial and human resources can negatively affect students' opportunities to obtain a quality education. Sixty-five percent of black and Latino students and 57 percent of American Indian/Alaskan Native students attended such schools during the 1993–1994 school year, compared to 27 percent of white students (Smith et al. 1997).

The executive branch has not worked to promote equality either. Since 1980 the civil rights division of the Justice Department has brought forward no new desegregation cases; meanwhile, the Education Department has phased out its civil rights operation. At the same time, changes in the nation's economic structure in recent decades and conservative government policies have contributed to a growing gap between rich and poor and a shrinking middle class (Harrington 1984; Lind 1995; Wills 1996),[11] making the possibility of improvement in the near future even more remote.

Behind much of the current resistance to demands by minorities for school reform is the unquestioned assumption that schools function as meritocracies, constituting a level playing field in which all students have essentially the same opportunities to succeed. Clearly the gross disparities in funding suggest otherwise. It is against this backdrop, in which unequal funding may translate into less money for resources, lower salaries for teachers, crumbling buildings, lowered morale for students and educators, and messages to minority parents that their children are being "written off," that debates about the schooling performance of minority children take place.[12]

Perceptions of Opportunity and Minority Community Relations to Schools

Within anthropology, two important lines of reasoning have emerged in addressing minority student performance in schools, and they look in opposite directions. One focuses on what happens *within* schools that contributes to minority students' lack of success, the "cultural difference" approach (which also challenges the myth of schools as meritocracies). The other focuses on what happens *outside* schools, the "cultural ecological" approach put forward by influential anthropologist John Ogbu (1978; 1987; 1988). In reviewing the two approaches I argue for attention to both the ways in which school practices and assumptions empower particular groups who enter school with more "cultural capital" than their nonmainstream counterparts (taken up in Chapter 5), and also to the significance of a group's sociohistoric experiences and the contemporary dynamics of power relations between minority and mainstream communities in explaining minority community orientation to the schools.

One consequence of the unequal treatment of minorities historically is visible in minority community relations to schools. As the works of anthropologists focusing on macrostructural analyses of school–community relations document, oppressed minorities do not share the faith of middle-class white communities in their schools. In laying out his argument Ogbu points to a significant body of literature demonstrating intergroup variation in minority students' educational achievement: African Americans, Mexican Americans, Puerto Ricans, and Native Americans perform relatively poorly in public schools whereas more recently arrived minorities, such as Punjabi and Chinese immigrants, are more successful. Not only are there significant differences among groups, but the performance of any given group appears to vary in differing contexts, depending on its relationship to the dominant society. The Burakumin, for instance, an oppressed and stigmatized minority in Japan, fare poorly in Japanese schools but are academically successful in the United States, where they are perceived as Japanese and lose their status as a distinctive stigmatized group (DeVos 1973).

According to Ogbu (1978; 1987; 1988), explaining such variable outcomes requires adopting what he terms a "cultural ecological" or "perceived labor market" explanation that looks to the history of each group, the group's relationship to the dominant society, and the cultural adaptations that develop in response to occupying a "castelike" status. Ogbu divides minorities into distinct groups based on their histories of incorporation into the United States (and likewise in other national contexts): castelike, autonomous, and immigrant minorities. African Americans, Puerto Ricans, Chicanos, and Native Americans are "castelike" involuntary minorities. They share a history of forced incorporation into the United States, have been victims of prejudice and discrimination, and have faced "job ceilings" throughout much of their time in the United States, limiting their upward mobility regardless of the amount of education they attain. Autonomous minorities—Jews and Mormons in the United States, for instance—possess a distinctive ethnic, religious, linguistic, or cultural identity but have no history of social, economic, or political subordination in the United States; such groups perform adequately in schools. The third category, voluntary "immigrant minorities," are those who have come to the United States more or less willingly to seek a better life. They are likely to experience problems resulting from their cultural and linguistic differences, but they generally fare well in schools. These include Chinese (Ogbu and Matute-Bianche 1986), Central American (Suarez-Orozco 1987), and Punjabi[13] (Gibson 1987) immigrants.

The important contrast is between immigrant and castelike minorities. Immigrant newcomers to the United States have as their primary reference point their homeland communities; although they may face prejudice and discrimination in their new home they tend to rationalize it, seeing it not as a permanent feature but as something to be expected given their status as newcomers. In considering their lives in the United States they are likely to look back to their lands of origin. They perceive people there as worse off, but if all else fails they know they can return to their homelands.

Involuntary minorities, on the other hand, have as their reference point mainstream American society. They are longtime residents and citizens and correctly perceive that, regardless of how hard they struggle, they have as a group been denied the same opportunities for success in the United States that have been accorded Euro-Americans. Ogbu argues that these people are distrustful of public institutions such as schools, and doubt that hard work in school will pay off. "Secondary" cultural characteristics that develop after their entry into the United States, such as dialect differences and styles of dress, become markers of identity that are maintained in opposition to the mainstream society. They may develop alternative folk theories for getting ahead that incorporate particular survival strategies designed to allow them to circumvent, reduce, or eliminate economic, political, and other barriers to success.[14]

Ogbu's work points to the significance of community–school relations, understanding community both as a specific local site, and as a general historical community. He underscores the need to consider the historical and sociocultural contexts in explaining intergroup relations to schools and differences in minority school performance. He links labor market conditions, socially shared perceptions growing out of the common experiences of minority members, and individuals' thoughts and actions.

Puerto Ricans in many respects fit Ogbu's "involuntary minority" characterization. As colonial migrants they have a status level unlike those of immigrants from other nations, more closely resembling African Americans, Chicanos, and Native Americans. In migrating to the mainland they experienced pervasive racism, discrimination, and cultural conflicts, which, along with structural changes in the economy, effectively blocked their upward mobility as a group. The colonial legacy of forced Americanization and the assimilationist orientation of most of the schools attended by Puerto Rican children both on the island and on the mainland (e.g., Hidalgo 1992; Rodríguez 1989), alongside possible misunderstandings growing out of cultural and linguistic differences between school and home (e.g., McCollum 1989; Zentella 1985), are possible sources of distrust and might decrease perceptions of the legitimacy of schools.

As we will see in the following chapter, in Arnhem it was "involuntary minorities" (mostly Puerto Rican) that most strongly expressed their sense of alienation from the schools. They argued that racism was pervasive and that the schools further contributed to minority student failure through exclusion and denigration of students' cultural identities and language. The groups that Ogbu would term "immigrant minorities" (Costa Ricans and Asian Americans) did not contest the efficacy of the schools in providing educational opportunities for their children. It was overwhelmingly members of the Puerto Rican population in Arnhem who challenged the popular perception of schools as meritocratic institutions affording all groups equal opportunities for upward mobility. Their challenge, as we shall later see, also finds support in the literature that questions the role of schools in the production of unequal educational outcomes.

Anthropologist John Ogbu's cultural ecological approach usefully draws attention to the significance of the larger sociohistoric context in which oppressed minority community orientations to schooling are shaped. Certain areas, however, remain underanalyzed, including intragroup variability, the role of class, and the influence of local conditions. Jay MacLeod (1995), for example, tracks a group of working-class black male adolescents who profess faith in the American dream and conform to school expectations and compares them to a group of working-class white male adolescents who exhibit oppositional identities and reject the American dream. Douglas Foley (1991) describes middle-class Mexican Americans who exhibit oppositional identities but succeed academically. Ann Locke Davidson's findings of minority youth who are "both pro-academic and oppositional" (1996:61) also challenge the notion that oppositional identities are necessarily incompatible with school success.

Ogbu also measures success in terms of existing school criteria and not the adequacy of the system to address diverse needs. The ways in which school practices may contribute to the production of unequal educational outcomes (see, for example, Davidson 1996; Erickson 1987; Fine 1987; Foley 1991; Kohl 1994) remain underanalyzed, though more recently Ogbu has begun to address such issues (e.g., Ogbu and Simons 1998). Some schools or programs have been found to be more successful with diverse youth (cf. Mehan, Hubbard, and Villanueva 1994; Meier 1995), and culturally compatible pedagogies have produced greater student engagement (e.g., Heath 1983a; Moll and Díaz 1987). Student resistance also is not accorded the possibility of being a valid and affirmative response to stigmatized identities and pedagogies that leave students feeling "left out" and "pushed out" of schools (e.g., MacLeod 1995; Walsh 1991; Zanger 1994; Zentella 1997). That the "cultural capital" of mainstream students is privileged in schools and the symbolic resources of nonmainstream students are devalued is left largely unquestioned. A different tradition of ethnographic research has paid greater attention to this matter, an issue we shall return to in Chapter 5.

In Arnhem both community–school relations and the treatment of cultural and linguistic differences emerged as important dimensions of the educational arena. The community conflict over ethnic and racial prejudice and schooling illustrates the very differing relationships between school and community that exist for Arnhem's white and minority communities, a matter to which we will now turn.

4 Telling Stories

> They [seniors] say that their parents or grandparents came from Poland, Ireland, and that kind of thing, Italy, and when they came here they could not speak English either, but it gave them no excuse not to try, go to school, try to be the best you can, try to learn the American ways. . . . Their grandparents, their parents worked hard in these mills and stuff to see to it, that they got educated. Their parents, grandparents, were not trouble, they did not go on welfare, they were not shown any special favoritism, they were not given anything, in other words. And they don't think the Puerto Ricans should be either. They should have to try like everybody else. If they can't try then get out. They have no patience for the idea that you come here and go on welfare.
>
> —Paul Bowers, Euro-American teacher, lifelong Arnhem resident, age fifty-four

Racialized groups are frequently evaluated for their fitness as members in the national community from the perspective of the "immigrant analogy" or "ethnic myth" (Steinberg 1989). This assumption rests on the premise that "there are no essential long-term differences—in relation to the larger society—between the *third world* or racial minorities and the European ethnic groups" (Blauner 1972:5). All ethnic groups are seen as similarly situated in terms of the structures of opportunity.

Despite sustained challenges beginning in the 1960s and 1970s, in recent years this assumption has taken on a new life in public discourse. Although arguments for the genetic inferiority of racialized groups that once provided legitimation for societal and educational inequalities may no longer be acceptable in the mainstream (Omi and Winant 1994), these inequalities are now ascribed to the cultural and linguistic practices of poor Americans of color (see, for example, Gregory 1993; Steinberg 1989; Urciuoli 1996). Frequently the "immigrant analogy" underlies arguments against the government's "coddling" of racial and linguistic minorities through various government-sponsored programs. It fails to recognize the relevance of a history of racial oppression for understanding the stubborn persistence of racial and economic inequalities in contemporary society. It assumes that racial inequalities can be eradicated through eliminating individual acts of racism attributable to individual attitudes and prejudices. Most problematically, within such discourses the failure of a particular group to achieve parity with other ethnic groups situates the responsibility for failed upward mobility within the group's culture or its individual members' behaviors, thereby averting attention from the differing historical trajectories and structural constraints that confront contemporary racialized groups.

These discourses, in turn, provide a rationale for social policies and legitimation of the existing system of inequities. It becomes essential, therefore, to examine the discourses that construct economically marginalized groups as somehow defective or pathological, or that deny the relevance of the experiences of racialized groups in explaining persisting inequities, in order to find out how people come to accept these assumptions and reject evidence to the contrary.

Contemporary struggles over public school curricula and programs are also, in part, struggles over the validity of this immigrant analogy. "Safe" differences among groups, in the wake of the "new ethnicity" of the 1970s, today are permissible. Not surprisingly, multicultural curricula in the schools has most frequently tended to take the form of celebrating diversity, what critics label "heroes and holidays," "foods, festivals and famous folks," or in England "saris and samosas" approaches. These celebratory moves have frequently evolved into advocacy of cultural pluralism and identity politics, and such forms of multicultural education have been criticized for their failure to address issues of "power, hegemony, and oppression" (Kenyatta and Tai 1997). However, multicultural education initiatives in the United States have also moved *beyond* "safe" differences (e.g., Banks 1991; Cortés 1991; Levine et al. 1995; Nieto 1996; see also Newfield and Gordon 1996). Leading advocates in the field refute popular visions of the nation as a color-blind land of equal opportunity for all. They advocate critical pedagogy and antiracist teaching, which incorporates a more inclusive history and literature curriculum that addresses the history of racial oppression in the United States.[1]

In Arnhem, events occurring late in the summer of 1991 gave impetus to a protracted public debate regarding the need for multicultural and bilingual education. In examining mainstream community and school discourse during this period I found widespread acceptance of the immigrant analogy, with ethnic success stories used by community "old-timers" to "discipline" those judged to have failed through a lack of hard work. The comparability of the Puerto Rican experience to that of earlier ethnic groups was taken for granted, with Puerto Ricans measured against earlier ethnic groups and found wanting. Problematically, within such discourses the continued maintenance of Spanish (including "Spanglish") among Puerto Ricans was seen as an indicator of the speaker's unwillingness to conform to "American" ways. Bilingualism was depicted as a threat to national unity and a key contributor to the lower socioeconomic status of the Puerto Rican community.

Close examination of the public discourse of minority community members and white ethnics in Arnhem reveals conflicting constructions of group identity and explanations for the social and educational status of minorities. Taken together, these are *telling* stories that I argue can provide important insights into what contributes to the current struggle over educational programs and curricula in the nation's schools. To that end, I offer and analyze in depth the stories told by two individuals—one a Latina community organizer,[2] the other a Polish-American senior citizen. I also construct and contrast the collective stories about "being" American as told by Euro-American seniors and minority speakers in the community, using discourse analysis to provide each group's interpretive framework. As Puerto Rican mainland migration out of large metropolitan areas and into smaller, more homogeneous communities accelerates (e.g., Stains 1994), struggles over culture, language, and identity issues such as those taken up here become increasingly common, problematic in their polarizing consequences and failure to address underlying issues that drive the stubborn persistence of racial and ethnic inequalities.

Background to the Debate in Arnhem

In the 1970s the Arnhem school district began offering English as a Second Language (ESL) classes in the city's schools. Policies, practices, and administrative commitment to the program were uneven throughout the 1980s. The ESL high school teacher, for instance, "lost" his classroom at one point and was forced to work in the library. Another time the high school program was cut back and the teacher was assigned to work part time in a school across town. In 1990 junior high school ESL students attended class only on alternate days when not taking gym class.

By 1991, when the community conflict erupted, 17 percent of the district's students were Latino, 2 percent African American, and 1 percent Asian American. Except for one African-American teacher, the teachers were Euro-American; roughly half had grown up in Arnhem. Prior to the intense debate there was little talk among these teachers of how schools might best adapt to the changing student population. The school district did take some initial steps in the direction of addressing the needs of Latino students: it offered an introductory course in Spanish for teachers and scheduled a presentation by speakers from the organization "Culture Link" to sensitize teachers to the needs of culturally different students. The Culture Link session, however, backfired. During the presentation teachers began to ignore the speakers, converse among themselves, and in some instances even walk out on the speakers. Teachers angrily reported afterwards that the speakers had failed to address students' and parents' responsibilities in ensuring educational success, instead laying the blame for unsatisfactory minority school performance—"once again"—at the teachers' feet.

As early as 1989, meanwhile, a local Latino community agency had detailed in a "Latino Community Needs Assessment" report its growing concerns about the education of Latino youth in the district. This report and a subsequent one issued in 1991 stressed the need for the district to acknowledge and affirm diversity and to work toward ameliorating differential educational outcomes along racial and ethnic lines[3]:

> Latino students [in Arnhem] have a drop out rate that is twice that of non-Hispanics [12.3 percent for Hispanics and 5.1 percent for non-Hispanics]. The long term goal of all involved parties is for these [Latino] children to be able to succeed in the school environment, yet be able to retain their cultural values and traditions. . . .
>
> If standards used to instruct Spanish-speakers (or by that matter non-English speakers) are, or appear to be, inferior to those utilized among native speakers, a significant population of students become alienated. . . .
>
> Addressing this problem will not only boost the self-esteem of a growing minority population, but enhance the well-being and future of the entire society. . . .
>
> Too often, Latino students are given the strong and intimidating message to, "Speak English, forget Spanish!" In this sense, they are made to feel ashamed of their native language. . . .
>
> The fact that the mainstream curriculum is geared almost a hundred percent towards white European history, traditions, and ideals, only serves to devalue the importance and essence of the Latino heritage and its contribution to modern society. . . .
>
> Presently, there is a substantial lack of qualified bilingual personnel on staff within the school system. As a result, Latino parents who cannot speak English feel isolated and unconnected with the school system and with their child's educational career. . . .
>
> Educational standards for secondary school Latino students are often inferior to those of other students. . . . Minority and low income students are not being encouraged to pursue Regents and Honor programs. . . .
>
> As the New York State Social Studies Syllabi states, fostering pride in cultural achievement is a step toward building self-esteem and self-confidence. If Latino students continue to see that their culture is not appreciated, it is unrealistic to expect progress in their educational achievements. . . .

The report was unsuccessful in convincing school board members or school officials of the need for significant change, however.

The Conflict Erupts

Conflicts within the community came to the fore late in the summer of 1991 as a result of a local school board member's public response to proposed revisions in the New York State social studies syllabus (see Sobol 1989). John Marris, a Euro-American[4] senior citizen, Ivy League graduate, and former fiscal officer of a local carpet factory, had recently been elected to the school board by a strong senior citizen turnout on a platform advocating fiscal conservatism.[5] When asked by a journalist how he felt about the strong multicultural emphasis in the recent New York State Education Department report on the need for social studies reform,[6] Marris stated that he hoped minorities who had made "genuine contributions" would be included in history lessons, but

> you have to understand that some contributions have been disasters. The Spanish people in South America, for instance, can't run a country without total chaos. You don't find that in Western civilization because people there are reasonably intelligent and know how to do things.

His response, printed in a newspaper article covering the New York State Education Department recommendations, made page one of the local paper. Marris's comments were immediately challenged by members of a local Latino community agency. A letter to the editor pointed out that Hitler's Germany was also part of "Western civilization," and that the United States had played an active role in supporting Latin American dictators. Within the Latino community Marris became a symbol of bigotry and insensitivity, a view supported by the editorial staff and the reporter of the local paper covering the debate, as well as by many in the Euro-American community.

Despite demands by members of the Latino and African-American communities[7] at the next board meeting for an apology, Marris continued to insist that his comments were not intended to be a reflection on the local Latino community. Several days later, when asked by a local journalist to comment on the public outcry over his remarks, he said that he had canceled his vacation plans: "I'm afraid of vandalism. Some of the younger Hispanics—high on drugs—may decide to retaliate because I haven't issued an apology for my earlier comments" (*Arnhem Record*). Minority community leaders [8] (one African-American woman and several Latinos) subsequently demanded his resignation from the school board. He steadfastly refused to step down.

At the next board meeting approximately twenty-five Latinos from the community, many waving picket signs, crowded into the packed boardroom. Also in attendance were approximately the same number of Latino students from a nearby college who had carried out informational picketing at the high school and talked with local Latino students earlier in the week. The minority contingent (overwhelmingly Latino) ringed the board table, making numerous impassioned speeches, demanding Marris's resignation, and arguing for changes in educational programs and policies that would better serve the needs of the minority community.

Regional newspapers, sensing a newsworthy event, began to provide extensive coverage of the growing conflict. Marris ultimately apologized for his remarks about *local* Latinos, saying at the same time that his error was in making the statement to the reporter. Refusing, however, to apologize for his original comments, he again insisted that he had said nothing wrong and that his statements were not intended to be a reflection on the local Latino community. Further, he did not think the comments were relevant to his ability as a school board member to serve all students equally well.

At the following board meeting the angry Latino audience was joined by approximately the same number of Euro-American senior citizens. Within the largely conservative senior citizen population Marris had quickly become a martyr, symbolic of the hardworking American (white) community that they felt had borne the brunt of attacks by minorities in recent years. In angry, impassioned speeches, Marris supporters attacked the local Latino population. The public session, usually only twenty minutes long, had to be stopped after an hour, and then only when one of the board members proposed a public forum be scheduled to air community grievances.

The Public Forum and Its Aftermath

The public forum was held in the local high school auditorium and televised live by the local cable station. Roughly one hundred people attended, slightly more than half of them local Euro-American senior citizens. Several off-duty police officers hired by the school district were stationed outside the school building and auditorium during the forum, and their presence heightened an already tense situation. Approximately fifteen to twenty Latino university students were present, and roughly twenty to twenty-five local minority community members, most of them Latino. Each speaker was required to sign up in advance of the opening of the meeting and was given three minutes to state his or her views. In all twenty-nine individuals spoke, including seven Euro-American senior citizens on the school board and from the community,[9] five Latino high school students and seven Latino university students, three minority community leaders, two Euro-American religious leaders, and four middle-aged Euro-Americans, three of whom spoke in support of minority proposals.

The conflict played out at this public forum and the school board meetings remained front-page news for several weeks and a heated topic of debate in letters to the editor of the paper and on the local radio talk shows for several months. Various seniors were regularly consulted by the local media for their opinions, in large measure due to their voting power, their claim to legitimacy as community spokespersons (having been "born and raised here"), and their control of the school board and power in local government. The Latino population, with little power locally, received support from the local Latino community agency and Latino college students who had become interested in the debate. In response to letters from minority community members the New York State Education Department also became involved, sending a team of investigators to look into charges that the educational needs of minority (in particular Latino) students were not being adequately met.

As is often the case, local participants and the media both framed the two sides as being in polar opposition to one another,[10] (Euro-American) "seniors" on one side and "Latinos" (or oftentimes "minorities") on the other. The most vocal members, those who gained the ear of the media and sought to win others over to their side, represented themselves as speaking for all their members. It is safe to assume that was not in fact the case. I use the terms "Seniors" and "Minorities" (capitalized) when referring to these group representations, reserving the lowercase form for discussions of each of these groups.

Studying Stories / Constructing Frameworks

The personal narratives we construct from past events in our lives and our reconstructions of the stories we hear growing up are important mechanisms for revealing our "presentation of self," both to ourselves and to others (cf. Benmayor et al. 1988; Goffman 1959). The stories we tell help us organize and make sense of our world and where we fit into it. They have strategic value as we attempt to move others to see our own visions of ourselves and our world.

Given that one's reading of the past is shaped by present circumstances, and one's experience of the present is shaped by knowledge of the past (Connerton 1989), we can anticipate significant differences in the narrative content of Euro-American senior stories and racial minority stories. For groups from differing structural locations in society such stories come to "mean" differently, both in content and in function (Benmayor et al. 1988). If we look at the narratives of Euro-American seniors, on one hand, and Latinos and African Americans, on the other, as revealed in their public discourse (letters to the editor, and public meetings), we can trace some recurring themes. These themes also turn up in other printed materials and in public speeches, interviews, and radio talk show callers' comments. In these we can see the content areas that are significant to the speakers and the semiotic building blocks that comprise the conceptual framework through which they make sense of their worlds (Agar 1983; Woolard 1989). These public discourses reveal the interpretive frameworks through which Arnhem residents understand the conflict and help us to understand the community's responses.

The Senior Story

Much that was central to the Senior perspective as it was articulated in public texts is revealed in a letter to the editor written by a Polish American resident. The letter appeared after two months of angry charges and countercharges in the media and at public meetings.

> To the editor:
>
> There is no need to debate or question which language should be spoken in these United States as the universal language. It is to the benefit of all nationalities to speak English, so that all can understand each other. . . .
>
> The ambitious . . . built America. . . . They faced ridicule and name calling and survived . . . worked . . . for a few coins per hour. . . .
>
> They asked for nothing. They spoke their native tongue in their homes, communities and business places. They had no modern schools, they learned to speak English from their co-workers . . . and [in the] streets.
>
> My mother taught me to read and write Polish as a child. She sent me to a one-room schoolhouse to learn to read, write and spell English. . . .
>
> The Indians . . . [lost] their land by force. Today the Indian nation speaks English. Their native tongue (I presume) they speak among themselves. . . .
>
> It should be essential that all immigrants go to school to learn English, so they can read and write, to vote and converse with their fellow men. . . .
>
> If language becomes an issue, there will be hard feelings amongst all. . . . There will be the danger of dividing these United States into sections like Europe. Stand together and be an immigrant American under one God, one government, one flag and one universal language—English. Many speak English the world over. . . .
>
> Let us lay aside our personal enmities. . . . (*Arnhem Record,* September 30, 1991)

Visible throughout the text are widely recognized American symbols: the immigrant "muscle" and self-sacrifice that built the nation; the one-room schoolhouse of bygone and better days; the English language as a symbol of national unity and culture. By way of responding to Latinos' demands for a bilingual education program—never explicitly mentioned—the writer presents a romantic vision of earlier European immigrants to which he negatively contrasts, largely by implication, current Latino (im)migrants.

Through the use of the past tense and reference to bygone days, the author attributes virtues of hard work and self-sacrifice to earlier immigrant groups. He then shifts to a discussion of today's immigrants without attributing such characteristics to them. Immigrants of the past went to school to learn English, but immigrants today, by implication, do not. Unlike immigrants of the past, he implies, current newcomers arrive expecting too much, making too much of discrimination, asking for special favors, trying to change the country (language) rather than accept it and find ways to fit in. Finally, by referring to local Latinos as "immigrants," although 75 percent are Puerto Ricans (all U.S. citizens and many of them second- and-third generation mainlanders), the author situates Puerto Ricans as "not" Americans, a group that has yet to earn its place and be accepted into American society. In his closing paragraph he asks "us" to "lay aside our personal enmities," although those acting on their "personal enmities" appear in his narrative to be Latinos.

A close reading of the text also reveals that behind the author's initial statement in support of English as the universal language lie several unspoken presuppositions. The author argues that native languages should be taught and maintained only in the privacy of the home and ethnic community; *even the Indians,* wronged as they were by white settlers, speak English in public and their native tongues in private. Choosing to make language an issue, like the Latinos who are never mentioned, will divide the nation's people and destroy America. Implicit here is the assumption that an intended outcome of bilingual education programs is the replacement of English with Spanish, and that acceptance and support for the maintenance of speakers' Spanish language abilities cannot coexist with acceptance of English as the "universal language." Latinos who demand bilingual programs are threatening national unity, symbolized by the "*one* God, *one* government, *one* flag and *one* universal language" (emphasis added).

Interpretive Framework of Seniors

While minority community leaders viewed the comments by John Marris as an opportunity to gain the public's attention and recognition of the need to change the ways the schools were dealing with minority youth, Seniors used their public outcry and the concomitant attention it received as an opportunity to censure the "minorities" not only for their "rowdy" public protests and their "harping" on the issue of racism, but also for their "gimme, gimme" attitudes and lack of success in the local schools and community. Marris became the symbol of the hardworking (white) population being scapegoated by minorities for what were ultimately the minorities' doings. A cryptic letter to the editor published a month after Marris's original comments encapsulated that position:

> The musical, *The Music Man,* there was a song about trouble in River City. The trouble has moved to the "Friendly City." The time for the silent majority to be heard is now. We are not going to let Mr. Marris become the victim of a "witch hunt." (*Arnhem Record,* September 25, 1991)

Recurring throughout their public discourse was the constant use of terms that set minorities apart from "mainstream" Americans. Seniors spoke of "those people" and "you people" in ways that markedly contrasted minorities unfavorably with "us" (Americans), usage that was frequently remarked on by minority community members. This dichotomization, which persisted throughout the texts, is visible through analysis of the themes that run through Senior discourse.

Several major interrelated themes emerge from analysis of the public discourse of Seniors, then, within which Latinos—and to a more limited extent, African Americans—were contrasted unfavorably with Euro-Americans. The quotations below are representative of public pronouncements over the three-month period following Marris's original statements and are grouped into several themes. (Some could be placed under more than one theme and illustrate the interrelatedness of the themes.) All statements were made by seniors in the community, who are overwhelmingly of southern and eastern European origin.

Theme 1: Assimilation Keeps America Strong. Seniors voiced strong support for cultural and linguistic assimilation, maintaining that their own parents had publicly abandoned their homelands, culture, and language for the greater good. Latinos, the "newest" immigrants, were censured for their alleged refusal to conform to the culture and language of the nation, which Seniors claimed was necessary for American unity. If there *is* bias against Latinos, Seniors asserted, they bring it on themselves:

> *School board member, public forum:* Keep your heritage and language, speak Spanish at home or with your friends, but learn to

speak English in school and the outside world if you want to succeed. [Loud applause from audience.] Whether you like it or not, this *is* an English-speaking country. . . . I myself am learning Spanish because I want to. You have to *want* to learn English.

Letter to the editor: The promotion of multiculturalism as public policy is antithetical to our national ideal of unity through cultural assimilation. . . . Witness the problems, the notoriously ethnocentric, acculturation resistant Hispanics have entering the American mainstream, to realize this [revising the state's social studies curriculum to make it more inclusive] is indeed a flawed policy initiative.

Caller to local talk show, discussing local Latinos: They refuse to join in, here, in a lot of things. They come here, they want their own ways, they want to change our ways. And our ways is our ways, and if they want their own ways, they should go back to wherever they came from.

Theme 2: "Attitude" Problem. Senior texts frequently portrayed Latinos/Minorities as lacking in motivation and expecting handouts, in sharp contrast to their own parents, who they felt had labored to make this city (read nation) great and asked for nothing in return:

Talk show caller: Enough is enough with the "gimme, gimme" attitude and "you owe me" attitude. I've had it.

Speaker #13, public forum: Arnhem is a wonderful city and affords many opportunities to everybody who wants them. . . . [But] I can't understand why the Hispanic population doesn't *want* to be educated. . . . Do you think that . . . [European immigrants] were just handed everything? No, they worked hard.

Letter to the editor: [Hispanics] seem to feel that they are owed something. . . . [They should] exercise their rights and return to their native homeland. America, love it or leave it.

Letter to the editor: The economy . . . is not only the fault of our leaders but . . . those who demand that the government owes us a living. Our oldsters remember how we made our own way and shouldered our own problems.

Theme 3: Equivalence of Experience/Denial of Racism. Latinos/Minorities were repeatedly censured for making a "big to-do" about racism and discrimination. Seniors either denied the existence of bias, claimed they and/or their parents had faced similar bias without complaining, asserted that it was no different in Arnhem than elsewhere, or claimed that minorities brought it on themselves by adhering to their old ways and to each other.

Letter to the editor: To orchestrate an attempt at his [Marris's] ouster is a classic example of an overreaction by a hypersensitive minority to a small and imagined slight.

"Guest column" writer: Certainly we all agree these incidents [racial epithets shouted at minority students] are cruel and worthy of our contempt, but are they racist? . . . Controversy sparks angry name calling. . . . We have no more prejudice or racism than you will find in any similar community.

Retired teacher, public forum: If there's been racism in Arnhem school district, maybe I'm naive, I don't know about it. I didn't feel it. . . . The Italians were called guineas and wops, so what's new, what's the difference?

Letter to the editor: But where were the voices when my ethnic group was being demeaned, laughed at and called dumb names? . . . As I see it, both Jimmy the Greek and Marris are victims of circumstance. Saying what came to mind but never thinking it would come out the way it did, it seems to me . . . Mr. Marris will never live it down, the people won't let him. And that is unfortunate, too.

Local talk show, caller #4: When I was goin' to school I'd go "Oh you dumb pollock, you guinea, you dumb wop" or this or that. We never had discrimination. . . . The more you people are on this, the more the pot is boiling.

Local talk show, caller #5 (responding to questions posed by guest host, an African-American community leader):
Guest host: Do you think bias exists in this community toward various ethnic groups?
Caller: I *do* not. I *do* not.
Guest host: You don't think there's maybe one person, or two persons in this community who may be racist? . . .
Caller: I don't think so. No.

Local talk show, caller #7 (speaking to talk show guest host; caller has insinuated that the guest speaker must be making up charges of racism against herself and her daughter):
Guest host: Do you believe, when I say that my child has been called a nigger in this community, do you think that is possible that did happen?
Caller: It may be possible, but let me tell you something. Just like the one lady said, they were all—what are the Italian people called? Grease balls, wops, and everything like that.
Guest host: Does that make it right?
Caller: No it doesn't make it right, but did they make a big fuss over it, and have trouble in the community over it? . . .
Caller: I think it's been carried too far. . . . I think it's turning a lot of people that did like the Costa Ricans, the Puerto Ricans, the Hispanics, I think it's turning them the other way a lot.

Theme 4: Public Comportment. Closely related to theme 3, this theme spoke to public behaviors. Latinos were depicted as "rowdy" and "out of line" picketing and "raising a ruckus" over issues of racism, behaviors portrayed as harming both the community's reputation and ethnic relations:

Speaker #4, public forum: You have a right to protest. But you also have an obligation to live peacefully within the rest of the community. So to sit down and discuss in a quiet manner . . . Wild cat demonstrations are not the way. They only tend to polarize the community and make a gap between Hispanics and non-Hispanics.

Speaker #8, public forum: [Have] meetings, but let's keep it quiet, let's keep it to ourselves.

Speaker #9, public forum: Now I notice today, all the rowdies aren't here. The Hispanic community is well behaved . . . not like they were on the last board meeting, with signs and everything else. . . . I sympathize with you people, but not when you're rowdy. Not when you're cracking up.

Speaker at school board meeting (quoted in *The Arnhem Record*): The board should come to an amicable agreement so at every meeting it isn't a mob like this against Americans like me—although you people [Hispanics] are Americans.

Local talk show, caller #6: He [Marris] presented, unfortunately, the excuse for *you people* to break loose. And you have done that. And I think that you might better use your energies, your efforts, toward making a better city, and a better living. Now, I have seen thousands of people come into this city, grew up with Polish, Italian, played with them, never went into their homes, knew my place. They made great citizens. . . . I'm American for going on four hundred years. And very proud of it. . . . There's some great people among your people, but they do not agree, and they are not taking part in it.

Theme 5: Insider/Outsider. Seniors characterized government agencies and people from outside the city (e.g., Latino college students) as "outsiders," who had no business being involved:

School board member, public forum: I do *not* want to listen to anyone . . . not from the Arnhem School District. . . . This is a family matter.

Speaker, public forum: [Directed at Latinos] Let's keep it quiet, let's keep it to ourselves. . . . Arnhem is a good place to work . . . [and] to live.

Theme 6: Dividing and Destroying Arnhem/the Country. Euro-Americans, according to Seniors, made this city (and nation) great. The actions of minorities are destroying all they worked so hard for:

Speaker, school board meeting: The same people trying to get him [Marris] out are the ones you see in the police report every night in the paper.

Letter written to Latino community activists and read at school board meeting: [You people are responsible for] 90 percent of all troubles in Arnhem. . . . You people aren't wanted here—go get welfare somewhere else.

John Marris, letter to the editor of the Arnhem Record: Uneducated millions [in Latin America] are risking their lives to cross borders in hope of a better life up here, while North Americans fear loss of their own jobs while trying to pay for better education for all.

Local talk show, caller #6: Having been born and brought up here, and having lived here for many years, and saw [sic] a lovely area, a lovely city, and my heart is broke to see what is going on. People, thousands came into this city, they came because of the industry. They made a living. They—they built beautiful homes, owned homes, worked hard for that purpose. And they kept the city nice. And kept it along. Why do the Latinos, as they like to be called, I believe, and the minorities, why did they flock in here? Again, do you realize *how* much is being taken out of the taxpayers' pockets, to teach so many of your people? This is—uh—part of the sore part.

Letter to the editor, the Arnhem Record: Arnhem is being held up, stripped of its dignity, and subjected to an unwarranted inquisition. . . . Based on mainly anecdotal evidence, this cabal of minority women have built a bonfire of racism, bigotry and prejudice where scarcely a flicker of flame actually exists . . . [and] their rabble-rousing accusations [to the State Education Department] have sullied the good name of the entire community. . . . [The State Education Department] if they're unbiased . . . [will] vindicate the one-time Friendly City's stellar reputation and restore the historically unblemished record of friendship, tolerance and harmony Arnhemites have always lived by.

Senior Symbols

Within the course of the community debate it became apparent that particular events, practices, and people took on diametrically opposed meanings for the two sides. The polyvalent nature of these symbols can be seen in excerpts from the videotape of the public forum and in the tapes of radio shows and public meetings. Reference to these emotionally charged events, practices, and people encoded a set of meanings that acted as a sort of "shorthand" to permit the speaker to quickly gain audience support in his or her attempt to move people to action. Among Seniors (to be contrasted later with Minority usage) the following meanings pertained:

John Marris: Symbol of white Americans wrongly under attack by minorities, scapegoated by them when the real problems are within the minority communities.

Spanish language: Symbol of Latinos' unwillingness to "assimilate." Language of exclusion; public use of it symbolizes the speaker's intent to exclude non-Spanish speakers. Metonymically, it stands in for the decline of the United States in recent decades as a result of the entry of "mobs" of illegals and other foreigners "swamping" the country and turning it into a "jungle."

New York State Education Department (called in by minority community members to investigate charges of racism in the schools): Symbol of "big government," meddling by outsiders, loss of control of state and federal institutions to minorities.

Latino (higher) dropout rate: Symbol of Latinos' lack of caring about their children.

Bilingual education, multicultural education: Symbol of how far the United States had "gone down the wrong track" to "cater" to the demands of minority communities; symbol of state's institutions "butting in."

Metaphors

Metaphors that served to situate the minority community negatively were frequently used by Senior speakers. Metaphors, as James Fernandez emphasizes, are significant in the process of defining others in relation to ourselves: "Language has devices of representation at its disposal, mainly metaphor, by which pronouns can be moved about—into better or worse position—in quality space. . . . There is an important social use of metaphor involving the occupancy of various continua which in sum constitute a cultural quality space. Persuasive metaphors situate us and others with whom we interact in that space" (1986:13–14). Seniors situated themselves at the opposite ends from Latinos on several continua, which, taken together, constitute what they define as important domains of experience in American society. The Seniors' metaphors operated to place minorities (Latinos and African Americans, with Asian Americans never acknowledged) in an unfavorable light, implying by metaphoric predication that they were endangering the community (and thus national) well-being. Minorities, for instance, were said to be "holding up" Arnhem and "stripping" it of its dignity; they were using Marris's comments as an opportunity to "break loose"; they held "wild cat demonstrations" and were "cracking up." Minorities had "broke" their (Seniors'/Americans') hearts, welfare was a "sore spot." Latinos, such metaphors suggested, were improperly socialized and harmful to community well-being.

A recurring metaphor cast Arnhemites as "family." Seniors repeatedly put forth the statements "we are family" and "Arnhem is a wonderful place to live." Minorities/Latinos were censured for going public with their complaints, taking "family" matters into the public domain and in the process blemishing the city's reputation. Their actions made them "not family." As Phil Cohen notes in examining similar European discourses, "Domestic metaphors and images of privacy are frequently used in constructing commonsense arguments for the exclusion of those who are held not to belong within the public domains of the body politic . . . when and wherever resentment is expressed by self-proclaimed 'natives' against immigrants and ethnic minorities. . . . The power of this kind of statement derives in part from the ease with which the boundaries of state and nation are pinned to those of the neighbourhood and family within the single rhetorical space of race" (1996:68–9).

Conceptual Framework of Seniors

Seniors, then, put forward as a universal model for incorporation into the American mainstream what they perceived to have worked for them. Their model drew (sometimes contradictorily) on both what social scientists have variously termed an "assimilationist," "Anglo-conformity," or "melting pot" model, taken for so long as the appropriate metaphor to describe the "making" of the American people, and on the self-conscious assertions of ethnic pride that reflect the "new ethnicity" appearing among Euro-Americans by the 1970s (Novak 1971). Conformity, accepting hard knocks, and hard work are the ingredients that ensure success, which is ultimately what made Arnhem great; with success also comes acceptance as an American.

We see in their arguments that their claim to being American is rooted in the story they share of a struggling, self-sacrificing immigrant past and their own hard work, through which they and their children succeeded in achieving social mobility and, by extension, national greatness. As Richard Alba's sociological study (1990) of ethnic identity among whites in a nearby metropolitan area suggests, ethnicity for Euro-Americans continues to be salient. What we are witnessing, however, is the original ethnic divisions among those of European descent being replaced or supplemented by a "Euro-American" identity, with emphasis on the shared immigrant experience and social mobility as setting them apart from "nonwhite" ethnic groups.

> Never mind that the historical experience of the Irish in the potato fields, the Italians in the villages of southern Italy, and the Jews in the shtetls were so different. . . . All this gets muted in favor of the similarity of the immigrant experience as it is embodied in the "we came, we suffered, we conquered" myth, which by now has gained legendary proportions. And all of it without a single reference to race. Instead, the quintessential American experience is defined in terms of immigration, its burdens, and the ability to overcome such burdens through sacrifice and hard work. They are the real Americans, the only ones worthy of the name. It just happens that they're all white. (Rubin 1994:192)

As should become apparent, this Euro-American "national origin myth" contrasts sharply with the stories put forward by minority spokespersons.

Seniors correspondingly positioned minorities as operating from opposite, and negative, ends of the various continua of criteria used to trace their successful entry into the American community: Purposeful diversity rather than conformity; complaining rather than accepting hard knocks; low motivation and expectations of handouts instead of hard work. These qualities in turn lead to failure rather than success, and rejection instead of acceptance into the American community. The actions of "those people," as seen by Seniors, helped explain both troubling changes in the United States in their lifetimes and the lower social, economic, and educational statuses of minority groups.

The Minority Story

Minorities responded with a counterclaim. Their discourse reveals a contrasting interpretation: their difficulties achieving success are rooted in the nation's racism and exclusion of their language and culture, which they maintain to be their entitlement as Americans. This perspective was eloquently expressed by Latino community activist Virginia Colón at the public forum, where she spoke in support of calls for a school district more responsive to Latino students' needs. Her narrative, which was frequently interrupted by applause and cheers from Latinos in the audience, paints a picture of the exclusion of minorities and asks the listener to consider the consequences:

> My name is Virginia Colón. . . . *Primeramente, quiero empezar por decirles que hay mas gente en los Estados Unidos que hablan español que muchísimos países. En fin, el derecho ajeno es la obligación de todos, incluídos ustedes que están presentes aquí esta noche.* [First, I want to begin by telling you that there are more people who speak Spanish in the United States than in many countries. So

> the obligation of all to respect others includes you who are present here tonight.]
>
> You know, I used to live in Kansas, and I remember the first time I went to a restaurant and I ordered my usual BLT—I love BLTs, I have a passion for BLTs–and the waitress told me, "I'm sorry we don't serve niggers here, you'll have to go." . . . What happens to kids who didn't have the skills that I had to get through that? . . .
>
> People have labeled this discussion . . . hostile. This is called dialogue. People have labeled this . . . racial preference. It's called diversity. People have . . . label[ed] it un-American. It's democratic . . . the foundations that this country has been built on. . . . Every time I hear a student have to . . . [say] "I am an American," it's because we once again are not included. . . . Let's make sure . . . all of us here today represent each star on that flag.

Colón initially switches to Spanish, emblematic of her identification with Latinos in the audience and affirming their right as Americans to use Spanish in public discourse. Her message, intended for Spanish speakers, was not repeated in English, though on the surface it addresses the Seniors. It stakes out the claim that Latinos are here in force, they needn't apologize for who they are, and they are entitled to respect. "Kansas" and "BLTs" are quintessentially "American"; Latinos can be different and at the same time as "American" as the nation's heartland and BLTs.

Colón's narrative also depicts Latinos as being forced to confront the ugliness of racism in their most formative years. The speaker's innocence and eager anticipation when entering the restaurant are juxtaposed to the ugliness and exclusion she encounters, symbolic of immigrants' anticipation of life in the United States and their encounters with the reality of racism. Using alliteration for greater impact—"dialogue, "diversity," "democracy"—she puts forward a reinterpretation of events that Seniors have condemned, turning a positive light on them. She concludes with an appeal to all the flag represents.

Interpretive Framework of Minorities

The themes found in this narrative—the United States as benefitting from diversity, minority rights to "difference," and the long history of racism and exclusion that has held minorities back—also recur throughout the Minority discourse. The number of local Minority spokespersons speaking out was small, however, in contrast to the number of vocal Seniors. Latino spokespersons connected to the Latino community agency active in the dispute, the New York State Education Department, and the state university's Latino student community generally articulated positions on bilingual and multicultural education shared by much of the Puerto Rican academic community based in New York City (e.g., Vázquez 1989) and by supporters of versions of multicultural education that have as an important objective the empowerment of minority youth and communities.

Theme 1: Difference as Entitlement: Diversity was portrayed as a positive quality, an entitlement and something to be proud of:

> *Speaker #7, Latino college student, public forum:* Nowhere in the U.S. Constitution is English the official language. . . . They left it open so that people who wanted to come . . . didn't have to worry about speaking English to fit in. . . . The "English Only" movement in this country is only gonna damage the greater culture . . . 'cause we're such a mixture of many, many cultures.

> *Latino community agency leader, newspaper interview:* We should learn from other ethnic minorities who regret that they can't

speak their native language, whether it is Polish, Italian, or Lithuanian. We don't want our children to have that same regret.

Theme 2: Racism as Damaging. The racism experienced by minorities is qualitatively different from that experienced by earlier groups experienced. Prejudice, discrimination, and insensitivity have historically held minorities back, and continue to do so.

Speaker #14, Latino high school student, public forum: The self-esteem of Hispanic students is suffering in our schools, because we hear every day of negative messages about who we are and why we are here. . . . We want to achieve . . . to organize as a group . . . [to] deal with the prejudice . . . constructively.

Speaker #24, Latino high school student, public forum: I would like to say that I am very proud of what I am. [Loud applause from Latinos in the audience.] I . . . have been called "nigger" and . . . [other words] I don't care to repeat. . . . [If you] want the children of the community to succeed, why are you continuously putting us down?

Speaker #18, Latino college student, public forum: We [students] . . . would like to propose that a stronger, cultural-oriented curriculum be formulated for the purpose of educating and alleviating racial tension. We, as an oppressed people. . .

Theme 3: Exclusion. Though they are as American as everyone else, white America excludes and treats minorities as the Other, in the process damaging their self-esteem.

Speaker #19, Puerto Rican college student, public forum: For you to come here and tell us that we're not Americans . . . to expect us to listen to Mr. Marris . . . [and then] expect Latinos to wrap ourselves around the American flag, then maybe you have to analyze yourselves. . . . Stand up and support the idea of Latinos.

Latino community leader (newspaper interview): Without that information [ethnic contributions to the United States], children are handicapped—they are defenseless—and information about their heritage is needed to arm them. . . . If they hear nothing . . . then they think, "I must be nothing."

Whereas Seniors argued that the gaps between the Latino and Euro-American communities—in terms of both ethnic polarization and economic and educational status—were brought on Latinos by their own doing, Minorities reversed causality: student failure is rooted in bias and rejection that has its roots in their "otherness" for white Americans. *Difference,* a stigma in the Seniors' framework, is inverted to become a positive factor, an entitlement rooted in appeals to the Constitution and the nation's longstanding espousal of the ideals of tolerance. Breaking the cycle of failure for minority youth, Latinos argued, requires a multi-pronged approach that severs the connections between *difference* and *bias* and *rejection,* through education and use of the state's institutions. The low self-esteem of minority youth, a consequence of their experiences with bias and rejection of their cultural, racial, and linguistic differences, can be countered through positive acknowledgment of minority cultures and languages and the sense of empowerment they will experience in understanding the roots of their low status in the United States. An integral element in such a schema is the advocacy of bilingual and multicultural education programs that promote the desirability and legitimacy of linguistic and cultural diversity and the empowerment of minority youth and communities (e.g., Banks 1991; Cummins 1989; Levine et al. 1995; Nieto 1996).

Visible in these excerpts from Minority texts is much that Senior and Minority spokespersons share: the importance of education, of being self-sufficient, of succeeding, of contributing to community well-being.[11] Analysis of the various public texts of minority speakers and writers also documents the quite different symbolic import that the people, actions, events, and practices held for Minority speakers:

John Marris: Symbol of whites' insensitivity and biased attitudes toward the minority community.

Spanish language: Symbol of ethnic identity, affirmation of selves, code for "in-group" membership.

State Education Department:. Symbol of the "proper" role of government to serve as a watchdog agency to protect minority rights and guarantee them an educational environment that maximizes educational opportunity.

Latino (higher) dropout rate: Symbol of school and community failure to adequately educate minority youth.

Bilingual education, multicultural education: Symbol of community's willingness to address minority needs and wishes and to positively affirm their presence and value to the city (and nation).

Story Telling as Telling Stories

There is in the construction of both the Senior story and the Minority story a dialectic operating between past and present. The history and current circumstances of the group to which the letter-to-the-editor-writer belongs—descendants of southern and eastern Europeans—differ significantly from the experiences of most Latinos, African Americans, and Native Americans. In turn, significant differences, as Connerton (1989) and Benmayor et al. (1988) anticipated, emerge in the narratives of these two groups.

Seniors, raised on an ethos of ancestral sacrifice and hard work as the essential ingredients for upward mobility *and* having achieved something of the American dream (tenuous though their hold may be on it), unproblematically link hard work and conformity to white ethnics' successes in climbing the social class ladder. One consequence is to defend the individualistic "up by their own bootstraps" view of the American system and to situate themselves as resoundingly part of the mainstream white middle class, with its connotations of progress and order. For members of struggling minority communities for whom the "rags-to-riches" story has rarely applied, stories of hardship and discrimination "mean" differently. Linking racial oppression, past and present, to contemporary ethnic and racial socioeconomic inequalities helps explain their current position in the social hierarchy and inspires members to challenge both the status quo and Seniors' classification of them as part of the "paradigmatic poor" (see Urciuoli 1993).

While social mobility has long been a reality in the United States, as in other class societies, opportunities for upward mobility have been constrained by factors other than individual "will" or degree of talent. Given the dominant ideology, however, Americans rarely acknowledge the presence of such constraints.

> What is unique about the American system is its ideology. Where European cultures have tended to emphasize traditional ranks and statuses, and to present themselves as more rigid in class terms than they really are, the United States has glorified opportunity and mobility, and has presented itself as more open to individual achievement than it really is. . . . Because hegemonic American culture takes both the ideology of mobility and the ideology of individualism seriously, explanations for nonmobility not only focus on the failure of individuals (because they are said to be inherently lazy or stupid or

whatever), but shift the domain of discourse to arenas that are taken to be "locked into" individuals—gender, race, ethnic origin, and so forth. (Ortner 1991:170–71)

Individuals who do achieve upward mobility ascribe their success to individual qualities, ignoring the larger forces that promote or constrain upward mobility. Arnhem's seniors are members of a generation of Americans that achieved unprecedented upward mobility in the post–World War II era of economic expansion. Declines in the manufacturing sector and corporate "downsizing" beginning in the 1970s have since translated into economic and social dislocation for many working-class and middle-class whites (Thurow 1995). Those seeking to climb the social class ladder today, unlike in the 1950s and 1960s, increasingly confront the downwardly mobile and those who cling precariously to their middle-class status. Sandwiched between their parents, who came to the United States as desperately poor immigrants, and their baby-boomer children, who represent the first postwar generation to be downwardly mobile (Newman 1993), Seniors look to explain the changes that have rocked their world.

As analysts of ethnicity within the context of the nation state highlight (e.g., Chock 1989; Williams 1989), ethnic groups are forced to vie for a legitimate place in the nation against the state-backed race/class conflation. "All bloods," Brackette Williams notes, "are not equal, but the precepts of nationalist ideologies demand that all subordinated groups bleed equally for the nation" (1989:436). As the most recent to achieve membership in the group that is ideologically defined as the "real producers" of the national patrimony, white ethnics in danger of losing economic ground turn their anger against those they believe to be less entitled to such rewards (people of color), given their "lesser" contributions to the making of the nation (see, for example, Fine et al. 1997; Newman 1993; Rubin 1992).

The greater economic stability that accompanies their rise to middle-class status carries with it a moral evaluation: "The link between control and cultural self-respect is definingly important. Being middle-class is a generic, and morally loaded, cultural identity, representing the triumph of individual virtue which includes good money management. The ideal ethnic comes in as working-class, but immediately embarks on the course of progress. By contrast, being poor means a lack of control" (Urciuoli 1993:206; see also Hochschild 1995; Newman 1993).

In staking out their claims to legitimacy white ethnics use criteria said to have built the nation: individual struggle and a willingness to suffer in the short term for long-term gains implicitly promised to their posterity if not themselves. To that end, white ethnics insist that minority groups adhere to the rules and standards of competition that they perceive themselves to have followed, and insist on their having to earn their place in the nation.

Visible in the Senior story is what Urciuoli (1996) characterizes as the differences between "ethnicized" and "racialized" discourses. In the American "imagined community" (Anderson 1983), the unmarked normative or generic American is white, middle class, and English speaking (also see Oboler 1995). This normative person stands in opposition to all categories of origin difference but furthest from racialized difference. "Racializing" discourses frame group origin in natural rather than cultural terms, in which "[r]acialized people are typified as human matter out of place: dirty, dangerous, unwilling, or unable to do their bit for the nation-state" (Urciuoli 1996:15). "Racializing discourses talk about unindividuated populations that differ fundamentally from whites in values, habits, language, character, and aspirations. Examples include the scientific racialism of the 1800s, the anti-immigrant writing of the early 1900s, and much of the writing on the culture of poverty and the underclass in the mid-late 1900s. In such discourses, racialized groups are seen as collectively, inherently, and unchangingly flawed" (Urciuoli 1996:17).

"Ethnicizing" discourses, on the other hand, frame group origins in cultural terms, in which cultural or language differences are not conceptualized as problematic. Ethnicization serves as a sort of mediating discourse between the unmarked middle-class Anglo and the nonwhite, poor, and culturally or linguistically deficient portrayed in racializing discourse. White ethnics today are talked about in ways that place them squarely within such a middle-class order, despite their own marginalized positions in the U.S. social order well into the 1930s and 1940s (di Leonardo 1992). As Puerto Ricans move with increasing frequency out of large metropolitan ethnic enclaves into smaller "whiter" communities such as Arnhem they confront more directly this moralizing discourse of exclusion that locates their lack of social mobility in their cultural and linguistic practices and personal choices. These discourses place the blame for poverty on individuals rather than on the outcomes of racial hierarchies, profound economic changes, and the historic exploitation of Puerto Rican labor that evolved within the context of the colonial relationship of the island to the United States after 1898 (see Bonilla and Campos 1981).

Language maintenance, meanwhile, has also become a lightning rod for moral evaluations of those groups not able to achieve such mobility. Ethnicizing discourses frame foreign languages as acceptable for certain purposes, for instance as justifiable in public places when they function to reinforce the cultural authenticity of a public performance. Racializing discourses, however, "equate language difference with disorder, with images of illiterate foreigners flooding the United States and refusing to speak English or hordes of the underclass speaking an accented English with 'broken' grammar and 'mixed' vocabulary" (Urciuoli 1996:18). Such images were woven throughout much of the Arnhem Seniors' discourse.

Attacks on language maintenance such as those outlined here and as put forward by proponents of English-only measures ignore the historic and sociopolitical realities and the cultural affirmation that underlies the continuing existence of Spanish among Latinos in the United States (Flores, Attinasi and Pedraza 1981; Urciuoli 1996). Such arguments may attract traditionally liberal voters who accept the uninformed argument that Spanish-language speakers are "prisoners" of language and special-interest politics (see Woolard 1989); more often they serve as a smokescreen for concerns about the "browning" of the United States (Attinasi 1994; Crawford 1992; Zentella 1988). Further, they have insidious consequences. "Silencing, or linguistic suppression, is the ultimate dehumanization through language. Both dialect suppression and language prohibition exclude speakers from dialogue with the culture of power. . . . [The ideological effect] is to reinforce the mistrust of non-English languages, speakers, and cultures. . . . Those who support language diversity are thought to be un-American, and those who speak other languages are seen as deviant and dependent, rather than as bearers of a precious human resource" (Attinasi 1994:334–5).

Public morality, as staked out by Seniors, was violated by Puerto Ricans both because they clung to their native language and because they did not struggle hard enough to achieve educational and economic success. Missing, Seniors argued, was the willingness of minorities to ascribe to the work ethic and the "rugged individualism" they themselves had exhibited. These Senior discourses did not generally reference *all* local Latinos, however. Both in community and school discourse, Costa Ricans, who make up 12 percent of the local Latino population, were typically framed as the "good Latinos," conforming to the patterns followed by earlier European ethnic groups. Indeed, the two groups were often depicted as representing opposite ends along a continuum of "acceptability" to the Euro-American community. Costa Ricans are hard workers; Puerto Ricans are lazy, settling for welfare and dependency. Costa Ricans keep up their homes; Puerto Ricans let their homes get run down. Costa Rican men like to have a good time, but settle down when they marry; Puerto Ricans exhibit perpetually irresponsible sexual behavior. Costa Ricans value family and act responsibly; Puerto Ricans act irresponsibly. Costa Ricans care about education; Puerto Ricans don't. Costa Ricans are law abiding; Puerto Ricans are into drugs and crime. Costa Ricans are willing to adopt community values; Puerto Ricans keep to their own people and don't adopt U.S. values and language.

That Costa Ricans, too, are "Latinos" and have achieved a modicum of economic stability is seen as further evidence of the willed lack of success of Puerto Ricans. Not unlike the earlier ethnic Jewish "exceptions" (Steinberg 1989) and "model minority" Asian Americans (Takaki 1993:417), Costa Ricans' successes are used to cast aspersions on those groups who have not achieved upward mobility and to deny the need for government programs such as affirmative action or welfare. Ignored are the differing histories and experiences of the Puerto Rican and Costa Rican populations: Costa Ricans in Arnhem were "whiter" and had more economic and educational resources, contributing to their greater relative success and the greater likelihood of their coming to be viewed as an "ethnic" (not unlike Italians and Poles) rather than a "racial" group.

In evaluating local Puerto Ricans, white ethnics draw on the hegemonic European immigrant success myth, in which all groups start from the same point and are assimilated into the national fabric by dint of hard work, sacrifice, and a willingness to conform to "American" norms. Also emphasized is the shared immigrant experience and social mobility as setting Euro ethnics apart from "nonwhite" ethnic groups, and the "imagined community" these Euro-Americans construct places them squarely within the American national myth of the "self-made man." It also situates Puerto Ricans as individually and collectively responsible for their failure to achieve widescale upward mobility. As Margaret Wetherell and Jonathan Potter underline in explaining a similar phenomenon in New Zealand, such constructions, whether in social science or lay discourse, are problematic for their potential to "become bound in with practices which sustain power relations" (1992:148). These hegemonic constructions provide a ready rationale for opposing projects intended to ameliorate the socioeconomic disparities that increasingly divide Americans, most problematically along racial and ethnic lines.

For many mainstream Americans, as this analysis suggests, recent demographic and social changes have been conflated with the nation's political and economic downswing in recent years, so that the blame for such changes is not infrequently projected onto the increasingly visible minority communities (see also Rubin 1992; Weis 1990). Unacknowledged in the public discourse in Arnhem are both the factors that enhanced white ethnics' upward mobility—

including the expanding postwar economy, the earlier successes of the union movement, and government largesse that benefitted white ethnics—as well as (among the Seniors) those factors that have historically impeded racial minorities' upward mobility. Unacknowledged by either side is the significance of the changed economy.

In challenging dominant discourses minority communities put forward an expanded vision of what counts as "American," pushing at the borders to incorporate groups marginalized by such constructions. The assumption that all ethnic stories are the same—that is, that the "Senior" model applies equally to all minority groups and that only the names of the groups change—has been successfully challenged by a new generation of scholars (cf. Nash 1974; Nelson and Tienda 1985; Portes and Rumbaut 1990; Rodríguez 1989; Rosaldo 1989; Steinberg 1989; Takaki 1993). Their historical analyses and ethnographic studies highlight the need to consider the significance of factors including race, class, educational background, changing economic conditions, the communication and transportation revolutions, and the reception of immigrants in the new country when seeking explanations for interethnic differences in "succeeding" in the United States. The understandings generated from such studies, however, have yet to make their way into mainstream "folk" explanations, including, as in Arnhem, those of people holding local power. Their support—along with that of teachers—will be vitally important if substantive changes are to take place. If we are to better address the issues that divide Americans along ethnic lines and move toward a more equitable and just society, the creation of greater opportunities for dialogue and public forums for the telling of American *stories* will be essential.

5 Dangerous Discourses

> When someone with the authority of a teacher, say, describes the world and you are not in it, there is a moment of psychic disequilibrium, as if you looked into a mirror and saw nothing.
> —Adrienne Rich, "Invisibility in Academe" (1986:199)

The moment of self-nothingness Adrienne Rich describes points to the role of definitions, knowledge, and exclusion in American education. It concerns the way in which both the stories told and the stories silenced in schools are part of a selective process of self-recognition and self-formation that implicate apparently neutral questions of school knowledge in heated ongoing debates about cultural identity and social conflict. An often-asked question in this debate is whether and how school knowledge builds on and affirms some identities while destabilizing and negating others. A less frequently asked question is how teachers perceive and participate in this debate.

After the NYSED investigation Arnhem's English teachers were asked to rethink their literature choices as part of a program for multicultural change. In this chapter I analyze English teachers' specific responses to these pressures for change. In the discussion I bring forward both the "upfront" and the tacit concerns, the rarely directly verbalized but always problematic issues that pervade multicultural education programs. The upfront concerns are what people publicly and repeatedly say; the tacit concerns are alluded to, mentioned in passing, or left unsaid. I analyze both the directly said and the hinted at because multicultural reform is controversial, and controversy is both dangerous and promising. The "language" of multiculturalism and inclusion unproblematically suggests "opening up" and "broadening" our visions of ourselves, our history, our literature canons, our classroom teaching styles, and the like. However, multiculturalism is also clearly a threat to many because multicultural curricula have the potential to challenge the silences that exist in schools around issues such as race and class.

The silences are important, however, for existing arrangements both within and outside of schools. They are the routine taken-for-granteds and the exclusions of contrary perspectives that allow social actors to ignore contradictions in their lives and crises in their institutions (Murphy 1970). Put another way, they are part of a social etiquette that allows existing inclusions and exclusions to go unremarked, and thus to appear natural. Challenge to silence is dangerous. It destabilizes common-sense understandings (e.g., that problems of racism and class stratification are matters of individual morality and effort) and therefore is threatening, especially in a situation of mounting conflict. We must acknowledge that teachers, like their students, enter the schools as raced, classed, and gendered actors. The significance of this fact when urging and implementing multicultural reforms in schools is that while breaking school silences may "open up" the schools for previously excluded groups, it threatens other identities.

The issue of the relationship between ethnic and racial (and to a more limited extent, class) identities and schooling outcomes has received considerable attention among academics promoting multicultural education approaches in the classroom (cf. Banks 1997; Davidson 1996; Jacob and Jordan 1993; Nieto 1996; Phelan and Davidson 1993; Weis 1988). Ogbu's "cultural ecological approach," discussed in Chapter 3, addresses possible issues behind the resistance to schooling exhibited by some minority youth. Here identity issues are constructed as part and parcel of the sociohistoric experiences of the group and result in students' unwillingness to work at achieving academically. Ogbu measures success in terms of existing school criteria and not the adequacy of the system to address diverse needs; the ways in which school practices may engender resistance and disengagement (see, for example, Davidson 1996; Erickson 1987; Fine 1987; Foley 1991; Kohl 1994) are not adequately addressed.

One area of focus among multicultural educators since the 1960s that *does* critically consider school practices attends to the subject matter taught in schools and posits that an exclusionary ("Eurocentric") curriculum may be implicated in the complex relationship between ethnic and racial identity and academic engagement. Schools are understood to put at a disadvantage particular groups through the curriculum taught; much of this focus has been on history/social studies and literature texts (e.g., Banks 1991; Harris 1992).

These contemporary challenges to the history and literature canons in public schools have their roots in the increased attention to racial and cultural bias that emerged during the civil rights movement. On the literature front, beginning in the 1960s analysts pointed out that children's and adolescents' literature—both that used in the public schools and such literature in general, was filled with stereotypes, distortions, and omissions. As Nancy Larrick (1965) documented, only four-fifths of 1 percent of the five thousand children's books published between 1962 and 1964 by members of the Children's Book Council included mention of contemporary African Americans. These early analyses, initially focusing on African Americans and women (e.g., Lieberman 1972), were soon broadened to incorporate other marginalized groups including Native Americans, Chicanos, Puerto Ricans, and Asians (e.g., Costo and Henry 1970; Council on Interracial Books for Children 1975, 1976). An underlying assumption of these critiques was that such literature not only reflected, but also taught and reinforced, negative images of people of color, causing harm both to those misrepresented and to those assimilating the distorted perspectives (see Lindgren 1991).

A modest trend toward culturally diversifying children's literature did emerge in the 1970s, only to weaken in the conservative 1980s (Barrera, Liguori, and Salas 1992). Despite recent assertions of a "huge demand" for multicultural titles (Jones 1991), both the quantity and the quality of available multicultural children's literature are still viewed by minority writers and multiculturalists as inadequate (e.g., selections in Harris 1992; Lindgren 1991). Studies of literature instruction in schools also indicate that the literature canon has changed "with glacial slowness" (Applebee 1990:67). Analyzing responses from a random sampling of 650 secondary schools across the United States, Applebee concluded that literature selections taught in the classroom continue to remain narrowly defined. "In the present survey, only 16 percent of the selections chosen for study during a five day period were written by women, and only 7 percent were by non-White authors. The narrowness of the selections is particularly troublesome given some 20 years of emphasis in the professional literature on the need to move beyond traditional selections, to better recognize the diverse cultural traditions that contribute to contemporary

American life as well as to the broader world of which we are a part" (1990:67).

Even if proceeding with glacial slowness, change is afoot. Across the nation, to varying degrees, English teachers are now being asked to reexamine their literature choices to better reflect and more accurately portray the multicultural reality of the United States. The effort to introduce such texts into the nation's classrooms has not gone unchallenged. Attempts to alter traditional school canons have been caught up in battles over "political correctness" (e.g., Hymowitz 1991) and have led to charges that broadening the curriculum to include the voices of the marginalized ultimately promotes ethnic particularism (see, for example, Gray 1991; Ravitch 1990).

How individuals "on the ground" perceive and participate in the debates about multicultural education is less well understood than the rationale for such educational changes. In the following pages I focus on this "local" question, arguing that to integrate the voices of previously unheard groups is not a simple or straightforward process of substituting one set of curriculum selections for another. The NYSED recommendations to the Arnhem school district included attention to classroom and library books, and it was the leadership of the English department leadership that most actively worked to incorporate more "multicultural" texts into classrooms, in the process providing me an opportunity to witness teachers' responses firsthand. Because the community and institutional contexts, as well as teacher perceptions and understandings of the larger debate, are essential to understanding those responses, I turn first to teachers' general responses to the community debate, and the NYSED visit. I then move on to chart and analyze English teachers' responses to pressures to change their own literature selections.

Teacher Backgrounds and Explanations for School Failure

Almost 90 percent of the nation's teachers are white, and teaching in classrooms with a growing percentage of students of color (Sleeter 1995). Arnhem is no exception. In the Arnhem Junior High School (grades seven and eight), 20 percent of the six hundred students are Latino, 2 percent are African American, and 1 percent are Asian. All administrators and fifty-nine of the sixty teachers (1991–1992) are Euro-American; 44 percent[1] are of Italian or Polish heritage. Almost half of them grew up in Arnhem (at a time when the minority population was significantly smaller); most of the remaining teachers and administrators come from nearby towns and cities.

The distribution of Arnhem's teachers and administrators by gender tends to parallel the findings from data gathered on U.S. teachers in general (Sleeter and Grant 1988). Sixty-five percent of the teachers are female, and the two building administrators are male. All the English and reading teachers, all the language teachers, all the special education teachers, and all the "home and careers" teachers are female. Males predominate in the areas of math (five of seven) and technology (four of five), and comprise half the social studies (three of six) and 40 percent (two of five) of the science departments.

The average age of the junior high school teachers is close to forty. Many on the staff were hired to meet the needs of the district during the years in which the baby boomers passed through the schools; with a declining student population and budget cuts resulting in teacher layoffs, the average age of teachers in Arnhem, as elsewhere, has risen steadily over the last two decades.[2]

The vast majority of the teachers indicate that they surpassed their parents educationally. Sixty-two percent of their parents had a high school degree or less (with 17 percent of the fathers, and 12 percent of both parents combined, leaving high school before graduation); only 21 percent of their parents had four-year college degrees. Among the teachers, many acquired their degrees at state colleges in the 1960s and 1970s, a period of rapid expansion in the numbers of college graduates. They see themselves as having achieved a degree of upward mobility, to have "made it" into the middle class, and they generally view themselves as professionals—though many feel they are not accorded the respect and status of other professionals.

Arnhem teachers, caught up in the maelstrom created by John Marris's remarks, had much to say about the issues at hand, though as a whole they were reluctant to become publicly involved in the community debate. Many school personnel became defensive about school practices when charges of unfair treatment of minority students surfaced at the beginning of the 1991–1992 school year. Most who spoke publicly on the matter denied the existence of bias toward minority students in the schools.[3] While research on explanations for minority school performance indicates that what takes place in schools plays a significant role in producing unequal outcomes for minority youth (e.g., Cummins 1989; Gillborn 1990; Heath 1983a; Jacob and Jordan 1993; Nieto 1996), many of the local teachers feel otherwise. They subscribe instead to an alternative model to explain minority school performance: causality is attributed to students' impoverished home lives and a lack of motivation.

"In all my years teaching, I only heard the word 'spic'

once," a twenty-five year veteran teacher in the junior high school insisted. "I treat all my kids the same. I don't want to know where they come from, it doesn't matter," said another when asked about the significance of ethnicity in students' schooling experiences. "Any student who works at it can make it into the regents level," was a common response to questions about why Latino students were few in number in the higher tracks. Several teachers who disagreed or took issue with such statements acknowledged in private discussions that they avoided public discussion of their sentiments, either because of their concerns about being denied tenure or because they felt that they had to get along with the rest of the staff and did not want to create "hard feelings."

Several themes recur in teachers' conversations. Many teachers feel that there has been a decline in society's valuing of education, with both students and parents failing to assume responsibility for the children's education. Many emphasize being "color-blind" in their interactions with students. Finally, many see themselves as scapegoated in the process of assigning responsibility for educational failure.

Theme 1: Declining Student/Parent Responsibility. Teachers in interviews and faculty room conversations—with some important exceptions—tended to place the blame for higher Latino student failure rates on nonschool factors: the home environment, cultural "deficiencies" in the Puerto Rican community, or the individual student's "laziness." A typical response in one faculty room conversation was that of a long-time science teacher: "Kids today, they don't see the value like I'm saying, of an education. . . . It's a general attitude today. . . . Discipline is lacking not only in school . . . [but] in the social community." Another teacher chimed in:

"I've seen unwillingness on a lot of the kids' part, a lot of them are Hispanic, that don't care." Many veteran teachers in informal conversations contrast children in general, and minority students' behaviors in particular, to those of earlier generations of schoolchildren. In "those days," students were "respectful" and ostensibly worked hard to get ahead. They learned respect at home, and would risk a "thrashing" if they ever dared to "backmouth" teachers or create a problem in school. An English teacher's comments capture this view:

> I know that the only thing that they [my parents, children of Italian immigrants] knew of education basically was don't you dare ever come home with a red F on a report card, and that was their needs, and I remember her telling horror stories, that if they ever got yelled at in school, they would get it doubly at home, and reprimanded at home and be punished.

One teacher, among the very small number who held extremely negative views about Puerto Ricans, offered the following explanation for their academic performance:

> They don't have the same kind of priorities in the home environment. Their family tree and their ideas of the families is quite a bit different than ours. They don't see as having a traditional mother, father, brothers, and sisters. . . . We're not drawing the best of the Puerto Rican to start with. . . . The majority come here because the welfare payments are higher . . . [and] many of them are, come here running from the law. . . . It's just unfortunate the vast majority that we have in this system, don't come from that kind of [good family] life. They're coming from welfare families, and drug families and stuff like that. Their backgrounds, it's really the biggest problem. . . . It's the culture that they come from.

Spanish language maintenance is also seen as symptomatic of a lack of effort. This view was expressed many times in informal conversations, or in interviews with teachers. The sentiments expressed by Lisa Renaldi, a seventh-grade reading teacher, are not atypical:

Lisa: This attitude—where I don't want to do this, why do I have to do it. And you know there's no sense of motivation to do it.
Ellen: So it's an attitude kind of thing?
Lisa: Oh yeah. Because they have the smarts. Some people in ESL, they should be out [of] there. Like four years or five years, and they're just not trying, while somebody that just came in this country, was out of there after a half of a year. They picked up on it.

Teachers who attribute failure to a lack of effort do not include the newly arrived non–English-speaking students in their judgments; those students are frequently put into regular classrooms before becoming proficient in English, and virtually all teachers agree that for them the language barriers are significant.

Arnhem teachers' responses to students' use of Spanish in the school vary.[4] Among the overwhelming majority of teachers, the concerns articulated revolve around the issue of whether the use of Spanish in the schools reinforces the students' segregation from the mainstream and interferes with their opportunities to practice and master English. Spanish language usage and students' identification with the larger Puerto Rican community are not encouraged in the school, and are at times actively *dis*couraged. When I first entered the school and asked the librarian about books on the Latino experience or books in Spanish, she stated that there were none because she thought such books inadvisable, as they might interfere with students' identification as "Americans" and with their learning English. With the exception of the Spanish language teachers and a couple of the ESL teachers, none of the teachers speak Spanish.[5] Spanish language teachers are thus often called on to "interpret" when Spanish-dominant parents come to the schools (generally only to register their children or if there are behavioral problems). Notices did not go out to Spanish-dominant parents in Spanish until the subsequent New York State Education Department investigation in 1992 prompted a change in the policy.

A very small number of teachers do not see Spanish usage as problematic and are cognizant of some of the factors associated with Puerto Ricans' bilingualism. At the same time, an equally small number are extremely ethnocentric and openly demean Puerto Rican students' language and culture in faculty room discussions. One teacher commented (prior to the community debate) that "they ought to lock 'em up across the river in the caves and don't let 'em come out until they learn English," and after seeing an assembly by a Puerto Rican dance troupe derisively commented "Wasn't that a hoot?" Another talked about the "slut clothes" and "slut shoes" the girls wore to school, and a special education teacher said that giving Puerto Rican students writing assignments was always difficult because they didn't really have a "home" and "any real family life" to write about. Some teachers also tended to evaluate Spanish-dominant Puerto Rican students' classroom behaviors as reflecting their lack of interest in getting an education, failing at times to understand when the behaviors stemmed from language or communication difficulties. ESL students I interviewed, for instance, told of being reprimanded when they whispered to English-dominant friends to have them explain something the teacher had said. Misinterpreting their actions, teachers tended to label such behaviors disruptive (which of course did at times lead to intentionally disruptive behaviors, as students in turn lost interest). Puerto Rican parents, too, are criticized for failing to show up at school functions such as open houses, and for moving their children out of the district during the school year. Such actions, in teachers' views, reflect the parents' devaluation of the importance of their children's education.

A recurring theme running through teachers' comments is that earlier generations of immigrants relegated their native languages to the home (or completely abandoned them) and embraced American values and identity; in turn, they succeeded in becoming upwardly mobile and accepted in the community. Ethnic success stories from their own families or communities frequently accompany such discussions. As in the larger community, it is Costa Rican students who are often pointed to as the most recent ethnic "success" story.

A popular "true" story told to me several times throughout my stay in Arnhem attests to the power of this belief. The story was offered up when there was talk of the academic performances of minority students or discussion of Puerto Rican students' behavior. I first heard it from an administrator who was explaining to me why he thought Puerto Rican students were less successful in school. It was later told to me by, among others, a teacher angry with the New York State Education Department's investigation into the schools, which she felt would put the blame for minority student failure on teachers; a teacher in an English department meeting where minority student progress was being discussed; a school aide during a faculty room conversation in which teachers were discussing the "attitude problems" of several Puerto Rican students; and several more teachers in follow-up interviews on their responses to the NYSED proposals the subsequent year. According to the story, an immigrant student from Costa Rica/Hungary/Czechoslovakia (the country of origin varied) who had recently entered the school district had, after only months of being in the United States, achieved enough fluency in the English language—through hard work—to be able to leave the ESL classroom. In one version the story included the parents, who it was said had intervened to pull him out of the ESL classes where everyone was reputed to be "fooling around" and learning nothing. The student, so the story goes, had then gone on to become an academic superstar at the high school.

What does the story, and the context in which it was told, reveal? This stellar student serves, first of all, as an "ideal type": a student (and his parents) who values education, respects teachers, surmounts language barriers, and works hard—even harder than the typical American student with far fewer obstacles to overcome. He is linked to the national past by way of being an immigrant of the type said to have built the nation. What *doesn't* get said is equally significant: there is never any mention of the educational, linguistic, or class background of the student.[6] (A little detective work into the origins of this story revealed that this mythologized student was actually from Czechoslovakia. His father was a biochemist, and his mother was completing her college degree. The family had lived for a short period in Canada before emigrating to Arnhem.) What the story affirms is that educational success, and thus success in life, can be achieved by anyone willing to work hard enough at it—and, by implication, many Puerto Rican students were not willing.

Theme 2: "Color blindness." A view of the United States as a nation in which groups have encountered—and continue to encounter—oppression is not easily reconciled with teachers' visions of the United States as the "land of opportunity," a notion most teachers grew up with both at home and in their educational experiences. Teachers, as well as administrators, were uncomfortable talking about racism and discrimination. To dwell on such topics, several explained, would be to create conflicts between groups where none existed previously. A building administrator, for instance, vehemently denied the existence of racism among some students after community leaders drew public attention to several bias-related incidents in the building. Commenting on the matter he told a local newspaper reporter, "I don't want to label it and say an incident is anti-Polish or anti-Hispanic, they're just problems between kids. . . . Sure kids make slurs, but I will not accept the term 'racism.' Once you plant the seed then you're going to have a problem."

Observation of classes and interviews with teachers indicated a general unwillingness or uneasiness on the part of teachers to address controversial issues such as racism in the United States. Such conversations, it was feared, might "stir up trouble" among students if introduced into the classroom through literature or discussions of the community debate. One exception to the rule was a young white male high school teacher who did encourage students to discuss controversial issues in greater depth. But one African-American student in his class, though she considered him "cool" because of his willingness to talk with students about subjects such as the Rodney King verdict, angrily denounced him for his failure to "follow through" when racist talk surfaced in the classroom and the debate became heated. Rather than the teacher taking a stand against what the student felt was racist talk—an action that she felt would have been warranted—he brought the discussion to a close by saying only "We're all entitled to our opinions, we just have to respect others' opinions."

Many teachers are wary of practices that result in students being separated by ethnicity or race. They expressed discomfort, for instance, with Latino students clustering in the halls or on the school grounds before and after school (where Spanish and English were both used); with their separating along ethnic lines in classroom activities; and with their sitting together at lunch.[7] Teachers insisted that they wanted to treat all their students "the same." One said she didn't want to know if her students were Puerto Rican or Costa Rican because it might bias her; another worried that making allowances for ESL students' language problems by permitting another student to interpret might harm the students by embarrassing them about their "difference" and hinder their progress in learning English; a third teacher anglicized *Javier* to *Xavier* because "it would be better in the long run for him to have a more American-sounding name."[8]

Theme 3: Teachers as Scapegoats. Many teachers feel that they are being scapegoated for the poor performances of Latino students, as well as for declining student test scores in general. They tend to feel their dedication and professionalism are being questioned when issues are raised regarding their instructional practices. As previously noted, teachers felt they were being blamed by "Culture Link" speakers for poor minority student performance. Prior to publication of the NYSED report teacher talk revolved around how they would be blamed "once again" for student failure. Teachers breathed a collective sigh of relief when the report failed to place the blame on them.[9]

Teachers also feel that desired changes in educational practices are frequently forced on them without opportunities for their input. Long-time teachers could rattle off a variety of educational "whims" that had come and gone during their professional lifetimes (e.g., open classrooms, mastery learning, behavioral objectives, the Madeline Hunter method). One teacher wondered whether "multicultural literature" was only the most recent manifestation of the search for a magic cure for the nation's education woes.

In a situation of conflicting accounts and highly politicized debate about the treatment of Latino students and the adequacy of school curricula, teachers appeared apprehensive about speaking openly with outsiders about their sentiments or concerns. Nontenured teachers in particular were reluctant to publicly take a stand on issues, fearful that they might offend school board members[10] and be denied tenure, a particularly frightening prospect at a time when teacher layoffs throughout the region had become commonplace as a result of budget constraints. One teacher writing a paper for a college course, for instance, refused to acknowledge in the paper that talk generated by the local conflict motivated her desire to construct a curriculum unit incorporating Puerto Rican culture and history. She feared that by putting the local motivation in writing it might get back to school board members and endanger her future as a teacher. Another teacher, who felt that Latino students were in fact sometimes treated unfairly by certain teachers, was unwilling to give a NYSED investigator such information, fearing it might somehow affect his tenure with the district.

As one might imagine, in such a context the act of research itself became charged with ambivalence. Many teachers were initially reticent about letting me observe them in the classroom, though all teachers approached did ultimately allow me to do so.[11] Teachers were most apprehensive about my requests to audiotape classes and interviews, and despite reassurances of confidentiality some in fact refused to be taped. Those reluctant to put their thoughts and classroom interactions on tape included both teachers from promulticultural positions and those who vehemently disagreed with proposed changes.[12] In spite of the fact that the vast majority of the teachers were tenured and the numbers of tenured teachers dismissed in New York is almost nonexistent, many did not feel free to state their views openly. Some expressed concern that what they said could be used against them by administrators, board members, or vocal community members. Within this context, the NYSED investigation was awaited with great trepidation by members of the staff.

The New York State Education Department (NYSED) Investigation

The six-member NYSED site research team assigned to investigate the district spent three days in Arnhem observing and talking with teachers, administrators, students, parents, and other community members and gathering school documents for review. The report they subsequently issued was prepared with several initial assumptions in place. Drawn from recent research and theory on teaching culturally different students (cf. Grant 1992; Nieto 1992; Oakes 1985), these assumptions included: (1) that institutional practices such as ability tracking adversely affect disadvantaged youth; (2) that role models such as minority teachers benefit minority students; (3) that curricula and school practices ought to include and value the culture and language of minority students; and (4) that greater parental involvement in schools would benefit minority youth.

In Arnhem the team found—as they would have in many New York communities—almost no minority personnel, little in the curriculum drawing on Latino culture or language, and a disproportionate concentration of Latino students in the lower educational tracks. The ensuing NYSED report called for numerous reforms designed to better meet the needs of minority students, including detracking, addressing racial prejudice, cultural sensitivity training, hiring more bilingual and minority personnel, improving school–community relations, and curriculum reform. Arnhem had clearly been found wanting, but in both the initial press conference on the findings and the subsequent report, the NYSED emphasized that the situation in Arnhem was not exceptional.

Many teachers, administrators, and board members felt unfairly attacked, however, and they complained that the district had been singled out. References to the NYSED investigation as a "witch hunt" with predetermined findings abounded:

> "I've been in the schools talking to a lot of the teachers and every one of them said they expect the state to give us a report that is 95 percent negative," school board member Jim Barker said. "I do too—they're not coming to tell us what a great job we're doing." (*Arnhem Record,* November 11, 1991)

It was a sentiment also widely expressed in the community, in particular among the senior citizens:

> Make no mistake about it, when an academically accredited, conservative, white middle class school district is being whipped into conformity by a team of Albany-based liberal ideologues enforcing a multicultural, minority-obsessed agenda, the witch hunt label applies. (Letter to the editor, *Arnhem Record,* November 5, 1991)

Community resentment notwithstanding, the superintendent (a former Spanish-language teacher and lifelong resident who had risen through the administrative ranks of the school district) led a massive effort to respond constructively to the report. Teachers, community residents, NYSED representatives, and university personnel met intensively for six weeks and produced a large document outlining programs to be implemented to make the schools more responsive to minority student needs. Implementation, however, was another matter; as my research findings indicate, teacher responses were ambivalent.

Local Responses to Challenges to the Canon[13]

In contemporary multicultural reform projects, multicultural literature has often been cast as "one of the most powerful components of a multicultural education curriculum, the underlying purpose of which is to help to make the society a more equitable one. In light of that purpose, the choice of books to be read and discussed in the nation's schools is of paramount importance" (Bishop 1992:40). Arnhem's secondary English teachers were encouraged to reevaluate the literature canon in the context of concerns raised in the NYSED report and by local minority spokespersons. Before discussing the responses of the teachers to challenges to the literature canon, however, it is important to establish what the teachers were already using and why.

The literature selections that teachers in the junior high English classrooms use includes a mutually agreed-on core of stories and texts for each grade and track level, with the remaining texts selected at the individual teacher's discretion. Teachers had agreed, for instance, that all students except those in the "modified" (lowest-level) track would read the play *The Diary of Anne Frank* (Goodrich and Hackett 1989). "Regents" and "honors" track students, who go on in high school to take state-constructed regents exams and earn the more prestigious regents diploma, read the novels *The Call of the Wild* by Jack London (1931) and *The Red Pony* by John Steinbeck (1973). No novels are mandated for the bottom two tracks, "nonregents" and "modified." The remainder of the literature selections, primarily short stories and poems, are drawn from literature anthologies. The "silver" edition of *Prentice-Hall Literature* (1989) is used by honors and regents students; the "red" edition of *Globe Literature* (1990) with nonregents students; and the *Scope English Program Reading Anthology* (Gardner 1979) with the modified students. Reading teachers have fewer constraints on their choices and seek out "high interest/low reading level" selections from several sources. This curriculum falls clearly within the bounds of traditional literature nationwide (as analyzed, for example, by Applebee 1990, 1991).

When asked to explain why they included particular selections, teachers stressed authorization, appropriateness, and familiarity. Their reasons included the following:

- The department mandates some works
- They have to use the books that are available
- They personally like a particular piece—it moves them
- They feel comfortable with the piece and understand it
- The story holds students' interest
- The story teaches something important to the student—for example, the harmful consequences of prejudice and discrimination (*The Diary of Anne Frank*)
- The story includes characters facing some of the same problems as the students[14]

- It is a piece with which all students should be familiar
- The reading level is suitable for the students
- The topic is appropriate for young teenagers
- The literature ties in well with the social studies curriculum
- The story contains "universals" that all children can relate to—for example, "coming of age" struggles
- The literature shows the "human" side of history

Concerns about Multicultural Literature

Prior to 1991, with the exception of Sandy Totten, a new teacher who stressed multicultural perspectives in the classroom, English/reading teachers were generally not acquainted with the body of research and theory arguing for a more inclusive curriculum. There was, however, considerable discussion of the topic during the 1991–1992 school year as an outgrowth of the conflict in the community over Latino students' educational needs and the subsequent NYSED investigation. Two of the monthly English/reading department meetings were devoted to the topic of multicultural literature. Several teachers attended the New York State English Council conference on multicultural literature, or a regional conference that featured teachers from nearby districts talking about their uses of multicultural literature in the classroom, or both. In response to the local conflict over the school of Latino students, the school district also arranged for Nicholasa Mohr, a popular author whose books reflect her experiences growing up Puerto Rican in New York City, to give a presentation to the students. The introduction of her books into the school in anticipation of her visit generated considerable discussion about multicultural works.

The teachers' concerns about multicultural literature that I bring forward were expressed both directly in department meetings and in interviews and informal discussions over the course of the school year, as well as indirectly in the teachers' choices and treatment of literature in the English classroom. I group these concerns into four categories[15]: knowledge issues, practical issues, canonical issues, and "danger" issues. The first two are discussed briefly, the latter two at greater length.

Knowledge Issues: "What Is Multicultural Literature?"

Despite a recent proliferation of journal articles and books and coverage in the popular press on the debates around multiculturalism and the literature canon in universities and schools, most of the teachers were initially unclear about such matters. Recurrent questions included "What *is* multicultural literature?" "Which books should I be using?" "How do I define African/European/Asian literature?" "Don't we do it already because I teach a book with all black characters/ because I teach the works of authors from Russia and other countries/ because I include poems from Maya Angelou and Langston Hughes?"

Teachers were also concerned about the "fuzziness" of the culture concept. "What is culture?" "Whose culture are we supposed to teach?" "How do you teach 'culture' when it's always changing?" One teacher repeatedly stressed that she was not a history teacher, hadn't studied history and culture in school, and as a result didn't feel confident talking about other cultures with her students.

Practical Issues: "How Am I Supposed to Fit It into the Curriculum?"

Closely linked to questions of "what" were questions of "how." "How do I find the time to do all the reading?" "How am I supposed to fit it into the curriculum when we barely have time now to do the requirements, with all the emphasis on testing and skills?" Because funds were earmarked for the purchase of such texts, the usual problem of accessing new materials in the face of budget constraints was not imminent.

Canonical Issues: "Good Literature"

Teachers did not generally subscribe to a rigid "canon" of literature that would serve as the sole arbiter of which selections they used in the classroom, but they were concerned about offering students "good literature." Teachers frequently alluded to the importance of exposing students to "good literature," but found its qualities somewhat ephemeral. As in the old saying about art, "I know it when I see it," they relied on their ability to recognize it when they saw it, much as one teacher did when asked whether classroom materials should be representative of the diversity of the U.S. population:

> Yeah—proportionately. I don't think you have to do it disproportionately, out of a sense of guilt, a collective sense of guilt. I mean you can feel a thumping "Yes!" in a room when teachers all read one book and say "It's great." I've seen all my colleagues, all of them say, "This is terrific.". . . When you look in somebody's eyes and they say its a good book, yeah, it's a really good book.

As these remarks suggest, good literature was something that teachers intuitively agreed on, and criteria for "good" literature included widespread acknowledgment of its inherent "quality."

Teachers also emphasized that good literature contained "universal" themes. Several teachers voiced uncertainty about whether "multicultural" literature, which they tended to see as something separate from "traditional" literature, would be considered "good literature" and have "staying power" in the future. Teachers with higher track students worried that their students might "lose out" by not being exposed to the classics, particularly if they were expected to know them in order to do well in high school and college. That is, there was an implicit or explicit contrast operating between a vaguely formulated but strongly felt literature canon, with its high quality and universal themes, and multicultural literature, of lesser quality and particularistic themes.

Answering the question "Why should we teach multicultural literature?" also requires addressing the question of who should be the audience for multicultural literature. Because of the local conflict, the demand for it in Arnhem was largely perceived as having grown out of the need to be more "inclusive" in the curriculum for the benefit of minority students. In junior and senior high school departmental meetings and at regional conferences, the importance of incorporating literature written by authors of color into the teaching of "American" literature came up several times. Usually at least one teacher was likely to raise the issue of whether, in the name of "equity," the history and literature of other ethnic groups, such as Italian and Polish Americans, would also need to be deliberately included.

Danger Issues: "Don't Get Students 'All Stirred Up'"

The final set of concerns, those that are in some ways both the most important and most problematic in attempts to expand the literature curriculum, are what I label the "danger issues." These are the concerns that, by virtue of their very nature, are often least adequately addressed or confronted in the literature on multiculturalism. These issues are often intimately connected to concerns already addressed above, but are less likely to be acknowledged. Thus, for instance, the question "Why should we be teaching multicultural literature?" may be answered by talking about the need for "inclusion" and valuing "cultural pluralism," but to leave it at that is to fail to acknowledge the political edge of the debate and the questions of power that surface in the process of "reframing" our histories and literatures. The concerns brought together here were often hesitantly mentioned by teachers as a side comment, or hinted at; rarely were they openly and directly addressed. Sometimes it was the very *lack* of talk that led me to infer teachers' unwillingness to engage their students in talk about particular topics.

"Language" Issues. Teachers were concerned about the use of obscenities in the multicultural literature selections they examined. Many considered such terms—in particular, slang references to sexual organs—totally unacceptable in school texts and rejected texts solely on that basis. They felt that including such terms was inappropriate for a number of reasons: it might appear that the school sanctioned the use of the terms; they were unprepared to deal with students' reactions to the terms; they would be embarrassed saying such terms aloud in the classroom; they were morally offended by the language; or they would "get into trouble" with administrators and parents because of the language. As pointed out earlier, teachers, like their students, enter classrooms as raced, classed, and gendered actors. In the "language" issues we see a double effect of gender: avoidance by female teachers of "profane" language and the

gendering of school as a place where the vulgar realities and words of life are not to be allowed.

Social Problems. The literature written by minority authors about the minority experience in the United States may well include topics that middle-class mainstream teachers are ill prepared to discuss, or indeed even acknowledge: drug use, gangs, teen pregnancy and sexuality, AIDS, and violence. While such issues are not exclusive to any ethnic group or particular class, they are often linked in teachers' minds (as in general public perception) with impoverished inner-city residents, the majority of whom are thought to be people of color. Arnhem teachers tended to avoid discussing such topics. One teacher, for instance, chose not to use a student magazine issue that included a play about AIDS. Students were also aware that some issues were not "school" topics: a Puerto Rican ESL student, for instance, trying to explain what the Spanish word *trafico* meant in English to a group of ESL students, hesitantly said "like drug *trafico*" while darting glances at the teacher to assess her response to his answer. In avoiding "social problems" we see what is likely a class-based avoidance of social realities: delinquent peer groups, sexuality, and drug abuse are not exclusive to any particular social class, but the ability to avoid public discussion of them may be a uniquely middle-class achievement.

Threats to Authority. Multicultural literature often draws on the experiences of oppressed national minorities. It introduces into the classroom perspectives and experiences of individuals from social backgrounds that differ from those of most school teachers or from those depicted in traditional school literature. Teachers were often uncomfortable with multicultural literature selections that depicted key societal institutions or their representatives—the courts, police, schools, teachers, churches—in a negative light. For example, one teacher rejected *Nilda* (Mohr 1973) for use with her students because in the novel neighborhood children defy the police and turn on a fire hydrant on a blazing hot afternoon, and because a Catholic church camp the main character attends is depicted negatively. In another case a teacher chose not to read "The Wrong Lunch Line" (Mohr 1986a) because in it the children talk among themselves, mocking authority figures in the school.

Teachers also felt that their own authority in schools was eroding. Recent incidents of teachers being reprimanded for their verbal treatment of minority students in Arnhem and elsewhere were popular topics of faculty room conversations. Stories abounded about "attitude problems"of particular students and teacher run-ins with them. Following one incident, in which a district teacher was suspended without pay for a month after making comments to a student that the school board deemed inappropriate, a long-time teacher angrily stated that teachers might as well paint bulls' eyes on their backs so they could be "picked off" more easily.

Some teachers felt that discussing the kinds of issues frequently raised in multicultural literature might also "rock the boat" and get students "all stirred up." One teacher described how she had read the introduction to the play *The Diary of Anne Frank* to her students but studiously avoided discussing Nazi theories with them because she worried how "all that talk about the superiority of blonde hair and blue eyes" might provoke controversy in her classroom, given the political situation of Euro-American/Latino polarization going on beyond school doors.

In summarizing teacher responses to multicultural literature, it was not "cultural difference" per se that was at issue with the avoided texts and topics, since most teachers would subscribe to the notion that celebrating "diversity" was a worthwhile endeavor "if it didn't go too far." "Too far" meant many things: challenging the existing literature canon; questioning underlying social assumptions endorsed by teachers (e.g., that police, schools, and churches are fundamentally benign for *all* social groups); or questioning their own position as arbiters of classroom language and discipline.

A Classroom Case Study: Margaret Lane

The issues brought out in the preceding pages illustrate general concerns of teachers regarding the incorporation of multicultural literature into the classroom. Margaret Lane, whose approach to the English classroom is described below (and in more depth in Chapter 6), was one of the teachers most reluctant to adopt a multicultural curriculum and approach in her classroom. As we will see, her classroom is a model of what Miller (1992) and others describe as the "authoritarian classroom." Because her style has long been the norm in classrooms, her traditional approach merits examination; it raises questions about how "difference" can be introduced into classroom discourse.

A diminutive, reserved woman with curly gray hair and glasses, Margaret Lane brings to mind the image of a caring teacher in a Norman Rockwell painting. She is Irish American, and attended a private Catholic college to earn an M.A. in American literature before beginning teaching in the mid-1960s. Unlike the majority of the city's teachers, she is not originally from the area, nor does she reside in the community. She brings twenty-five years' experience and a more traditional approach to her teaching of the English language arts.

Mrs. Lane uses short stories in her eighth-grade nonregents class; ten of the eleven stories she taught over the course of the school year had white males as the major characters. The eleventh involved a white male narrator telling the story from his perspective of how a "girl pitcher" saves the day for his team (circa 1950s). Only through reading the required play *The Diary of Anne Frank* do her students encounter a central female character or narrator.

Mrs. Lane had been under pressure to move from her primarily grammar-based teaching approach (with average and lower-track students) toward a more literature-based curriculum, but has consistently resisted doing so. She is reluctant to accept criticism and guards the prerogatives of seniority. When a college student, a man in his thirties who had returned for a teaching degree, observed her class and then made a suggestion to her about something she might want to try in class, her angry response (in describing the incident to this researcher) was that he had no right to tell her–a twenty-plus-year veteran–how to teach. She speaks with pride of her reputation with administrators and parents as an excellent teacher, and the basis on which she has traditionally been given the honors-track class.

Mrs. Lane feels that her opportunities to teach literature have consistently eroded over the years because of the need to prepare students for state competency exams and because of declining student skills. She explains her emphasis on grammar in the nonregents tracks, and the students' consequent lack of writing opportunities and exposure to literature, as a result of the need for them to improve their basic skills before moving on to incorporate more reading and writing in their learning. Students in her eighth-grade nonregents class that I observed did not write any essays until mid-January, when they were provided with the "proper form," a standardized five-paragraph format long popular in

English classes.[16] While her regents-level students read two novels, and her honors section in addition wrote book reports and worked on a "heroes" unit, her non-regents students focused on grammar, short stories, and fill-in and short-answer exams. These pronounced differences in classroom experiences are particularly significant for Latino children: whereas 77 percent of the white eighth-grade students were in regents and honors classes, only 45 percent of the Latino students (with 2 percent "honors") were similarly situated. Almost a quarter of the Latino students were in the lowest-level, "modified" track. Mrs. Lane is adamantly opposed to the ideas of detracking and teaming, both of which were scheduled to be implemented in the school the following year in preparation for the transition to a middle school.[17]

Mrs. Lane's literature selections include "classic" pieces she feels students should be exposed to such as Homer's *Iliad,* "The Legend of Sleepy Hollow" by Washington Irving (1963), and works by Robert Frost. She also draws on adventure and "fun" stories that she believes students like and "morality tales" such as "The Man Without a Country" (Hale 1963) that hold a message for students about traits such as courage or patriotism. She draws from stories she has used in past years, and did not substantively alter her literature choices in response to the discussions around multicultural literature. These stories are incorporated into theme units developed in her early years of teaching that she feels worked well in past years.

In Mrs. Lane's nonregents class there is little opportunity for, or evidence of, student involvement with classroom literature. Questions tend to be lower-level recall questions, and students either follow dutifully along or "drift off" in class until called on.[18] There are few calls for students to "engage" with the texts, to draw connections between their own lives and those in the literature.

During my observations, Mrs. Lane subtly reinforced lower-track students' awareness of their ranking in school and the larger society, though she intended her statements to make them proud of their accomplishments and to motivate them. In one instance, speaking to an eighth-grade nonregents class and discussing the results of a spelling test given to all eighth graders, she announced that she "was pleasantly surprised . . . (because) some of you beat out some of my honors kids. Yeah!" On another day with the same class, she ignored the contrast between levels when students mentioned it:

Mrs. Lane: You guys are doing better than my first-period class. My first period class was dead.
Jamie: Aren't they honors?
Mrs. Lane: What does that mean?
Tom: They're smarter than we are.
Mrs. Lane: [No response to statement.] I asked them what did you do—sleep till 11:00?

Mrs. Lane also accepted the assumption that the nonregents track meant technical training with a clear sexual division of labor, as when she discussed the local high school's vocational program:

Mrs. Lane: They've got quite a carpentry shop up there. And they've got a program for you gals.
Karin: Cosmetology.
Mrs. Lane: Right. Many times people look down upon those who work with their hands. Don't—do they make a lot of money?
Students: Yes.
Mrs. Lane: We need these people.

The messages she sends to the students are straightforward and traditional: that nonregents students performing well is unusual enough to be pointed out; that nonregents students are destined for the vocational program at the high school; and that the programs are gendered, with boys pursuing carpentry and girls pursuing cosmetology.

Concerned that she not be out of step with other teachers and feeling pressure from the supervisor to alter her classroom practices, Mrs. Lane did introduce the works of Puerto Rican author Nicholasa Mohr to her students. Though she expressed concern that the author's stories were "particularistic" and not likely to appeal to non–Puerto Rican students, she read two of Mohr's short stories to students prior to Mohr's visit to the school. However, Mrs. Lane did not discuss the stories extensively, incorporate them into exam questions, or add them to the list of readings covered during the year for students to draw on in answering their final exam questions.

In her classroom response to the stories Mrs. Lane disparaged the vernacular used by the main characters and telegraphed to the students her own discomfort with ethnic differences. In the following example, taken from a grade eight regents-level classroom discussion, she reads from background material about the author and from a Mohr story entitled "Once Upon a Time . . ." (1986a; note the treatment of vernacular idiom as well as of Spanish and English differences):

> I want to give you a little background about Nicholasa Mohr, so that when she comes next week to talk to you people, you know something about her. [Reading aloud:] "Nicholasa Mohr was born in Manhattan, where she grew up in *El* ____?____?" [Pauses.] The word begins with *b* [Points to the two Latino students in the classroom.] You Hispanic students have some insights here? [No response from two students. Long pause.] *Barrio*. She grew up in *El Barrio*.

> [Later in the same class, reading aloud from "Once Upon a Time. . . ":] "'What do you think?' asked the second girl. 'Should we tell somebody what we seen [a dead body]?'" [Addresses class, in an astonished tone of voice:] *Seen*? [Continues reading:] "'. . . We better not; then they'll ask us what we was doing up on the roof and all,' said the first girl." [Addresses class:] These kids haven't had Mrs. Lane's grammar class yet.

Like many Americans, Mrs. Lane is uncomfortable with the use of vernacular in literature, as shown by her response to "seen" and her comment about grammar. She is also uncomfortable with Spanish in the classroom, as shown in her treatment of the place name *El Barrio*.

Mrs. Lane indicated that although she thought there were "universal" themes in Nicholasa Mohr's stories, the "specific ethnicity" of the characters (primarily Puerto Rican) was a problem, as students would not relate to the texts. She framed the texts as "Puerto Rican" literature, explaining to her class that the author had taken up writing because she realized there were "no books for Hispanic students, who are different." In an interview before a follow-up class discussion of a Mohr story, Mrs. Lane maintained that none of her students had displayed any interest in Mohr's books. After the subsequent class discussion of the short story by Mohr, however, all of the female students requested a copy of the order forms for purchase of her works.[19] In another (nonregents) class, ten of the fourteen students present (including both males and females, and all five of the Latino students) requested order forms.

Mrs. Lane attempts to avoid conflict and heated discussions in her classroom. Her questioning style is to solicit one-word or one-sentence factual answers, thus limiting students' opportunities to voice their own opinions or give full responses. She is aware that some students harbor racist sentiments, but in the classes I observed she attempted to ignore prejudicial remarks by students said loud enough to be heard by teacher and students but quietly enough to be ignored if the teacher chose to do so. In the following example Mrs. Lane is attempting to elicit the meaning of the spelling word "emancipation" from her students:

Mrs. Lane: What's the "Emancipation Proclamation"?
Russell [African-American male, calling out]: That's social studies!
Paul [white male, under his breath but audibly]: Freed the niggers.

Mrs. Lane appeared not to hear Paul. Miguel, a Puerto Rican student sitting two rows away from Paul, was visibly angry and shot a hostile look at him but said nothing. After the bell rang Miguel walked over to Russell, his friend, and asked him if he had heard what Paul said. Russell shrugged ("So what's new?") and Miguel muttered angrily, "I'm not a nigger," a response that suggests his identification with African Americans. Mrs. Lane later admitted to me that she had heard the remark but didn't want to "make a scene."

These very selective excerpts from Margaret Lane's classroom illustrate the traditional nature of her literature selection, her avoidance of issues of inequality and prejudice, and her linguistic prescriptivism. But I also emphasize that in these respects she is a perfectly normal, good teacher of her generation. As noted above, she had for years been assigned honors classes, and only in recent years has she begun to seem somewhat out of step with trends in English education. She was the most resistant to changes in the junior high school, but not atypical of several other long-time teachers; to varying degrees, many exhibited the same qualities.

Exclusion and the Classroom Teacher

> Knowledge is neither neutral nor apolitical, yet it is generally treated by teachers and schools as if it were. . . . Every educational decision made at any level, whether by a teacher or an entire school system, reflects the political ideology and worldview of the decision maker. . . . It is important to understand that as teachers, all the decisions we make, no matter how neutral they seem, may impact in unconscious but fundamental ways on the lives and experiences of our students. (Nieto 1992:219)

As Nieto suggests, a multicultural curriculum has been encouraged as a primary means of making schools more inclusive, as a way of breaking the silences and acknowledging the political nature of educational choices. Yet failure to acknowledge the teacher's importance in delivering that curriculum may mean that adopting a more "inclusive" curriculum or text produces little significant change. Urged to broaden their classroom literature selections, teachers in Arnhem drew on their own experiences and popular understandings in ways that silenced particular discourses—for example, by omitting particular types of selections, avoiding classroom discussion, or subtly reinforcing societal biases. These practices were not intended or understood to be harmful to particular groups. But without being encouraged to examine the ways in which they contributed to school practices that marginalized particular groups of students, little of consequence was apparently accomplished in actual curricular or classroom reform.

There is little in the educational biographies of Arnhem teachers, or American teachers more generally, to predispose them toward embracing the merits of a more inclusive literature curriculum that challenges cherished assumptions about matters such as equality of opportunity and acceptable public cultural expressions. Most teachers are Euro-American and, in a society that is largely segregated, have limited exposure beyond "food and festivals" to other U.S. subcultures. Many of the teachers grew up on the stories told by community Seniors and achieved a degree of social mobility that allowed them to believe that they and their white peers' progress came through individual hard work alone; within that framework upward mobility is available to those who succeed educationally and work at it.

Most current teachers also acquired their degrees prior to both the proliferation of research attesting to the role of cultural difference in the creation of unequal educational outcomes and the recent challenges at the university level to the literature canon. Recent graduates are unlikely to have fared a great deal better, since teacher education programs have been slow to incorporate a significant multicultural focus (see Grant 1992; Nieto 1996; Ramsey et al. 1989).[20]

Cultural differences in the classroom can form the basis for the dialogic, reflective thinking that all students need to learn, but only if new stances toward texts, collaborative reflection, and sustained dialogue are actively sought in classroom literature discussions (Miller 1992). The dominant metaphors of teaching work against this dialogic orientation, however. On their way through our educational system, teachers have passed through classrooms dominated by what has been termed a "banking" (Freire 1970) or "transmission" (Cummins 1989) model of education, in which the teacher is understood as the dispenser of a preset body of (elite) knowledge and the student the passive recipient of an education. Teachers "possess" knowledge; students lack it. Teachers are understood as, and expected to be, the "authorities" on a fixed body of knowledge (Applebee 1993;

Giroux and McLaren 1988; Hirsch 1987). They are not encouraged to see knowledge as socially constructed and themselves as lifelong learners. They have had little if any exposure to a model of "critical literacy," which "invites teachers and students to 'problematize' all subjects of study—that is, to understand existing knowledge as an historical product deeply invested with the values of those who developed such knowledge" (Shor 1986:420).

In addition to the cultural backgrounds and professional socialization of many teachers, there are the conditions of work to consider, both daily conditions and those held over the longer term. The nature of teaching traditionally has been that teachers are isolated behind closed doors, with only students as an audience; when administrators enter to observe classes, it is almost always for evaluative purposes. Opportunities for teachers to observe their peers and reflect on their own teaching are virtually nonexistent (Cuban 1984). Teachers in Arnhem are not required to take classes once they have acquired a master's degree (as is the case in New York in general), and typically have funding to attend at most one educational conference per year. Exposure to new information and group discussion is likely to be limited to department meetings, an annual or biannual "Superintendent's Day," after-school workshops, in-service courses, and the teachers' own initiatives beyond the school doors. In Arnhem, as elsewhere, department meetings are frequently taken up with more mundane concerns–paperwork, scheduling, and the like. While several English/reading department meetings in Arnhem had been used one year to begin to explore what a multicultural education might involve, and how tracking might put certain groups at a disadvantage, department meetings were virtually eliminated the following year when the position of department head was abolished for budgetary reasons.

Serious curricular reform requires careful attention to the conditions (and consequences) of change. There is little, however, in the existing service network for teachers that provides such sustained attention. Conference days and after-school workshops may be useful means of introducing a topic but constitute little more than lip service without adequate follow-through. In-service courses, when run by teachers' centers, are more likely to be oriented toward teachers' concerns and needs, but many teachers never avail themselves of such courses for a variety of reasons. They may perceive no benefit because the financial remuneration is minimal or they may complain–with some justification–that the professors are "eggheads" with no idea what classroom realities are like. Outside presenters, while tackling difficult issues, must be aware that most teachers feel embattled and are therefore quick to reject what looks like uninformed criticism. As mentioned earlier, many teachers disliked what they perceived as the hectoring tone of the Culture Link workshop, and many resented the outside imposition of NYSED-driven reforms.

Paradoxically, although certain outside authorities were questioned, others were taken for granted. Arnhem teachers' responses to the question of how they make literature selections point to some of the many ways in which schools function as conservative institutions. Teachers indicated a reliance on "experts" (e.g., editors of anthologies) in making their choices; selected among pieces they themselves had enjoyed; and attempted to include selections that had a "good message" embedded in them.[21] Whereas authorities and "outsiders" demanding changes were rejected, other authorities had been assimilated into the taken-for-granteds of teaching and curriculum. Criteria of "enjoyable" stories with "good messages" can also be problematic. Although the moral optimism of a "good message" is appropriate for educational endeavors, as an unexamined category of common sense it can block engagement with texts that explore the more difficult and painful aspects of American life.

Given the homogeneity of the English/reading teachers' racial and ethnic and class backgrounds, and the remarkable homogeneity of the literature curriculum nationwide (Applebee 1990), these teachers' selections were likely to reflect and support a very particular view of the world. When left unexamined and not raised to a conscious level, such views unavoidably excluded other voices, especially those of students of color and working-class students. Following Michele Fine (1987), I suggest that this exclusion or silencing is pervasive, affecting students, teachers, and the general sense of what can be discussed in school settings. "Silencing" is basic to educational institutions:

> Silencing constitutes a process of institutionalized policies and practices which obscure the very social, economic, and therefore experiential conditions of students' daily lives, and which expel from written, oral, and nonverbal expression substantive and critical "talk" about these conditions. . . . Yet simple, seamless pronouncements of equal opportunity and educational credentials as the primary mode of mobility are woven through the curriculum and pedagogy of urban high school classes. Silencing constitutes the process by which contradictory evidence, ideologies, and experiences find themselves buried, camouflaged, and discredited. (Fine 1987:157)

Institutions are constituted by negations as well as assertions, by hidden curricula as well as overt curricula, by what is unsaid and excluded as well as what is said and included. In Arnhem, despite open consideration of what literature gets taught in the classroom, silencing occurred in a variety of ways. It occurred through omission of particular topics and selections (e.g., by defining "quality" narrowly); through failure to use the literature to create an environment in which students could safely bring their own lives and perspectives into the classroom (e.g., by avoiding social problems literature); and through subtle reinforcement of racial, class, and gender hierarchies (e.g., by simply accepting gender categories in vocational education and by ignoring openly racist comments made during lessons).

"Naming" is what Fine calls the opposite of silencing. It is critical talk about "the very social, economic, and therefore experiential conditions of students' daily lives" (1987:157). In her study of an inner city school Fine discovered that naming was something educators studiously avoided. Instead they smoothed over or ignored the social contradictions that students' daily lives presented (see also Shujaa 1991). A similar case for silencing or avoiding naming can be made for Arnhem, whether the issue is recognition of different groups through organizations, the social studies curriculum, or simply the treatment of students. For instance, Latino students at the high school asked to set up a school club for minority youth where they might meet to discuss their encounters with prejudice and discrimination and find ways to confront such issues and generally provide support for each other. The request was turned down and instead a "multicultural" club was officially established with the mission of encouraging students to value diversity. Diversity was divorced from underlying issues of inequality and power.[22]

There is a powerful and understandable desire among teachers to want to believe that the United States has been a land of opportunity for all, and that all groups have encountered essentially the same barriers. It has been problematic to acknowledge prejudice, discrimination, and racism in the classroom; yet that is essential in discussing the literatures and histories of the oppressed. An Arnhem social studies teacher teaching about immigration, for instance, asked his Puerto Rican students to understand their experiences as equivalent to those of turn-of-the-century European immigrants, who had struggled so that their children or grandchildren would "have it all." The possibility that racial hierarchies and changing economic conditions might have a bearing on the Puerto Rican community's economic and social locations was never raised. Nor were the students asked to examine their parents' or their own experiences and test them against the teacher's contention that "we all face the same problems" as newcomers. Other teachers also systematically elided discussion in classrooms of the local controversy about racism on the school board and in the school system because it was "too hot" a topic. They were concerned that including unflattering portraits of the United States today would somehow "demoralize" students or leave them angry and hostile. As members of the "majority group" teachers frequently felt defensive and attacked.

Many teachers, as also noted, emphasized that they ignored "race" and "ethnic differences" among students. They spoke of how they didn't see differences among their students, how they forgot their students' last names after a few weeks, how they treated all students the same, how they didn't want to know who was "Puerto Rican" and who was "Costa Rican" because it might prejudice them. While such teachers believed that to be "color-blind" was desirable, because it meant that they treated all their students fairly and impartially, "the opposite may actually be true. That is, to see differences, in this line of reasoning, is to see defects and inferiority. Thus, to be color-blind may result in *refusing to accept differences* and therefore accepting the dominant culture as the norm. It may result in denying the very identity of our students, thereby making them invisible. . . . Being color-blind can be positive if it means being *nondiscriminatory* in attitude and behavior. However, it is sometimes used as a way to deny differences that help make us who we are" (Nieto 1992:109).

When teachers deny differences such as race or language that may be integral components of their students' identities, they block out qualities that the students' parents or communities may view positively (e.g., Paley 1979; Zentella 1981). The unwillingness of teachers to acknowledge differences in the classroom also constitutes silence—a common American uneasiness with the ugly fact that "difference" is frequently evaluated negatively. Like Fine (1987) and Shujaa (1991), I found that certain topics and discourses were typically avoided or omitted in classrooms, faculty discussions, and school texts, constituting a pervasive silencing that in the process negated or denied the lived realities of many of the district's students.

School observations and interviews in Arnhem suggest that the presence or absence of a diversity of voices in the libraries and classrooms matters for many at-risk minority youth. One seventh-grade Puerto Rican student, catching a glimpse of a book I was carrying entitled *Puerto Ricans: Born in the U.S.A.* (Rodríguez 1989), expressed genuine shock that there were books about—or by—Puerto Ricans. The visit of Nuyorican author Nicholasa Mohr to the local junior high school likewise engendered considerable excitement among the Puerto Rican students.[23] Her presentation to the students included numerous Spanish phrases and "insider" jokes and references Puerto Rican students responded to immediately; in this instance they had the "cultural capital" that made it possible for them to appreciate her storytelling at another level, and they enjoyed it immensely. Their rapt attention to Mohr's presentation and the way they approached her at the book-signing and reception suggest that her visit had special significance to them.

Teachers' encounters with and responses to the multicultural selections that reflect the lived experiences and perspectives of working-class and ethnic cultures are instructive. Those who challenge the traditional canons and the consequences of such canons at the university level—for instance, academic scholars who are feminists, ethnic studies scholars, or historians of social movements–are ideologically aligned and politically committed to challenging a status quo that works in multiple ways to marginalize and silence particular groups. But when we transfer the challenge to the literature canon of the public schools, we ask teachers who may have no such orientations, understandings, or commitment to become involved in the task. What transpired in Arnhem points to the need for teacher educators to recognize that incorporating multicultural literature into school curricula and encouraging the introduction of a "dialogic pedagogy" (Miller 1992), a crucial step toward moving away from the silencing that has characterized much of students' educational experiences, is an inherently dangerous process, for it challenges some of the most basic and cherished assumptions about knowledge, schooling, and opportunity in the United States.

6 Inclusion and Exclusion in the Classroom

Mrs. Lane [reviewing worksheet on selecting the appropriate verb form for a sentence]: This is the one I cringe at: "I *seen* that movie last week."

Mario Rivera [Puerto Rican student explaining in English class how a native Spanish speaker might carry over Spanish pronunciations into English]: Sometimes your grand—my grandmother, my grandmother says, instead of "yellow" she says "jellow."

Among the areas of inquiry considered in the search for explanations for unequal educational outcomes has been the classroom environment itself. "Cultural mismatches" between student and teacher, with subsequent calls for "culturally appropriate," or "culturally congruent" instruction, were an early focus beginning in the late 1960s. Increasingly, however, such alterations are viewed as only one element in creating classroom communities that enhance nonmainstream students' opportunities to succeed academically. Multicultural educators have called for greater attention to how traditional classroom practices work to marginalize nonmainstream students. Gloria Ladson-Billings urges the adoption of culturally relevant pedagogy that "provide(s) a way for students to maintain their cultural integrity while succeeding academically . . . (and learning) to recognize, understand, and critique current social inequities" (1995:476); Sonia Nieto calls for "affirmation, solidarity, and critique," underlining that "racism needs to be confronted head-on" (1996:355); and Sharon Nelson-Barber and Terry Meier stress the need for teachers to create classroom environments that "grant voice and legitimacy to the perspectives and experiences of those who are different from themselves—communities that do not require students to surrender personal and cultural identity in exchange for academic achievement" (1988:5). Such works suggest that teacher responses to students' linguistic and cultural diversity, particularly with domestic minority students who may have less reason to accept the legitimacy of the schools, may be important in establishing the trust needed for nonmainstream students to consent to learn.

The English teacher's classroom is arguably one of the most crucial sites in which the validity of minority students' home culture and language or dialect may be contested or affirmed. It is in the English classroom that students are exposed to "great" writers, and to the topics deemed worthy of studying. It is also in the English classroom that judgment may be passed on students' home languages and dialects, as expressed in their spoken and written language.

My own observations of English teachers' classrooms over the course of a school year revealed significant differences in how nonmainstream students' cultural and linguistic practices were treated, as well as in students' accompanying willingness to enter into classroom participation.[1] I have chosen here to highlight excerpts from the transcripts of two teachers' classrooms that point to the significance of the classroom encounter for Puerto Rican students. Margaret Lane, introduced in the previous chapter, represents a more traditional approach to the teaching of the English language arts. Her classroom is contrasted with that of another junior high school English teacher, Sandy Totten, whose teaching more closely aligns with that advocated by multicultural education proponents. Both teachers taught the same grade and track levels. Here I examine how the classroom environments the two teachers construct—through literature choices, classroom pedagogy, interactions with students, and responses to linguistic and cultural diversity—work in ways that either affirm or exclude the voices and lives of nonmainstream students. If education that is culturally inclusive and empowering has the potential to play an important role in enhancing the likelihood of students from oppressed groups in society achieving educational success, such practices necessarily bear close examination.

Research on Classroom Practices

Before addressing the particulars of the two classrooms it is useful to consider some of the frequently cited research linking classroom practices to student outcomes. The myth of schools as meritocracies rests on an unexamined assumption that all children are equally positioned to take advantage of the educational opportunities the school offers; yet the cultural or class backgrounds of students may enter into their opportunities to achieve in school in subtle ways. Anthropologists examining classroom interactions have pointed to the ways in which differences between the culture of the classroom and students' homes contribute to interactive difficulties and negative evaluations by teachers of students' abilities. The likelihood of these differences contributing to interactive difficulties, and subsequently to resistance by students to school learning, is further enhanced when societal evaluations that stigmatize nonmainstream cultural or class practices are operating.

Before examining the value of such anthropological works, however, it is useful to consider how these cultural differences in schools can better be conceptualized as the "cultural capital" of the dominant classes. Pierre Bourdieu's work (e.g., Bourdieu and Passeron 1977) highlights the ways in which formally meritocratic educational institutions contribute to the reproduction of inequality through legitimation of the linguistic and cultural resources of the dominant classes. These resources become "cultural capital" in school settings. As Michele Lamont and Annette Lareau note in reviewing Bourdieu's work, the power exercised through cultural capital "is first and foremost a power to shape other peoples' lives through exclusion and symbolic imposition (Bourdieu and Passeron 1977 [1970], p.18). In particular it is a power of legitimating the claim that specific cultural norms and practices are superior. . . . The capacity of a class to make its particular preferences and practices seem natural and authoritative is the key to its control" (1988:159).

Individuals acquire different sets of linguistic and cultural competencies through their class (and ethnic or racial) backgrounds, and these are privileged to a greater or lesser extent in schools to the degree to which they conform to those of the dominant mainstream culture. "Distinctive cultural knowledge is transmitted by the families of each social class. As a consequence, children of the dominant class inherit substantially different cultural knowledge, skills, manners, norms, dress, styles of interaction, and linguistic facilities than do the sons and daughters of lower-class origin. . . . Schools and other symbolic institutions contribute to the reproduction of inequality by devising a curriculum that rewards the *cultural capital* of the dominant classes and systematically devalues that of the lower classes" (Mehan et al. 1994:93).

What goes unrecognized is the extent to which "talent" and school success are inextricably linked to the amount of accumulated cultural capital students bring to schools.

> Because the social conditions of its transmission and acquisition are more disguised than those of economic capital, it (cultural capital) is predisposed to function as symbolic capital, i.e. to be unrecognized as capital and recognized as legitimate competence. . . . The initial accumulation of cultural capital, the precondition for the fast, easy accumulation of every kind of useful cultural capital, starts at the outset, without delay, without wasted time, only for the offspring of families endowed with strong cultural capital: in this case, the accumulation period covers the whole period of socialization. It follows that the transmission of cultural capital is no doubt the best hidden form of hereditary transmission of capital. (Bourdieu 1986:245–6)

The legitimization in schools of middle-class forms of knowledge, ways of speaking, and ways of relating to the world privilege those who enter the schools already familiar with such forms; from the very outset students from minority and working-class communities are put at considerably greater risk of failing.

Rather than focus on institutional mechanisms perpetuating unequal outcomes, much of the early research and theory attempting to account for differential schooling outcomes posited genetic, linguistic, or cultural deficits—or some combination of the three—as reasons why certain groups performed poorly in school. Early twentieth-century arguments that southern and eastern Europeans were genetically inferior to northwestern Europeans and "native" American stock were more easily laid to rest than assumptions of genetic inferiority of the "nonwhite" races; these alleged genetic differences were frequently used to justify separate and unequal educational facilities and programs for such groups (Menchaca and Valencia 1990). The assumptions of genetic inferiority are now summarily dismissed by most members of the academic community as flawed, as noted earlier. Less easy to lay to rest, however, has been the "deficit" or "deprivation" approach, which locates the responsibility for minority children's poorer academic performances in the language "deficiencies" and cultural orientations and values learned in minority students' homes and communities. This explanation was readily accepted by many educators, fitting as it did so well with societal attitudes toward ethnic and racial minorities and allowing the underlying assumptions driving the schools to remain essentially intact. The role of schools, according to this perspective, was to provide the necessary compensatory education to help children overcome their handicaps. White middle-class culture and language is the norm; minority children's cultural backgrounds and language are assumed to be deficient and pathologic (e.g., Heller 1966).

Within this framework, language deficits were held to be a key reason for the poorer performances of minority students in schools. Carl Bereiter and Siegfried Engleman, for instance, described the language of poor and ethnically diverse children as "inadequate for expressing personal or original opinions, for analysis and careful reasoning, for dealing with anything hypothetical or beyond the present or for explaining anything very complex" (1966:32). Poor minority children were said to be disadvantaged by their lack of verbal interaction in the home, evident in school contexts by their apparent difficulty in responding to teacher questions.[2] Black English was purported to be an ungrammatical and inferior version of Standard English.

Linguistic deficits were also attributed to language minority students. The frequent intermingling of their native language and English, code switching, was viewed as an inability to master either language adequately (Carter and Segura 1979), and the dialects of Spanish-speaking students from Mexico and the Caribbean were considered evidence of language deterioration. Puerto Rican students were corrected in Spanish language classes with the intent of teaching them "proper" (i.e., Castilian) Spanish (Zentella 1985).

The introduction of an anthropological perspective on culture and language differences, incorporating a cultural relativist position that recognized the legitimacy of all cultures and languages, significantly began to shift the debate around educational failure and the role of schools in addressing minority educational performance. It was the works of sociolinguists that undermined the claims of adherents of "language deficit" explanations. Upon examination Black English turned out to be a complex linguistic system with its own rules (Labov 1972); social context and power relations were shown to influence language usage (e.g., Labov 1972; Leacock 1971); code switching was found to be rule governed, part of the linguistic repertoire of bilinguals and functioning as an additional communicative resource to be employed where deemed appropriate (Aguirre 1978; Bennett and Pedraza 1988; Gumperz 1982; Marlos and Zentella 1978; Poplack 1978). Minority children did not suffer from a "poverty of culture" (Leacock 1971); they were experienced participants in different but equally sophisticated and valid cultural systems (Keddie 1973). The problems lie not with the "inferiority" of the home cultures and languages children bring with them to schools but within the conflict engendered by the differences in cultural practices and expectations between mainstream school personnel and culturally diverse students.

Microethnographic studies support the thesis that cultural differences can contribute to communication difficulties between teachers and nonmainstream children and enhance the likelihood that teachers will misread students' interest and ability levels. We now know from ethnographic research that literacy activities and expectations in middle-class homes more closely conform to those of the school, conferring distinct advantages to mainstream students (see Cook-Gumperz 1986b). For nonmainstream students, traditional educational practices may work to their disadvantage. Shirley Brice Heath's work in diverse ethnic and class neighborhoods (1983a) aptly demonstrates how nonmainstream students' "ways with words" can come to differ strikingly from those in mainstream communities, where uses of language most closely parallel school expectations. Teachers she worked with, for instance, relied heavily on the sorts of "display" questions found in middle-class homes that ask the obvious: "And what did Johnny do when his sister took his bicycle?" The working-class black Trackton children Heath observed, meanwhile, had been socialized in communities that did not require children to routinely display information. At the same time, these Trackton children, socialized to creatively "invent" stories, responded enthusiastically in schools to stories read aloud to them, particularly those with fanciful characters and word play such as Dr. Seuss books. Working-class white Roadville children, on the other hand, successfully negotiated the literal straightforward questions they encountered in school, but floundered when asked to move away from such recountings and "make up" a story or put themselves in another character's place: "In Roadville, such stories told by children would bring punishment or a charge of lying" (Heath 1983a:296).

The general lesson to be drawn from Heath's particular example is that in a class-divided society in which minorities have largely been segregated from mainstream communities and workplaces, distinctive linguistic and cultural differences evolve that also tend to fall out along racial and ethnic lines. Mainstream students, as a result of school–home similarities, are privileged in classrooms over their working-class peers from the outset.

Studies of Native American populations have documented similar interactional difficulties across ethnic lines. Ronald Scollon and and Suzanne Scollon (1981), analyzing conversations between Athabaskan Indians and whites, found differences in anticipated lengths of time between speakers from the two ethnic groups. This in turn led to interactional difficulties. White speakers, accustomed to less time between speaker exchanges, frequently assumed that their Indian conversational partners had nothing to say and resumed talking without giving their Indian partners adequate opportunities to speak. For Indian children in classrooms with white teachers such differences, if unacknowledged, would limit opportunities for full participation in the classroom.

Greater cultural congruence between classroom organization and students' cultural backgrounds has also been shown to be more conducive to educational success for nonmainstream children (e.g., Delpit 1986; Heath 1983a; Trueba 1988). Susan Philips (1972; 1983) found that Indian children performed most effectively in classroom situations in which cooperation was emphasized over competition and sociality over individuality. Their reputation as language-deficient students who were essentially nonverbal and lacking in communicative skills was unwarranted, a product of differences between classroom teachers' expectations for students and the patterns of participation expected in the children's home communities. More compatible classroom styles in turn encouraged more active student participation, maximizing opportunities for learning. Teachers' awareness of communication differences, Philips points out, would help to diminish the likelihood of teachers holding low expectations for their students. Gerald Mohatt and Frederick Erickson (1981) also looked at classrooms with Native American students and found that teachers using language interaction patterns that most closely resembled those of their Native American students' home cultural patterns were more successful in raising student achievement levels.

Teachers can deliberately modify the classroom environment to more successfully foster culturally diverse students' access to classroom literacy activities. Kathryn Au and Cathie Jordan (1981), classroom ethnographers, found that native Hawaiian students' conversational turn-taking strategies in their homes differed from those used in their classrooms, creating impediments to student participation in the classroom. With the researchers' assistance, Project KEEP teachers working with native Hawaiian students adapted elements of Hawaiian cultural practices to their classrooms, including cooperative learning styles; more indirect praise; and aspects of "talk-story," which is characterized by "overlapping speech, voluntary turn-taking, co-narration and joint construction of a story" (Vogt, Jordan, and Tharp 1993:57). The outcome, subsequently documented by the researchers, was increased student classroom participation and achievement on standardized tests of reading.

There are also important pedagogical implications to be drawn from Heath's (1983a) work in schools, as discussed above. Teachers and students alike learned to use ethnographic techniques to reduce communication barriers between schools and communities and to explore diverse ways of developing and using language skills without devaluing those of students' home communities in the process; that is, nonmainstream children were invested with their own "cultural capital."

These various findings underline the importance of teachers' awareness of the potential for cultural differences to contribute to student difficulties in traditionally structured classrooms. Although sociolinguists have provided a rich body of research on the subtle classroom interactions that have the potential to contribute to nonmainstream students' difficulties in the classroom, however, cultural difference *alone* fails to adequately explain why minority students raised in the United States often perform less well than many groups new to the United States who are culturally and linguistically more different from the mainstream. "Communication mismatch" explanations are suggestive; they point to the subtle cultural differences that can put nonmainstream children at a disadvantage by cumulatively affecting their educational well-being. But interactive difficulties in the classroom are not driven solely by unrecognized cultural miscommunications and misreadings; there is also a strong evaluative subtext operating in classrooms that defines *whose* linguistic and cultural expressions and voices are permitted in classrooms (as in the larger society), in the process encoding important messages to students from stigmatized class or ethnic backgrounds. Speech patterns of regional speakers, ethnic group members, and lower-class populations, for instance, are consistently rated lower in terms of status and prestige than those of speakers of Standard English (Edwards 1982). These moralizing evaluations are not lost on speakers of nonstandard languages and dialects, as ethnographic studies in working-class Puerto Rican communities affirm: "The unmarked American represents a specific conflation of class, ethnicity, and race—white, Anglo, and middle-class. To most working-class Puerto Ricans, this figure represents the stereotypic white person, a figure of authority in workplaces, schools . . . [where] Spanish has no legitimate place. It is marked. Any sign of speaking Spanish or being Puerto Rican puts one at risk. . . . Spanish and indexes of Spanish become conflated with race (non-white) and class (poor)" (Urciuoli 1996:8–9).

Upon entering school Spanish-dominant Puerto Rican children quickly internalize the larger society's pejorative view of Puerto Ricans. Catherine Walsh found that Spanish-dominant students generally identified positively with their ethnic and linguistic heritage, whereas more English-proficient Puerto Rican students denied their heritage and defined "Puerto Rican" by using negative stereotypes such as "member of a gang, speaks only Spanish, dirty, drinks and smokes a lot" (1987:200). Ana Celia Zentella notes that most of the Nuyorican college students she worked with over a twenty-five-year period were "ashamed of their dialect and reluctant to speak it, moreso than other second generation Latino college students" (1997:298).

Teachers, as members of the mainstream, are likely to accept hegemonic assumptions about language. Ethnographic evidence points to the ways in which conflicts over the role of dialect and language in schools can contribute to disruptive classroom practices. For example, Ann Piestrup (1973) found that African-American elementary school children who were repeatedly corrected for speaking Black English actually spoke a more pronounced version by the end of the year; in classrooms in which the teacher did not negatively comment on their speech, the students' ways of speaking more closely approximated the Standard English spoken by the teacher.

Teachers' perceptions of student abilities have also been linked to their evaluation of students' use of non-Standard English in the classroom (Ramirez 1981; Seligman, Tucker, and Lambert 1972). James Collins (1988), for instance, found that discursive differences among African-American children in lower reading tracks (in their use of Black English Vernacular [BEV] pronunciations and the influence of oral narrative styles on intonational characteristics when reading aloud) entered into the teacher's evaluation of their reading abilities and prompted the teacher to focus on decoding skills and emphasize "correct pronunciation" rather than focus—as she did with high-level reading groups—on reading comprehension. Over the long term the students in the lower reading groups have fewer opportunities to read for meaning and are likely to remain in reading groups that focus on reading as decoding, and ultimately to be tracked into lower-level classes as they move through the school system.

Macrostructural analyses, which attend to the consequences of societal inequalities for minority student identity formation and relations to school, also suggest important forces operating in the classroom. As noted in the earlier review of Ogbu's work, these analyses posit that an oppositional social identity may emerge in response to minority treatment by dominant group members, and conformity to school expectations becomes equated with a loss of cultural identity (Cazden, Hymes, and John 1972; Collins 1988; Ogbu 1987; Walsh 1991). In such instances the significance of cultural difference for student achievement takes on a new and noteworthy dynamic: "Cultural difference can be thought of as a risk factor in the school experience of students and teachers; it need not cause trouble but it usually provides opportunities for trouble. . . . Those opportunities can serve as resources for escalating conflict that might already exist for other reasons, such as conflict between social classes, genders, or races" (Erickson and Bekker 1986: 175–7, cited in Erickson 1987). Hegemonic school practices can transform politically neutral cultural "boundaries" (e.g., non-Standard versus Standard

English pronunciations) into cultural "borders" (e.g., through an insistence on "correct" pronunciation) (Erickson 1987) that may engender student resistance and quite possibly loss of trust in teachers.[3]

As minority spokespersons and advocates of multicultural education have also pointed out, school *knowledge* is selective (cf. Harris 1992; Kohl 1994; Loewen 1995; Nieto 1996; Sleeter 1991; Swartz 1992). Proponents for change argue that that selectivity may act in ways that affirm or deny important aspects of minority student identity, including among them language practices, cultural practices, histories, and perspectives that may differ significantly from those of mainstream communities. Herbert Kohl (1994) describes the anger and withdrawal of Chicano students studying from a history text that ignored their presence in the Southwest, and subsequently their active class participation when he, as a teacher, openly acknowledged the book's omissions. School practices that demand adherence to mainstream linguistic and cultural practices and denigrate home cultures enhance the risk of fostering resistance from involuntary minority groups or, alternatively, as one study of academically successful African-American students found (Fordham and Ogbu 1986), of alienating successful students from their peers when their peers perceive them as "acting white."

Teachers willing to question such practices and assumptions can, however, create educational environments that enhance the likelihood of student assent to learning by attending to the political implications of such classroom practices. Hegemonic practices that leave unexamined the potential to further student resistance can be closely scrutinized. In addressing such matters from a linguistic perspective, Marcia Farr, for one, argues for a policy of "biloquialism" in teaching a multicultural population:

> Recognition of the differences between the linguistic and cultural resources of nonmainstream students and those that are needed for success in mainstream schools leads to decisions that are essentially political in nature. . . . Eradication, the traditional policy "long nourished in the English profession" (Fasold and Shuy 1970:x) assumes the undesirability of speech patterns associated with nonmainstream groups and attempts to rid students of these features, replacing them with more desirable "standard" ones. This, in fact, describes the status quo in most schools. . . . Biloquialism calls for the learning of new, standard patterns without eliminating the old nonstandard ones. . . . This pattern attempts to provide mainstream linguistic and cultural resources to nonmainstream speakers, while avoiding negative attitudes toward nonmainstream cultures and dialects. (1991:366)

"Whole language" and process writing approaches to teaching literacy are also educational innovations that can permit students to bring diverse "ways with words" and interests to the classroom; in the process the "cultural capital" embedded in traditional school assumptions and practices is reconfigured. As Harman and Edelsky note, the

> whole language approach is geared to the creation of texts for real use; it encourages multiple interpretations of existing texts-in-the-world; it honors and uses the language norms students arrive with; it not only accepts "alright" and "ain't" as linguistically legitimate, but it accepts differing discourses, identity kits, and worldviews; it focuses on the ideas students have rather than the ones they lack; it assumes the expansion of roles so that students teach and teachers learn; it sets high but flexible standards; it emphasizes language repertoires rather than right answers; and it fosters questioning, analyzing, speaking up, and writing down. (1989:396)

Ethnographic studies of classrooms in which process writing and whole language approaches are used with nonmainstream children have documented considerable student involvement in the classroom. A report by Luis Moll and Rosa Díaz (1987) on the success of a project working with low-performing, low-income Latino junior high school students describes one such situation. Teachers interested in developing students' expository writing were encouraged to use a process writing approach, which guides students through stages of writing (prewriting, drafts, feedback, rewriting), and to draw on issues relevant to the students' lives in establishing writing topics. The most powerful examples of student writing, they reported, were those that drew on community-related themes: in one instance students writing on "violence" (a part of their daily lives in the urban inner city); and in another instance writing on attitudes toward bilingualism, in which students moved out from student and family views to interview others in the community and school, compile results, and write a persuasive essay on the topic. An important point of such studies is that when the cultural and linguistic capital of the school is reconfigured in such a way as to allow students to draw more successfully on their own resources, greater success may be achieved with children who typically perform more poorly in schools.

Through their interactions with students, their responses to cultural and linguistic differences in the classroom, and their selection of curricular materials, then, teachers can affirm or exclude the cultural practices, perspectives, and experiences of nonmainstream students. For students who lack a "structural rationale" (D'Amato 1993) for conforming to school expectations, the classroom environment may be that much more critical as a site for providing the "situational rationale" for academic engagement:

> Children can have access to both structural and situational rationales for accepting school, to one but not the other, or to neither. The especial intensity and volatility of castelike minority

> children's resistance has to do with the fact that they typically have access to neither sort of rationale. Owing to the fact that their racial and ethnic experiences will not support structural rationales for accepting school, their resistance to school is always relatively intense from the outset; owing to the fact that their experiences at school will also typically not support situational rationales for accepting school—a quite different matter—their resistance tends to escalate to conflict. (D'Amato 1993:191)

While many factors that enter into the likelihood of students succeeding educationally are beyond the control of schools and teachers, ethnographic and anecdotal evidence strongly suggest that the classroom can be reconceptualized to promote greater likelihood of fostering such "situational" rationales.

Variability in Classroom Practices

Margaret Lane and Sandy Totten represent two contrasting approaches to the classroom and the teaching of English. In the course of many hours spent in their classrooms[4] I found significant differences in their relations with students, their responses to linguistic and cultural differences, and their selection and handling of texts. The dimensions of classroom practice that I highlight are categories selected as particularly relevant for nonmainstream students, based on the educational research literature examining the treatment of cultural and linguistic differences in classrooms.

The data included here are drawn from field notes, conversations and interviews (both formal and informal), and transcripts from the teachers' classrooms gathered over the course of the school year. Like many teachers, Margaret Lane was apprehensive about having her classroom and interviews taped.[5] Consequently, taped transcripts from her classes were only available for a three-week period near the end of the school year. In some instances short dialogues from Margaret Lane's classroom were reconstructed from in-depth field notes made during classroom observations. Taped transcripts from Sandy Totten's classes were available over a longer period of six months. Margaret Lane also never consented to being interviewed on tape, though we did have numerous informal conversations over the course of the school year. Thus the representation of the two teachers is necessarily unbalanced, and readers will lack the depth of insight into her educational decisions that is afforded us with Sandy Totten's greater openness. Margaret Lane's teaching is included not as an equally insightful analysis into her decision-making processes, but rather because many of the practices found in her classroom have been typical of English classrooms in past decades and offer a point of contrast to Sandy Totten's up-to-date educational practices.

Teachers' responses to students' language, styles of interaction, and the conservation or transformation of the curriculum, I argue, can affect student participation in the learning process. In comparing and contrasting the two teachers' classrooms I focus on general patterns of student—teacher interaction, assumptions about textual authority, and treatment of language difference.

The Traditional Classroom Teacher: Margaret Lane

Margaret Lane, introduced in Chapter 5, has traditionally been given the honors English class because of her reputation for excellence in teaching honors students a literature-based curriculum. Mrs. Lane is not routinely given nonregents classes; during the year in which I observed her she indicated that that was the first in several years that she had been assigned lower-track students. As noted earlier, she was concerned about the potential for taped classes or interviews to "fall into the wrong hands," and refused to be taped throughout most of the school year. In general her comments about teaching and her students were also quite guarded, making it difficult for me to have significant insight into reasons for the choices she made as an educator.

Mrs. Lane teaches junior high school English classes in the fortresslike brick three-story building that was once the district's high school, in a classroom that has been hers for fifteen years. Pictures of animals and authors neatly cover her bulletin boards, and her bookcases are packed with older editions of literature texts she has been unwilling to part with over the years. The tall ceilings, battered but clean desks, and tan tiled floors are like those in so many of the older schools scattered throughout the Northeast. Her windows, though, look out on a highway that runs along the river that played such a major role in Arnhem's earlier history; beyond, as far as the eye can see, extend the low treed mountainsides that make the region so picturesque to the drivers in the cars that whiz by on the interstate.

Mrs. Lane's classroom is teacher centered, and she presides over it in the style of a stern but loving "elder" who on occasion jokes with students about the subject matter at hand. Throughout the school year students sit in straight rows responding to her questions and directives from the front of the classroom. In Mrs. Lane's classes challenges to classroom order and her authority are largely muted. While Mrs. Lane despairs over students calling out without first being called on, her major "problems" with her lower-track students are not in classroom management issues (a frequently cited issue with nonregents classes) but rather in their failure to come to class with the appropriate materials, to study for tests, and to complete occasional homework assignments.

Mrs. Lane emphasizes form over process in student writing, teaches the traditional literary canon, and stresses knowledge about literature (literature terms, memorization of characters, author names, author intent, and so forth) over student responses to literature. In her lower-track class she devotes most of the classroom instruction to reading comprehension, grammar, vocabulary building, and spelling. Higher-track students, as she pointed out to me in an after-class discussion, need less time on these areas because they already have the basic skills she feels are essential to successful reading and writing.[6] Lower-track students in Mrs. Lane's class have few writing opportunities; because she felt it important that students use the "proper form" when writing essays, students were not assigned essay writing until January, well into the school year. At that point she introduced students to the standardized format, the popular "five-paragraph theme," to structure their writing assignments. When essay writing in the classroom did take place it revolved largely around preparation for the New York State Preliminary Competency Test, which typically asks students to write a business letter, organize facts provided them into a logical and coherent report, and write a composition on a given topic.

Classroom writing for her students consists largely of note taking, copying work from the board, or filling in answers to questions discussed in class. Students keep a notebook divided into four sections: one for spelling words; one for grammar; one a literature section with vocabulary lists and notes given in class on the reading selections; and one labeled "language skills," which is subdivided into topics such as alphabetizing, understanding analogies, and so on. Mrs. Lane's tests closely reflect what she teaches in her classes and consist largely of fill-in-the blank, matching, and short answer questions. A test brings closure to a discrete segment of classroom activities; in informal discussions Mrs. Lane commented that a student's success on the test serves as an indicator of the student's willingness to submit to the discipline needed for success in schools. As a consequence of her pedagogy, as advocates of "process writing" would be quick to point out, her students have limited opportunities to see themselves as "writers," to write extensively for communication in natural types of settings, or to bring their own experiences to their writing. Other classroom studies have documented, however, that such a classroom environment is not uncommon nationwide (e.g., Goodlad 1984; Langer and Applebee 1986).

Rethinking the Traditional Classroom: Sandy Totten

Sandy Totten, a first-year Euro-American teacher in her mid-thirties, professes to have no ethnic identification and laughingly defines herself as a "mutt." Dark-haired and with glasses that magnify her dark eyes and intense gaze, she is described by others in the building as a bundle of energy, never standing still. Mrs. Totten has a working-class background and identifies strongly with students "on the margins," having herself had a troubled adolescence that contributed to her dropping out of high school at age seventeen. She vividly recollects the pain of having once been told by a teacher that she was a "moron" who would amount to nothing, and feels that high teacher expectations for nonmainstream students within a supportive educational environment are critical to student success. During student teaching Mrs. Totten worked with a teacher well known in state education circles for her excellence in developing a multicultural literature program and a learner-centered classroom that incorporates reader-response approaches to literature and emphasizes process writing. This experience, she asserts, "turned her around."

Mrs. Totten does not have her own classroom and instead "rotates" among the classrooms because of her junior status. Like any teacher in such a situation she becomes frustrated trying to wheel a cart with the necessary books and materials around from one room to another through crowded halls between classes, and often arrives breathless to begin her classes. The lack of her own classroom also means that she is unable to display student writing and permanently rearrange desks the way she would prefer them, but she professes to being so happy to have the job that none of these things matters very much.

Student writing is encouraged from the outset in Mrs. Totten's classes. Unlike Mrs. Lane, who spends thirty to forty minutes a week on spelling words, Mrs. Totten does not make correct spelling an issue in her classroom, though she emphasizes that final drafts be as free from spelling errors as possible. She herself is a poor speller, something she openly acknowledges and that students tease her about:

Mrs. Totten [soliciting names of the five New York City boroughs from students]: Queens. [writes on board]
Mario: And Manhattan.
Carmen (a Puerto Rican student who has visited family in New York City): Manhattan is so changed.
Mrs. Totten: Manhattan's changed? Two *t*s in Manhattan? *e-n*?
David: a-n.
Mrs. Totten: a-n.
Mark: Jeez, Mrs. T., you're an English teacher and you can't spell.
Mrs. Totten: So? I can't spell. That's no big thing.

Overemphasizing spelling and correct grammar, Mrs. Totten feels, makes students reluctant to try writing because of their fear of making errors. She believes that improvements in spelling are more likely to grow out of increased exposure to the written word and students' correcting their own writing, rather than through memorizing spelling words or grammatical constructions in isolation from the written word. Grammar and spelling are addressed as they come up within individual students' writing (what Clay and Cazden [1990] metaphorically call "instructional detours"), rather than as a separate component of the program. (These are assumptions based in "whole language" approaches to writing.)

On occasion Mrs. Totten shares her own writing with the class, emphasizing that writing is a process, modeling the steps she herself takes in arriving at a finished product, and explaining how she deals with problems such as writer's block. Her students keep journals, writing at times on topics of their own choosing, at other times within a framework she provides (e.g., "Write about the most courageous thing you've ever done"). Students also practice other kinds of writing in her classroom, for instance, tackling research reports, constructing a dialogue between two individuals of their choosing, and writing thank you notes to speakers. Such assignments provide numerous opportunities for students to practice text conventions discussed in class, to use writing for communicative purposes, to bring their own experiences to their writing, and to draw on literature discussed in the classroom. Mrs. Totten believes that her students are most likely to be interested in writing well when the writing has meaning for them. She would have liked to encourage students to write on the issues raised in the community debate, but like many teachers she avoided discussion or writing about discrimination against the local minority community because of concern over possible repercussions for her tenure in the district.

While Mrs. Totten and Mrs. Lane teach the same grade and track levels, their approaches to the classroom in many respects differ significantly. Close examination of Sandy Totten's and Margaret Lane's classrooms over the course of my time in the junior high school reveals important differences in the two teachers' choices and treatment of literature and language in the classroom, and it is to these matters that we now turn. I begin with Mrs. Lane.

Choices and Treatment of Literature in the Classroom: Mrs. Lane

Mrs. Lane feels that her literature teaching over the years has suffered as a result of students' declining skills and motivation and the imposition of standardized tests that require she "teach to the test." Her regents-level students spend considerably more time on writing and literature than the nonregents class, but even in her regents classes she recently stopped teaching her prized "heroes" unit to students because she feels students need more time to master basic skills. Nonregents literature selections include approximately a dozen short stories selected from literature anthologies. Some are required for that particular grade and level (see Chapter 5), others she selects by balancing her sense of which "classics" she feels students need exposure to (e.g., "The Legend of Sleepy Hollow" or "The Man without a Country") with her sense of which pieces are likely to hold student interest. With the exception of two stories by Nuyorican author Nicholasa Mohr that Mrs. Lane read in preparation for Mohr's visit to the school, all the selections she uses but one (the play *The Diary of Anne Frank*) feature white male protagonists. In addition to the short stories, she also teaches a poetry unit that focuses on students' being able to correctly identify aspects of poetry such as rhyme schemes, verses, stanzas, and figurative uses of language.

In reading literature with her classes Mrs. Lane "walks" students through the text as she rotates reading from one student to another. Questioning is typically to ascertain whether students understand the literature at a basic level. Literature discussions follow a pattern commonly found in classrooms in which the teacher initiates a request for information, the student responds, and the conversational ball is returned to the teacher for teacher evaluation (e.g., Marshall, Klages, and Fehlman 1990; Mehan 1979). The result is that Mrs. Lane initiates and controls the direction of virtually all classroom talk. Students call out short phrases or one-word answers, with the teacher either ignoring incorrect or unsolicited responses, asking another question in her search for the correct answer, or using the answer to connect to another question as she assesses student understanding of the text. Knowledge is generally transmitted unidirectionally, with students cast in the role of "performers" (Lindfors 1987) during classroom recitations. The following transcript illustrates a typical classroom pattern, with the teacher initiating the questions and students calling out brief responses. (I use empty parentheses to indicate portions of the conversation that were inaudible):

Mrs. Lane: This is from a Robert Frost called—poem, excuse me, "The Road Not Taken." I've only got a few verses out of it for you [gesturing to poem written on board] but enough said so we can do it. It said, [reading from board] "Two roads diverged in a wood, and I—I took the one less traveled by. And that has made all the difference."

Hmm. What does it mean to diverge? "Two roads diverged in a wood."

Dan: They intersect together?

Mrs. Lane: [drawing on board] Well they intersected or two roads sort of came together. Here you are, walking along the woods, and all of a sudden here's a little ( ) path, and here's a road, and, there they are, and here's another one. "I took the one less traveled by."

Jennifer: Fork in the road.

Mrs. Lane: "And that has made all the difference." Which road do you take?

Jennifer: The right one.

Mrs. Lane: The right one, because it's what?

Jennifer: Less traveled.

Mrs. Lane: "Less traveled by." Does the person seem happy with that person's decision?

Alan: No.

Mrs. Lane: Read the last verse. "And that has made all the difference."

Alan: Yes.

Mrs. Lane: Yes. The person is satisfied that he, or she did this. . . . [continues to explain that the poem can be understood at the literal level as being about a journey through the woods, but also at a symbolic level] Yes, this represents life. You can either go on the path of life which most people don't go on, or go where most people have gone. [pause] It's *dangerous* to go any further than that, gang. [Explains how one student interpreted the poem to be about a football player being at a party the night before a big football game where he expects to be scouted by a college, and the player has to decide whether or not to go along with the crowd and use drugs at the party.] Is there [gesturing to poem excerpt written on board] a football player in that?

Melissa: Yeah, but if you think it's—
Students: No—No they're just—
Mrs. Lane: No. That's reading too much into a poem.

Student responses tend to be minimal, focusing primarily on attempts to ascertain the correct answers to questions initiated by the teacher. One consequence is that students are unable to create a conversational aperture in which to interject a challenge to the teacher's statements or to assert their own perspectives on the literature in question. Such discourse conventions are not unusual, as studies of lower-track English classrooms confirm (e.g., Marshall, Klages, and Fehlman 1990).

We see a similar response below in Mrs. Lane's handling of a "multicultural" text she incorporates into a lesson on poetry: close attention to the details of the text rather than to eliciting student responses to the literature or engaging students in critical thinking processes that might include exploration of how authors' biographies shape their texts, practices encouraged by those advocating the incorporation of multicultural literature into classrooms (e.g., Harris 1992; Jordan and Purves 1993; Purves 1991):

(Mrs. Lane has been discussing the difference between simile and metaphor, asking students to identify phrases as one or the other; one of the phrases is "Life for me ain't been no crystal stair.")

Mrs. Lane: The only thing I want you to consider as I'm reading is, what do you think about who is saying these words? No, I know it's me, that's not what I'm referring to. What I'm asking you, who is the narrator? What can you tell me about the narrator? The person who is speaking? That person says [reading from text]:

Well, son, I'll tell you:
Life for me ain't been no crystal stair.
It's had tacks in it,
And splinters,
And boards torn up,
And places with no carpet on the floor—
Bare.
But all the time
I'se been a-climbin' on,
And reachin' landin's,
And turnin' corners,
And sometimes goin' in the dark
Where there ain't been no light.
So boy, don't you turn back.
Don't you set down on the steps
'Cause you finds it's kinder hard.
Don't you fall now—
For I'se still goin', honey,
I'se still climbin',
And life for me ain't been no crystal stair.

Jonah: [calling out] Sounds like a grandfather.

Mrs. Lane: What can you tell me about the *narrator*? The speaker in this poem? What do you think?

Bryan: Somebody down South.

Mrs. Lane: Sounds like somebody down South. Right. What else can you tell me about this person speaking other than "somebody down South."

Jason: Old.

Mrs. Lane: Somebody maybe old. Of course that's a relative term. What do you mean by "old"?

Jason: Old of age.

Mrs. Lane: Old of age. [student and teacher laughter] Does old mean like thirty-five? Old mean like ninety-three?

Amber: No!

Mrs. Lane: What are we talking about here?

Jason: I mean like a grandfather. A grandfather's telling these things.

Mrs. Lane: Okay. Sixties, seventies, somewhere through there. Possibility.

Jason: A person who—a person who quit school or something.

Mrs. Lane: You're saying a person that didn't go to school. Okay what are you basing that on?

Jason: He—how he sounds.

Mrs. Lane: How the person is speaking, right. Using words that probably you would not use in educated language, right?

Jason: A person who's sort of, knocked up in life a little bit, doesn't want this person—a younger person—to do that.

Mrs. Lane: Good. Someone who's speaking to a younger person. And this older person has had not a very easy life of it, and this person wants to make sure that this person keeps going on, and he's fighting, making sure that that person's life is going to be really good.

Jocelyn: ( )

Mrs. Lane: What does that *tell* you about this person? What can you tell me about the person that's speaking? I don't think we even mentioned what sex the person is although some of you may have caught on. Male or female?

Students: Male/ Male/ Female

Tony: Unknown.

Sabrina: Who knows? Female.

Mrs. Lane: I'm gonna read it one more time, and then you tell me. [Reads again]

Sabrina: It's a girl.

Brett: They called him "honey."

Mrs. Lane: Okay. I think it's going to be more female, than male.

Brett: 'Cause fathers wouldn't call a boy "honey."

Mrs. Lane: Okay. First verse said, "Well, son, I'll tell you." Now, we could interpret this one of two ways. When the person says "son." What am I talking about?

Patrick: The son being the boy.

Mrs. Lane: Could be actually biological, the son of this older person. Right? Okay? Or, some people speak in terms of, "Well son," I'm sure you've had older people do that to you. And you're not even biologically related to this person. However, there seems to be such a closeness between these two individuals, it seems to be that they are related. Um, and now with regard to the sex of this individual, male or female, somebody mentioned the word—

Amber: "Honey."

Mrs. Lane: Right. Is this—is this going to be a male or female speaking?

Patrick: Male.

Students: Female/female.

Eric: How can you tell?

Mrs. Lane: To the young person as "honey?"

Eric: You never know.

Mrs. Lane: [speaking over student voices] Where down there it says, "For I'se still goin', honey." Now we assume that this person, the young person's not like five or six.

Patricia: How old?

Mrs. Lane: The person's probably gonna be a bit older than that.

Patricia: Thirteen.

Mrs. Lane: Why am I saying that? Gotta be at least thirteen, early teens, right? Why? What has the person wanted to do, that this older person is trying to break the person out of?

Jay: Climbing up a tree.

Andrew: [laughs]
Jay: [defensively] What?
Mrs. Lane: Trying to do what in reference to life? [Pause] Jack? Trying to do what [students laugh at his being chosen] in reference to life?
Jack: Um, go on in life?
Mrs. Lane: That's what the person does *not* want to do. The older person is trying to bring the person out of it, trying to make that person go on. [brief pause] This poem is entitled, "Mother to Son" people, not "Father to Son," but—"Mother to Son." It's written by Langston Hughes, and this is, Langston Hughes is a very popular, up-to-date black writer. He writes in all genres of literature. Short stories. He's written poems, he's written novels, he's written essays, things for newspapers, all kinds of things. Um, so once again, we'll have more, review on figures of speech before you take any test, but these are an important part of your notes. Speaking of notes . . .

Again we see classroom discourse controlled by the teacher, whose focus throughout the lesson is on moving students toward a "right" answer, practices that act to exclude students' knowledge and perspectives (Langer and Applebee 1986). Unasked are the sorts of questions that affirm students as capable of "making meaning" and critical thinking, such as asking them to relate the poem to their own lives; to speculate on how the author's background might be relevant in understanding the poem; to understand why the author of the poem chose to use "uneducated" English; or to consider whether the two characters might themselves represent a larger struggle.

While Mrs. Lane did not routinely incorporate multicultural literature into her curriculum, the political climate was such during the 1991–1992 school year that she did alter her usual selections. When Mrs. Lane learned that others were reading selections from Nicholasa Mohr's books with their classes in anticipation of Mohr's visit, she decided to also read aloud two of Mohr's short stories, "Once Upon a Time . . ." and "The Wrong Lunch Line" (Mohr 1986a).

"The Wrong Lunch Line," set in New York City in 1946, recounts the story of two high school students, one Puerto Rican (Yvette) and one Jewish (Mildred), who are close friends. Yvette, eligible for free school lunches, is invited by Mildred to go through a special Passover lunch line set up for the Jewish students. Mildred is attempting to explain to Yvette's Puerto Rican friends why they eat that particular combination of foods (matzo, no milk and meat together, and so forth) when a teacher approaches Yvette and singles her out in front of other students, demanding to know whether she is Jewish and should be eating the Jewish students' lunch. Yvette is called to the office, and later Mildred and Yvette are left feeling too uncomfortable to talk directly about the incident. The story closes with the following dialogue:

> "Boy, that Mrs. Ralston [the teacher who humiliated Yvette] sure is dumb," Yvette said, giggling. They looked at each other and began to laugh loudly. "Old dumb Mrs. Ralston," said Mildred, laughing convulsively. "She's scre . . . screwy." "Yeah," Yvette said, laughing so hard tears began to roll down her cheeks. "Dop . . . dopey . . . M . . . Mi . . . Mrs. Ra . . . Ral . . . ston. . . ."

Mrs. Lane read the story straight through, interjecting comments at two points:

Mrs. Lane: [reading from text] *Yvette lived on the top floor of a tenement, in a four- room apartment which she shared with her parents, grandmother, three older sisters, two younger brothers, and baby sister*. [pauses briefly] Good grief!

Her second comment came shortly before the end of the story:

Mrs. Lane: [Reading from text] *"Boy, that Mrs. Ralston is dumb," Yvette said, giggling*. [breaking off from text] Now here's the part where I don't agree with the author. I think it would have been better if she had left it off right about here. [Continues reading to end of story.] [Long pause] I didn't get the ending.
Becky: That's the ending?
Mrs. Lane: That's the ending. I think it was stronger before it got to this part. What message is the author trying to say to you?
[Brief exchange, teacher brings out point that Yvette is being judged by the way she looks, and adds that similar conflicts exist in the city today between blacks and Jews and blacks and Hispanics.]
Sonia (Puerto Rican): You know, the Jewish people wash with vinegar, and when they go by you they smell.
Mrs. Lane: Now who's being discriminatory?

At that point Mrs. Lane appeared flustered by the turn of the conversation. With only a few minutes left in the class she abruptly dropped discussion of the story and asked students to take out their notebooks and participate in an unrelated rhyming exercise for the remaining class time.

Three points bear mentioning here. We may first ask what the "hidden curriculum" conveyed in the above classroom scene might be. Mrs. Lane responds to the description of Yvette's living situation by following it with the parenthetical interjection "Good grief!" Yet the scenario Nicholasa Mohr incorporates into her story is certainly not unusual among working-class Puerto Ricans in New York City (or in Arnhem): a large extended family in cramped living quarters. Her comment marks the scene as exceptional and implicitly undesirable. Given that five of the students in her classroom were from working-class Puerto Rican families, and that a strong correlation exists between social class and tracking—students from working-class families are more likely to be in lower tracks—we can assume that some of her students are now, or have at one time, lived in similar situations. For working-class students the comment affirms their "otherness" without recourse to understanding the roots of class differentiation, shared immigrant experiences, or the strengths that may accompany such residential patterns, such as strong family ties.

Mrs. Lane also circumvents an opportunity to address students' stereotypes when she avoids taking up discussion of Sonia's comment about Jews. Mrs. Lane responds by saying "Now who's being discriminatory?" in a disapproving tone of voice, but silences any possibility of talk about the topic by switching to a totally unrelated classroom exercise.[7] Finally, Mohr's story could be used to provide students opportunities to reflect on similar situations (close friendships, discomfort talking about painful subjects, learning about customs of others that differ from those of your family, and the like.) The conversational exchange in the story between Jewish students and Yvette's friends about religious dietary customs offers opportunities to discuss cultural differences, similar rules in other religions, and so forth. Mrs. Lane also misses an opportunity to encourage students to form and support their own positions on the quality of the ending and the story.

Choices and Treatment of Literature in the Classroom: Sandy Totten

Unlike Mrs. Lane, Mrs. Totten is a strong advocate for multicultural literature selections in the English classroom. She had entered the school district already familiar (from her student teaching experience) with debates about the literary canon, and was responsible for arranging Nicholasa Mohr's visit to the school. During the school year she attended workshops on multicultural literature, whole language learning, and process writing.

Mrs. Totten's selection of texts for her students was made partly in response to her growing awareness of the ethnic and generational conflict in the larger community that included public disparagement of the Puerto Rican population. She believes that multicultural texts provide an effective means to explore cultural differences, to reduce student prejudices, and to validate cultural diversity. She began the school year with a thematic approach, exploring through literature selections from diverse groups what it means to be "American" with her students. In preparation for Nicholasa Mohr's visit she read and discussed several of the author's works with her students.

Mrs. Totten devotes class time to "walking" students through literature by having them read aloud, at times assessing students' understanding through the typical set of discourse conventions Mrs. Lane uses in her classroom (teacher initiation, student response, teacher evaluation), particularly when reviewing information covered in previous class discussions. Mrs. Totten, however, also encourages students to bring their own experiences and voices into the classroom literature discussions. She frequently begins such classes by arranging students in a discussion circle, where she joins them at one of the student desks rather than standing at the head of the classroom. Classroom discourse more often approximates what Tharp and Gallimore (1989) term an "instructional" conversation: students are likely to ask questions, introduce their own experiences into the discussion, and respond to one another's comments. Questions are often open ended, with no one correct answer. When students do ask questions or make an evaluative statement (even when unsupported by the text), their conversational overture, as we see below, is accepted and given consideration. Students are typically asked to support their statements or to examine the text to find out whether "textual evidence" supports or contradicts their statements, as we see in their discussion of Mohr's short story "The New Window Display." Mrs. Totten has just asked students to speculate on why the parents might want to take Little Ray, who is extremely ill, from New York City back to Puerto Rico, where he was born:

Mrs. Totten: Mario?

Mario: 'Cause it's warm over there. That's the advantage of being over there when it's all warm and not when it's cold.

Jerry: I know one.

Mrs. Totten: Okay, so you're saying the weather might be better for him. For whatever his ailment is. Jerry?

Jerry: Because there's not a lot of factories so there's not as much pollution.

Mrs. Totten: Okay that's another good point. So the air is—

Jerry: Clearer.

Mrs. Totten: So the air is clearer than here. And Matt?

Matt: He's in his own country.

Mrs. Totten: Well then, that's interesting. Okay you're saying that then maybe he's become ill because—

Matt: ( )

Mrs. Totten: I didn't hear it yesterday. I never heard that.

Jerry: [challenging Matt's inference that Little Ray will get better faster if he is "home"] Yeah, but it says that he didn't want to go back [looking through text].

Mrs. Totten: That he didn't want to leave?

Jerry: Yeah, remember it said that he didn't like that idea at all?

Mrs. Totten: Okay, that's pretty observant of you, Jerry, because if the text says, if the text actually says, that that's not the reason, then that's not the reason. We have to go by what it says here. So if they say Little Ray doesn't want to go back to Puerto Rico, then your [referring to Matt] comment about him being homesick isn't true, because it says so.

Rather than testing students' knowledge of why Little Ray's family plans on returning him to Puerto Rico at the end of the story, Mrs. Totten models the kinds of questions a proficient reader being drawn into the story might ask and encourages students to develop reasonable hypotheses and test them against the text as they move through it. Because there is no one right answer, students can generate several responses and end up considering a broader realm of possibilities. While Mrs. Totten could have pointed out immediately to Matt that the text contradicts his statement, instead she puts it "on the floor" to be examined. Jerry, another student, is able to point out the contradictory evidence in the text, possibly contributing to his own sense of empowerment in his encounters with literature.

In reading literature students were encouraged to bring their own experiences to the texts (without abandoning attention to the text itself). Mrs. Totten's selection and handling of several of Mohr's stories, as we see in the following excerpt, provided opportunities for Puerto Rican students to act as "cultural interpreters" for other students and thus contribute to building understanding of the text. Note the matter-of-fact manner in which ethnic and linguistic differences are handled, and how comfortable the Puerto Rican students appear discussing such matters. A student has just finished reading the following passage from Mohr's "The Window Display":

> Little Ray [who has recently arrived in New York City from Puerto Rico] was always with Papo, who had to look after him. In the four months since he had arrived, he had become the group's favorite. At first he had spoken no English, but now he was almost fluent. He spoke with an accent, which amused the other children, and he would get back at them by correcting their Spanish.

Mrs. Totten: Okay, does that make sense?

Students: Yeah/ Uh huh.

Mrs. Totten: He's learned Spanish, he's picked it up rather—or English—and he's picked it up rather quickly, but of course he has the accent, and sometimes that—

David (Puerto Rican): What accent?

Mrs. Totten: A little Spanish accent. Wherever you come from, you bring with you, the one—

Mario (Puerto Rican) [addressing David]: You know how you—

Carmen (Puerto Rican): ( )

Mario: Sometimes your grand—my grandmother, my grandmother says, instead of "yellow" she says "jellow."

Carmen: [chuckling] Yeah.

Mrs. Totten: You know something, sometimes you say "jes" instead of "yes," you say "jes." Now why is that, Mario?

Jeff: 'Cause he sits near Jessica. [laughter from students]

Mrs. Totten: No, why is that?

David: ( ).

Mario: 'Cause it happens to me, 'cause it just happens the "y" gets pronounced as a "j."

Carmen: Instead of saying "something" they go "some sings," like—

Mario: Some sings, some sings.

Carmen: Yeah. Some *seeng*.

David: Yeah.

Mario: Some *seeng*.

. . .

Mrs. Totten: Well it's just a little bit of a difference that you take from your native language into another um, into another language, and you have a little trouble making the—the switches. I know I'm not being too clear. In every language—in Spanish and English—the languages aren't equivalent all the time. Remember we talked about the "how," Carmen?

Carmen: [nodding] Yeah.

Mrs. Totten: Like you would say [in Spanish], "How is your school like?" instead of "What is your school like?" Just little switches, in the language, that just make it a little bit amusing to that person listening to you. Okay? So if I would—sometimes I find it a little amusing when I hear that. But I might say things in Spanish, that would make you laugh very hard. [Students laugh]

Tony: Like what?

Mrs. Totten: Like not—

Mario: Like um—you don't have the accent that we do.

Mrs. Totten: Well like my—my friend says, "The fingers ( ) my toes." And of course in English, "the fingers of my feet." And in English we call them toes. *Dedos de mi manos,* right? How do you say feet [in Spanish], *pies* [pronouncing as if the English word "pies"]?

Carmen: Yeah, *pies* [pronouncing pee-ays].

Mario: Pies [pronouncing pee-ays]. Making pies.

David: Pizza [pronouncing pee-ay-zah] pie.

Mrs. Totten: So it's just a language switch that doesn't con— that doesn't parallel.

Students eagerly offer examples from their own experiences growing up in a bilingual community that regularly moves back and forth between English and Spanish (Zentella 1981). Mrs. Totten has previously explained that she is taking Spanish lessons and wants to work toward being bilingual; she thus presents herself as a learner, and makes clear that she views students' bilingualism as a strength. Her Puerto Rican students—who some would label "language deficient"—incorporate a sophisticated play on words into their classroom discourse, making a bilingual joke of the differences between the pronunciation in Spanish and in English of the word *pies.* Carmen tactfully corrects Mrs. Totten's mispronunciation of the Spanish word *pies,* affirming that she has the right word and modeling the correct pronunciation. They talk comfortably about language use that in other contexts might have been marked "deficient."

In reading Nicholasa Mohr's stories, Carmen and other Puerto Rican students also became, like Little Ray in Mohr's story, the experts and final arbiters on Spanish pronunciations and translation, as we see below:

Jerry: [reading from text] *"To our dear departed Uncle Felix," Hannibal read, "from his loving niece and husband and children"* [pauses, clears throat, unsure of pronunciation of Spanish names Rojelia and Esteban; other students giggle]—

Mario: Carmen says she'll try that name.

Mrs. Totten: Yeah, Carmen, help him out.

Carmen: [pronouncing with Spanish accent] Rojelia.

Jerry: And—Esteban? [voice trailing off]

Mario: [correcting pronunciation] Esteban.

Jerry: [continues reading from text] *Esteban Martínez, and Gilberto, María, Patricia, and*—[breaks off] Consuelo?

Mrs. Totten: Uh huh.

Jerry: Para un gran amigo. I don't know. [makes a funny face, other students giggle]

Mrs. Totten: Which means what?

Jerry: I have absolutely no idea.

Mrs. Totten: You don't take Spanish, Jerry?

Mario: For a grand friend, for a grand friend.

Jerry: I don't take any language. [continuing from text] *Joey read from another wreath. Felix.* Umberto?

Mrs. Totten: Carmen or Mario, help him out.

Mario: Umberto.

Carmen: Umberto Cordero.

Jerry: [can't pronounce the Spanish words]

Carmen: De la familia Jiménez.

Jerry: Thank you. [continues reading]. Five—oh, *fifty thirteen Kelly Street, Bronx, New York.*

Puerto Rican students' comfort serving as "cultural interpreters" was also evident in classroom discussions of cultural practices:

Mrs. Totten: [reading from "A New Window Display," which describes a picture of the children's friend Little Ray as he appeared in his casket] *"His dark curly hair was oiled and combed and parted."* So he's looking his best.

Patrick (Euro-American): Oiled?! Why do they make him look nasty?

Mrs. Totten: Now, Mario [addressing Puerto Rican student], you put baby oil on your hair to make it look shiny, right?
Mario: I used to.
Carmen (Puerto Rican): That ruins your hair.
Mrs. Totten: It makes it—Does it?
Mario: That messes it up.
Mrs. Totten: Why? Your hair always looks so shiny.
Carmen: ( )
Mario: I put ( ) on it.
Mrs. Totten: I see.
Mario: I stopped because it messes it up. It makes it dry—
Mrs. Totten: It makes it dry?
Albert: It all falls out—
Mrs. Totten: Well, realistically, Little Ray [the character in the story who has died] will never have to worry about that, will he?

When Patrick expresses disgust at the idea of putting oil on Little Ray's hair, Mrs. Totten invites students to move from an evaluative judgment ("Why do they make him look nasty?") toward a position of cultural relativism, to recognize it as a different, but not inferior, culturally specific practice among some Puerto Rican males. In talking about the difference she also creates a space for Mario to modify her assumptions.

The environment Mrs. Totten creates in her classroom is such that her Puerto Rican students even appear comfortable joking about negative public stereotypes and images of Latinos, including the claim that had recently been advanced by local outspoken senior citizens that Latinos were swarming in droves to the city and threatening its well-being. In Nicholasa Mohr's short story "Mr. Mendelsohn" (1986a), an elderly Jewish man (Mr. Mendelsohn) is befriended by his neighbors, the Suárez family. Mr. Mendelsohn grows fond of his neighbors' children and tells them stories about "the good old days" in New York City when he was young. Mrs. Totten asks students if they have ever asked older people about the past, or if they know older people who talk about the "good old days." Several students respond with the stories their grandparents or parents tell, and Mario Rivera, a Puerto Rican student who participated in the first-day school boycott to bring attention to the needs of minority students, joins in:

Mrs. Totten: So have you ever heard a child asking someone about what things were like in their day?

Mario: Yes, I used to do it.

Mrs. Totten: Okay, tell me about who you asked. Who did you ask?

Mario: My grandfather.

Mrs. Totten: You asked your grandfather what?

David: How old he was.

Mrs. Totten: Let Mario finish.

Mario: How it was in New York City.

Mrs. Totten: How it was in New York City? And what did he tell you?

Mario: [jokingly] There was a lot of Hispanics. [students laugh]

Mario: No, he said it was a lot peacefuller there.

Mrs. Totten: It was more peaceful—there wasn't as much crime maybe as there is now?

Unlike many of the teachers, Mrs. Totten was aware of, and did not ignore, racist or derogatory comments students made about various groups, the likelihood of which was enhanced by the introduction of literature that included characters from varied ethnic and racial backgrounds. She encouraged students to think about how they might feel being the victims of prejudice and discrimination and to recognize their own stereotypes. She also talked openly with them about how she had felt encountering people's stereotypes about teenage dropouts, and asked her students to reflect on similar experiences through their journal writing.

In such an environment students themselves pointed out comments or actions they felt were indicative of prejudiced attitudes, as the following excerpt illustrates. Mrs. Totten asked students to predict what the children in "A New Window Display" (Mohr 1986a) would see when they walked up to the funeral parlor window (a regular routine of theirs, in which they observe the numbers of wreaths people receive and read and comment on the messages on the wreaths). Note Carmen and Mario's responses (both are Puerto Rican) to David's innuendos about Puerto Ricans. Carmen's family moves back and forth between Puerto Rico and the mainland, and Mario's parents were born in New York City. Mario participated in the school opening-day boycott to protest John Marris's public comments. David's mother is Puerto Rican and his stepfather is Euro-American. In classroom conversations David sometimes made subtle disparaging comments about Puerto Ricans.

Tom: He's gonna see a whole bunch of pictures up in the window.

Mrs. Totten: A whole bunch of pictures of Little Ray in the storefront window. Okay, there's one prediction. What do you predict?

Carol: The same thing.

Mrs. Totten: And you?

Students: Same thing/ Same thing.

David: Me.

Mrs. Totten: What do you predict?

David: I don't think he's gonna be on there, because he's not that popular. The flowers and stuff like that. He won't even take a picture of him because he's not that popular.

Mrs. Totten: Who's not popular?

David: Ray.

Amber: He is.

Mrs. Totten: He certainly is.

David: No, the whole world don't care about him.

Students: [overlapping]

Mrs. Totten: But now wait a minute, that's an interesting point that David has. He may be popular, you're right, he—

David: He's popular to his friends but not to anyone else.

Mrs. Totten: He's right.

Robert: Maybe his friends took pictures.

*David:*You see, you see—what do you know.

Jenny: And sent a lot of flowers.

Mrs. Totten: Now remember, the amount of flowers that gets to a person during their wake has to do with how wealthy their family is, because certainly people have to afford these.

David: And I don't think Little Ray's family is rich, because they live in Puerto Rico.

Carmen: [emphatically] *So*? That don't mean nothing.

David: Yes it does.

Carmen: No it doesn't!

David: Yes it does!

Carmen: No it doesn't!

Student: [overlapping]

Mrs. Totten: Wait a minute, wait a minute—we're getting loud. I'll tell you what we'll do—

Carmen: [angrily] It don't mean you're rich because you [live here?].

David: He's not rich because his family comes from Puerto Rico and he's living in New York State.

Students: [overlapping]

Mrs. Totten: Children, we don't want to fight here, we can debate. Let's do a raise of hands. No one talk while the person whose hand's raised. Jenny. Listen now. Listen now. Listen. Listen. Listen.

David: I'm sure, so leave me alone.

Mrs. Totten: Anyone who has their hand raised may speak, okay? But do not interrupt that person while they're talking. Mario.

Mario: It says, "Many neighbors had attended the funeral mass." So that makes him more.

David: No it doesn't.

Students: Yes it does/ It does.

Mrs. Totten: Now let me write that on the board. It says, "Many people—"

Jerry: Many neighbors.

David: What are neighbors but a whole bunch of people?

Mrs. Totten: Many neighbors attended. All right, that's textual evidence that a lot of people were at the wake.

Jerry: Family.

Mrs. Totten: Is that your point now? Okay, so you have a textual point you found something in the writing that says that many people went to that wake. David. You have a point to make?

David: Yes.

Mrs. Totten: So what is your point?

David: That just because neighbors went that don't mean the whole world knows that he—he's not popular, he's just a little, like, street kid.

Jenny: [a student frequently absent from school, a local "street kid"] So? You can be popular.

Mrs. Totten: So, you're right, you're right.

David: So if I go out and steal and stuff and I do all that stuff I'm popular because I do that kind of stuff?

Jeff: To the police you are.

Karen: ( )

David: And because I'm out on the streets?

Jenny: People know you—

Students: [overlapping]

Mrs. Totten: Raise your hands. Raise your hands. Okay. Now we're not talking about criminal activity. We're talking about popularity and who gets more flowers.

David: But his picture won't be up there because he's not popular.

Jerry: How do you know? How do you know?

David: Because I know, by reading the story.

Mrs. Totten: Shhh.

David: By reading the story, by reading the story.

Mrs. Totten: Okay, let somebody say something else, David. Okay Carmen.

Carmen: This don't have nothing to do with this but I just want to know why does David always have to be talking about Puerto Ricans when he's a Puerto Rican?

Jerry: Well how is he—

David: You're right, it has nothing to do with this.

Carmen: So why you always have to be talking about us if you're one of us?

David: You're right, it has nothing to do with this.

Mrs. Totten: Calm down, calm down. Carmen, what do you mean? What is he saying about Puerto Ricans?

Carmen: He's always talking about things.

Mario: He's always putting us down.

Carmen: That we're always getting in trouble, that just because we're Puerto Ricans we don't have money.

Mario: Yeah, like he just said that he steals—if he goes out and steals—he's not going to be popular and all.
Mrs. Totten: You see, I didn't catch that. Now he said that they steal—
Mario: He's always putting us down.
Mrs. Totten: Did he mean Puerto Ricans?
April: ( ).
David: I just said—
Carmen: You meant Puerto Ricans.
Students: ( )
David: Street kids I meant.
Mrs. Totten: You meant just street kids. Not Puerto Rican children?
David: Yeah ( ).
Mrs. Totten: Okay, he's clarified what he meant, okay? You did not mean Puerto Rican kids, you meant kids.
David: Yeah, I just meant street kids.
Mrs. Totten: Okay, you should clarify that. Because Carmen took it the wrong way. Okay . . . Carmen, did you have another point to make about this?
Carmen: [shakes her head no]

Carmen's and Mario's responses to both David's statement that Little Ray's family can't be rich because they come from Puerto Rico, and his implication that Puerto Ricans steal, speak to their awareness and sensitivity to negative stereotypes in the community. Rather than ignore the comment Mrs. Totten provides Carmen an opportunity to voice her concern and David an opportunity to explain himself, subtly putting him on notice that such statements are inappropriate.

Mrs. Totten, then, uses multicultural literature to draw on students' experiences and to explore and affirm their differing cultural backgrounds. Students often responded in unanticipated ways to such literature. Mrs. Totten recounted one such incident that occurred in her classroom. Puerto Rican students (one of the few in a regents-level class) who had said nothing in class all year excitedly explained to the entire class what a *coqui* (a small frog found in the rainforests of Puerto Rico) was when the word came up in a story. The next day the student came in wearing a T-shirt from Puerto Rico with a picture of a *coqui* on the front of it. Excerpts from early drafts of thank-you notes[8] written to Nicholasa Mohr by Puerto Rican students in Mrs. Totten's class after her visit to the school also suggest the significance of including literature written by nonmainstream authors for students typically considered "at risk":

> *Blanca Cepeda: Felita* [Mohr 1979] was enjoyable. It reminded me of when I used to live in N.Y. city And the story with "Mr. Mendelson" was very touching. It was very funny to. You made me love him then he died. You did that in another story with Little Ray. I'm Puerto Rican to and you make me more intersted, because you are to. You the first Puerto Rican writer I heard of.
>
> *Ana Cruz:* I read one of your books. The book that I read was *Felita*. I really liked it. I know that I liked it because that was the only book that I ever read. That was the only book that I read because I know how it feels. I liked your book so much that I bought *Going Home* [Mohr 1986b].
>
> *Julio Thomas:* What I really liked is that you are Puerto Rican. Why? Because I grew up here, and I grew up hearing that any hispanic growing up in the U.S, or just living hear, didn't have any chance. After seeing you I thought they were wrong.

At the same time these stories were not marked as stories about, or stories exclusively for, minority children. Mrs.

Totten encouraged students to find universal themes in the stories and to draw on their own experiences in making sense of the characters. Thus, for instance, she asked them what "stories" older family members passed down about "the good old days," or to write on what they would miss most about a relationship if someone close to them were no longer in their lives (as in "The New Window Display," in which Little Ray dies). Thank you notes to Nicholasa Mohr written by non-Latino students indicate that they, too, were able to identify with her characters and their experiences:

> *John Richardson:* When you read "Isabel and her New Mother" that is what kinda happend to me because I got a stepfather. It took me 3 yrs to get use to him. Did that happen to you? In "Shoes for Hector" that happen to me. My mother got me sandal shoes and I hated them. One time I almost through them in the garbag. When I read your stories it seems like it has already happened to me.

> *Pete Maratto:* Your stories are really fun to read because they are about kids our own age and we can kind of relate to them and what they deal with each day of their life. In the story "A New Window Display" when little Ray died, I could kind of relate to it because my cousin died and I felt almost the same way the kids did.

An important point to note in examining these two classrooms is that, although incorporating more multicultural selections into the classroom has been viewed as a mechanism for introducing all students to the diversity of the United States and enhancing minority children's self-esteem and academic engagement as they see themselves in their texts (cf. selections in Harris 1992; Lindgren 1991), introducing such literature into the classroom does not *in and of itself* achieve such objectives. Multicultural literature, as we saw earlier, can open up possibilities for students to introduce their own learned prejudices into classroom discussions. Teachers may be uncomfortable acknowledging and addressing those prejudices. Mrs. Lane was also uncomfortable with stories that opened up the possibility of discussing cultural and class differences. Her brief comment on Yvette's crowded living quarters carries a message we can assume the author did not intend.

Mrs. Totten's interactional style[9] with her students is not without risk. Providing numerous openings for students to interject their comments means that students can more easily disrupt the flow of conversation around the text. Three boys in her class occasionally used the opportunity to "get a rise" out of the teacher or other students (a not-uncommon phenomenon in any junior high school classroom), testing the lines between what was and was not appropriate.

In Mrs. Lane's classes, on the other hand, such distractions are unlikely to occur. For example, students may not sit with their friends or move out of their seats once the bell rings, and the types of questions asked in class limit their opportunities to wisecrack. Although some students called out answers without first being recognized by the teacher, they were few in number and their responses were generally shorter.

Mrs. Totten's students also frequently respond simultaneously to her questions or to statements made by other students. Mrs. Totten accepted such events so long as students did not extend their simultaneous outpouring of responses. Despite their potential to interrupt the flow of the classroom conversation, such events signified that students were actively following and involved in the classroom discussion rather than passively attending to what was going on in class.

Language Issues: Mrs. Lane

Mrs. Lane stressed grammar in her classroom and frequently incorporated grammar worksheets in her classroom lessons. In the process of encouraging her students to use Standard English, she also disparaged students' non-Standard English:

> *Example #1*: [Mrs. Lane handing back a test on present and past participles] Shame on you individuals that gave me "brang" and "brung"!
>
> *Example #2*: [Mrs. Lane going over worksheet on selecting the appropriate verb form for each sentence] This is the one I cringe at: "I *seen* that movie last week."
>
> *Example #3 (repeated from previous chapter):* [Mrs. Lane reading aloud from Nicholasa Mohr's short story, "Once Upon a Time. . ."] "What do you think?" asked the second girl. "Should we tell somebody what we seen [a dead body]?" [Addressing class, in an astonished tone of voice] *Seen*? [Continues reading]" . . . 'We better not; then they'll ask us what we was doing up on the roof and all,' said the first girl." [Addressing class] These kids haven't had Mrs. Lane's grammar class yet.

The comment on the characters' English was meant to introduce a note of levity into the class, but in the process it communicated to nonmainstream students that there is something inherently flawed with the way English is spoken in their communities. The text could alternatively be used as an opportunity to explore issues around language usage in different contexts.

Mrs. Lane also told me informally that she disapproved of Latino students' using Spanish among themselves when in school; such a practice, she felt, kept students from mastering the English language. As we have seen, she seemed uncomfortable with Spanish terms in English reading

two selections she read from Nicholasa
not have any Spanish language passages in
ny that she might have chosen did.
ner treatment of the English spoken by her
orking-class and bilingual students, her treatment of Spanish, her choice and treatment of texts, and her emphasis on the importance of school knowledge without acknowledging students' knowledge Mrs. Lane creates an environment in which nonmainstream students' lives, languages, and knowledges are marginalized or excluded. In the process students rarely have opportunities to talk about their own lives in the classroom and to draw on knowledge learned outside the classroom. Mrs. Lane, in turn, has little opportunity to learn about their world beyond the school doors. Mainstream students, too, lack opportunities to explore similarities and differences among their peers.

Language Issues: Sandy Totten

Mrs. Totten, in contrast, incorporates Spanish into classroom talk and values students' bilingual skills. She refuses to make student use of the vernacular an issue in student writing and talk, pointing out to students that in certain contexts—talking with friends, writing dialogue, and so forth—use of the vernacular is the language of choice:

Fred: [reading from text]—*"I guess then they"*—I guess they are really–*"are real late. Or they ain't coming. We better split or we are"*—going—*"are gonna be late," said Hannibal.*
Mrs. Totten: Okay, Fred—
Mario: "Gonna" and "ain't" are not words—you know that?
Mrs. Totten: Pardon me?
Mario: "Gonna" and "ain't," they're not words.

Mrs. Totten: But she's using them how in this piece of writing, Mario? Why are they okay in this?

David: They're Puerto Rican people.

Mrs. Totten: Nooo.

Mario: No, that's how we speak. That's how everybody speaks.

Mrs. Totten: Remember when you were doing stories and we used these [draws quotation marks on board]? What are those?

David: Quotions [sic]. Quotes.

Kerry: Quotations.

Mrs. Totten: Quotation marks. So if you're putting the writing inside, and that's what the person said, then that's okay, even if they say "gonna." All right? If it's inside the quota—

Mario: But "gonna"'s not a word.

David: Gonna, gonna.

Mrs. Totten: But the person *said* it. Now, Mario, if you said to me, "I'm gonna go to the store, I'm gonna go to the store," right—

Mario: Okay—

Mrs. Totten: and I want to quote you *exactly* the way you said it, I'm gonna [sic] have to use those kinds of words aren't I? Because if I change them—

Mario: It's not a quote.

Mrs. Totten: If I change them then we don't know exactly how Mario said it. I'll make him sound like me—and that's not how Mario sounded. And if I wanted—if I want people to hear, hear it in their head, okay, if I want them to hear how Mario sounds, I'm gonna use it the way it sounds, inside the quotation marks. And that makes it okay. Is that clear? Do you understand what I mean?

Treatment of language usage clearly emerges as a significant difference in these two teachers' approaches to teaching English. Teachers' assumptions about language, as David Bloome notes, may have important consequences for nonmainstream students:

> The official language of education (in the United States) is not any English but a specific English often referred to as Standard English.[10] Those who do not speak Standard English in school are often viewed as disadvantaged, less academically capable, or, more generously, needing to learn to code-switch into Standard English in order to be successful in the mainstream society. Whether there is or is not a Standard English . . . whether students who do not speak Standard English are or are not disadvantaged, less academically capable . . . (are less issues than that) educators, researchers, and others, take for granted Standard English as the language of education. . . . Perhaps as important as choosing English as the language of education, is the way that choice is enacted. African American and Hispanic students are often made to feel less academically capable and that their home, community, and culture are less valuable because they do not speak Standard English. (1991:48)

Pedagogy that supports the vernacular or home language while also moving students toward Standard English literacy (e.g., Attinasi 1994) has multiple benefits. It acknowledges the validity of the home and community language—in the process not reinforcing societal denigration and reducing the risk of oppositional behaviors—while also empowering students with the standard language skills that will permit them to participate more effectively in the public discourses that are redefining what it means to be an American in the twenty-first century.

In choosing not to mark non-Standard English usage as inferior and in envisioning students as writers regardless of how closely they adhere to reigning assumptions of what constitutes "good writing," Mrs. Totten affirms their sense of themselves as capable speakers and writers. Mario Rivera, the Puerto Rican student who raises the issue of whether "gonna" and "ain't" are words, offered an unsolicited evaluation of the effect of Mrs. Totten's classroom on his own sense of efficacy as a writer when I interviewed him the following school year:

Ellen: [responding to Mario Rivera's statement that he feels more open about his writing now] What do you mean by "open"?
Mario: Like I don't mind writing any more. Like writing stories and stuff. I used to get intimidated.
Ellen: What do you mean by "intimidated"?
Mario: Like if I have to write a story, I wouldn't be able to ( ). I couldn't put it down on the paper. I couldn't put what I wanted to. I would put something else.
Ellen: Why couldn't you put down what you wanted to?
Mario: Like it wouldn't make sense. I always like skip words or I'll put the wrong word down. I'll leave out a letter, or I'll spell another word.
Ellen: Uh huh, that's interesting that you can remember that. And now you have a different sense of it, now you feel more comfortable writing?
Mario: Yeah, I think it was Mrs. Totten that did it for me.
Ellen: How so? I mean, how did she get you to feel more comfortable about it?
Mario: She made me feel more better. She would always like say it was good, she says yeah I can do it, she gave me that little push I needed. And Mrs. Moskowitz [the reading teacher] helped too.
Ellen: And before what would happen, with earlier teachers?

Mario: I would take—they told me to do it and I'd take a long time to do it. I wouldn't do it or it would come in late.

Ellen: Did they act differently toward the writing? When they got it? I mean you said that Mrs. Totten like encouraged you, and said good things about it?

Mario: Yeah, she really gave me more attention to it.

Ellen: And what would happen before, when you turned in something?

Mario: Oh nothing, they would, they would take it. And they wouldn't really tell me anything about it. They would just give it back, tell me what I got and that's it. Or they would say what, like that word is wrong. Mrs. Totten she like points out, she helps me with it.

Ellen: How does she help you?

Mario: She would point out it [sic], and then she would tell me why it's wrong, and how it was wrong, and she would tell me what I could do better. Like she would just give me ( ), she would make me feel positive about it. More positive.

Ellen: How does she make you feel positive?

Mario: Like what she does and says to me. Like once she made us write a story. And then if something was wrong, she will tell me why it was wrong. And how—what I did to it to make it wrong. And she said, and then said, and then she started saying it was good though, she wouldn't just give me like the negative parts, she gave positive parts too, and the other teachers really wouldn't give me the positive, they would just give me the negative.

Toward Rethinking the Classroom

Both Margaret Lane and Sandy Totten want their students to become more proficient readers and writers, but their approaches in the classroom are driven by differing assumptions about language learning, relations to texts, and whose knowledge and ways of speaking are to be heard in classrooms. These differing orientations in turn significantly shape the classroom context in which their students encounter schooled literacy. Recent sociolinguistic analyses of language usage within the Puerto Rican community also support the value of the sorts of classroom practices modeled by Mrs. Totten.

> Classrooms that honor the usefulness, rule-governed nature, and validity of the dialects and ways of speaking that students acquire at home, instead of attacking them as ungrammatical or illogical, are more likely to expand students' linguistic repertoires successfully. . . . One immediate way of facilitating the adoption of new ways of using language is to allow students to talk more. . . . Given the discourse strategies that depend on code switching, the cultural significance of non-standard dialects, and the bridges they offer for crossing over into other ways of using language, it may jeopardize the linguistic and social development of children if their language is "corrected" in every part of the school day. (Zentella 1997:279–80)

That Mrs. Totten was profoundly influenced by her student teaching experience points to the importance of such educational opportunities for aspiring teachers. Teacher training institutions and student teaching experiences can provide students much-needed opportunities to examine literacy acquisition in homes and schools and explore the ways in which the languages and cultures of students can be excluded or incorporated into classroom learning and lessons to better foster student engagement and learning. Questioning the reigning assumptions about what constitute the most effective classroom practices for culturally diverse students also demands that teachers in training understand the societal forces that undergird much "cultural difference."

Promoting change among teachers already in the field is far more problematic. Mrs. Lane's adherence to traditional methods in English language arts instruction is not unusual (see, for example, Britton and Chorny 1991:110). Despite major changes in theory and research on language learning, as John Simmons notes, "it is traditional grammar and prescriptive, 'right-wrong' usage that continues to hold sway today in junior high English curricula" (1991:327).

The assumptions teachers bring to the classroom are shaped by their own cultural, biographical, and institutional experiences. Tracking students and large class sizes further increase the likelihood of teachers' continued reliance on "seatwork," objective tests, and grammar-based approaches to language learning to maintain a semblance of order and a reasonable work load. When administrative emphasis is on "orderly" and quiet classrooms, teachers may also be reluctant to experiment with new approaches that generate student "noise" and move the focus of students' attention away from the teacher.

With traditional approaches evaluation criteria are also much more clear cut; student mastery of grammatical conventions, spelling, and authorial intentions can be evaluated and used as a marker of student progress on tests intended to measure achievement, assuring teachers and the public that their students are learning—or not learning—what is being taught in schools. Use of these easily quantifiable indicators is premised on the assumption that learning—like inborn intelligence, intended to be captured by I.Q. tests—can be scaled and individuals measured against one another. This increasing dependence on standardized tests in public schools fosters the kinds of teaching we see in Mrs. Lane's classroom. The "back to the basics" movement that gained momentum in the 1970s meant both a renewed interest in "the grammar text, workbook, spelling list motif of yore" (Simmons 1991:329) and pressure for more standardized tests as a means of measuring students' "progress." In 1977, for instance, with the rise of statewide testing, the Warriner's series *English Composition and Grammar* broke all sales records (Simmons 1991).

American students today are tested more than children in any other country (Resnick 1982, cited in Johnston 1992); at the secondary level, students lose approximately ten instructional days per year to standardized tests, not counting classroom preparation explicitly *for* the tests (Johnston 1992:4). Increased reliance on such tests may actually be counterproductive. Alan Purves, for example, points to arguments against minimum competency tests for having "produced a circumscribing of the curriculum to a point where it merely prepared students for the test rather than being concerned with broad educative functions" (Purves 1984, in Farr and Beck 1991:494).

Educators and researchers, meanwhile, including among them advocates of "whole language" and "reader response" approaches, assail the ability of standardized multiple-choice tests to adequately and meaningfully evaluate student progress in the English language arts (cf. Farr and Beck 1991; Johnston 1992). The many critiques of such tests—ranging from the disempowerment of teachers to the consequences of labeling students who fall below the norm "failures"—are beyond the scope of this book (but see, for example, Johnston 1992; Miner 1991). If such practices are to be critiqued, however, educators (including both administrators and teachers) and teachers in training will need opportunities to examine the "commonsense" assumptions about testing—as well as language learning—that drive such practices.

At the same time, many current progressive theories

ignore or marginalize the underlying systems of domination that drive much linguistic and cultural "difference." As Carole Edelsky cautions, these theories

> can as easily support *avoiding* looking at white privilege, for example, as they support looking *at* it. Those progressive theories and practices are correct, I believe, but they don't go far enough. They don't actively and primarily–*as a first priority*–tie language to power, tie text interpretation to societal structures, or tie reading and writing to perpetuating or resisting. . . . [Our theories] act as though language expression and language processing, although socially situated and constrained by social conventions, are primarily acts of individuals. Our theories-in-practice fail to take as their central focus the way language learning and language use are tied not only to people's individual experiences but also to people's societal positions, to their structured privilege, to their greater or lesser power, and to the interests of the groups they represent. We can't hope to change what's societal if we keep backgrounding what's societal. (1994:254–5)

The school curriculum is not a neutral body of knowledge to be transmitted to students; the fact that we include and legitimate some knowledge and exclude others through the choices we make in school texts, tests, and talk needs to be raised to a conscious level among all educators and examined in light of its possible consequences for students. The taken-for-granted assumptions about language learning that long have undergirded traditional English language arts teaching are now being called into question; "whole language" or process approaches to writing and reader-response approaches to literature offer promising alternatives to traditional teaching methods in the English language arts and can provide opportunities for students to bring their own experiences and perspectives to their reading and writing. Multicultural literature in the classroom gives students and teachers the chance to explore diverse ways in the world in a context in which cultural and linguistic diversity are invited into the classroom.

But creating environments in which students' "ways with words" and experiences are seen as resources in assisting students as they build bridges to the larger world requires more than just introducing new methods of teaching into the English classroom. "Rethinking" schools also requires putting critique front and center. In a racially divided and stratified society, projects to assist white mainstream teachers in better understanding their own assumptions about race, ethnicity, and class, as well as the perspectives and issues confronting students of color, become essential to changing the status quo. Such projects can, for instance, involve teachers in exploring and charting the "funds of knowledge" (Mercado and Moll 1997) found in students' home communities. Carmen Mercado and Luis Moll found that teachers gained important insights from such involvement. They moved from cultural "deprivation" ideas to perceptions that students' communities possessed an "abundance of knowledge" and the students a wealth of interests, abilities, and experiences not readily apparent in the classroom. This project also improved the teachers' contacts with and understandings of family and community members. This new knowledge in turn affected teachers' pedagogical practices and their perceptions of their students' levels of competence. Educators can also attend more closely to community perceptions of critical educational issues. Pedro Pedraza (1997), for instance, points to the continuing emphasis on culture, language, and identity issues among Latino educators and activists and the marginalization of such matters in mainstream discourses on educational reform. We see the same outcomes in Arnhem.

What all substantive educational reform will necessarily require regarding decisions about classroom practices is attention to the inequities of the larger society and their consequences for students. In the sort of environment that closely interrogates the existing system teachers might also talk about *who* says "gonna" and "ain't" aren't words; *why* many Puerto Ricans caught up in the migratory stream are poor; and *how* local schools work in ways that serve the needs of some students better than others.

7 After/Words

> There's no denying that the multicultural initiative arose, in part, because of the fragmentation of American society, by ethnicity, class, and gender. To make it the culprit for this fragmentation is to mistake effect for cause. . . . Maybe we should try to think of American culture as a conversation among different voices—even if it's a conversation some of us weren't able to join until recently. Maybe we should think about education, as the philosopher Michael Oakeshott . . . has proposed, as "an invitation into the art of this conversation in which we learn to recognize the voices."
>
> —Henry Louis Gates, "Multiculturalism" (1995:7)

The myth of schools as meritocratic institutions, as the intermediary mechanism through which all Americans are provided equal opportunity to achieve success, functions as an important fiction, an imaginary resolution of the social contradictions inherent in a class-divided society with longstanding social divisions that fall out along racial and ethnic lines. "In a society marked by great disparities of wealth and power," note the editors of a recent collection of articles that closely examine the role of schools in reproducing societal inequities and the potential for change, "American schools have often been praised as a pathway to equality. But public education in our country has been marked by a cruel gap between rhetorical commitment to democratic ideals and practices that foster intolerance and inequality" (Levine et al. 1995:5).

We have now looked at both the fragmentation of American society as a way of explaining differing community relations to schools and the complexity and difficulty of incorporating minority voices into school "conversations." As we approach the twenty-first century, the voices of groups that have been marginalized throughout U.S. history are demanding their right to full participation in American society and to inclusion and attention to the needs of their children in schools.

For Puerto Ricans, as for other "involuntary" minorities (Ogbu 1987), their relations to schools have been shaped in large measure by a history of blocked aspirations, inequitable access to a quality standard of living, and the stigmatization that accompanies their marginality in society. But while the voices of the minority community members that emerged in Arnhem's public debate reflect their differing relations to schools, at another level they also reflect their faith in the *potential* of the nation's schools to effect social change. Rather than dismissing schools as important sites for the future well-being of their children, they argue that schools can become what they have long been in popular imagination: sites that foster opportunities for all children to succeed. More than that, they envision schools as important sites in fostering the creation of a more democratic common culture.

Although we cannot assess the perceptions of Arnhem's Puerto Rican community as a whole, the turnout of local Puerto Ricans at public meetings, my own interviews with a sampling of Puerto Rican parents[1] and those conducted by the New York State Education Department investigators, as well as an independent study of school–family relations in Arnhem (Galdámez 1993) suggest that the community did feel alienated from the schools and were aware that they encountered barriers because of their ethnic and linguistic backgrounds. Many parents expressed a strong desire that their children not feel ashamed of being Puerto Rican, one possible consequence of the negative stereotypes they and their children encountered in schools and the larger society. Lidia Perez, a long-time Puerto Rican resident of Arnhem, spoke for many when she told me with a trace of pain in her voice, "It would hurt me deeply for my kids to deny what they are, or to feel bad about what they are." Virtually all the Latino parents I talked with said they also wanted their children to keep their native language, though their reasons for doing so differed. Those with closer ties to the island thought it would make their children's lives easier when they were living in Puerto Rico; some saw bilingualism as advantageous for their children's economic prospects; many mentioned that without Spanish their children would be cut off from their Spanish-speaking relatives, and that Spanish was part of their heritage. ESL or bilingual education classes (the two terms were often conflated) were considered essential for helping non–English-speaking students make a smoother transition in school.

Many parents recounted incidents in which they felt their children or others' children had been treated unfairly in school because they were Latino. But at the same time, they also emphasized that they felt that their children's chances for success in school were better in Arnhem than in big cities, where gangs, violence, and drugs in schools would threaten their children's well-being. As with the concept of relative deprivation, the degree of alienation felt by minority community members may be relative to the conditions they have experienced elsewhere.

The divisions between communities separated by class, race, and ethnicity are not easily bridged. Educators in Arnhem, for instance, saw the lack of involvement by minority parents as a sign of their lack of concern about their children's education. Some teachers viewed the absence of minority parents at school events such as "parents' night" or their failure to set up appointments with teachers when their children did poorly in school as evidence of their disinterest in their children's educational well-being, a finding also reported by Galdámez (1993). Although the ESL teacher could point out the significance of the fact that only two of her students' families owned a car and many were uncomfortable entering the schools, most teachers often failed to recognize when class and ethnic differences entered into parents' involvement in school activities. Many Puerto Rican parents lacked ready transportation across town for parents' night—their neighborhood was more than two miles from the school. Many parents worked night shifts, and babysitters were needed if younger children were not welcome at the school. Their lack of familiarity with educational practices and policies also contributed to home–school misunderstandings. One parent I talked to, for instance, spoke with pride, reporting how her son was doing so well in school that they expected him to go on to college and become a doctor. What she didn't know was that he was in the nonregents track and not attaining the skills needed to succeed in college. Language differences complicated matters; the school did not send notices or school policies in Spanish, nor did they provide translators for events.

Current research suggests that the skills and resources parents have at their disposal, rather than differences in the desire to see their children succeed educationally, may explain class and ethnic differences in parental involvement in children's schooling, and that working class and minority parents may not feel comfortable in school settings when they themselves have not had positive or extended experiences in schools (e.g., Delgado-Gaitan 1991; Finders and Lewis 1994; Lareau 1989; Nieto 1996). School personnel can meet parents partway by moving from a "deficit model" when thinking about nonmainstream parental involvement to one that fosters trust and emphasizes how parents *can* become involved in supporting their children's educations (see Delgado-Gaitan 1991; Finders and Lewis 1994; Nieto 1996; Pedraza 1997). My conversations with several parents made it clear that establishing personal relations with school personnel is one important component of any project designed to foster better home–school relations. One parent who had moved outside the school district to a neighboring small town, for instance, spoke enthusiastically of how unlike in Arnhem, teachers in his children's new school met regularly with all parents. Another parent talked at length of how much he appreciated the elementary school ESL teacher's coming to his house.

The community debate and NYSED investigation prompted some important changes that could make a difference in community–school relations. The district did move to implement some of the suggestions proposed by the NYSED. They hired more bilingual aides and began sending home notices in Spanish. The Latino community agency began to work closely with school officials to set up after-school tutoring programs for Latino students. Such initiatives can be a step in the direction of laying the groundwork for better school–community relations.

Several of the parents I talked with also mentioned another consequence of the debate: Marris's comments made them even more aware how prejudiced many in the city were toward Latinos—in particular Puerto Ricans—and they were now more committed to changing the status quo.

> *Patricia Suarez:* Marris added salt to the wound. Arnhem is a very prejudiced little town—racist.

Roberta Renaldo: What Marris did—where I didn't vote before I vote now.

Julia Morales: My husband, the same thing. He was never a registered voter, and because of what Marris started, he said I'm going in. . . . I'm registered now. And I'll vote.

Sonia Diaz: It [Marris's comments] was something very rough. . . . It was very unfair too. We [Puerto Ricans] spoke a lot about racism, because that's what the whole issue was really about.

Several of these parents subsequently joined forces with a diverse group of residents concerned about polarization in the city and the growing expression of hostility toward the Latino and African-American communities, organizing the following year to elect a Puerto Rican minister to the school board and to replace the most intransigent board members.[2]

In the schools themselves there was no consensus among teachers when they were asked a year later whether the NYSED investigation had had a positive effect. Many, as we have seen, strongly resented the presence and evaluation by the NYSED. Asked what they thought about the NYSED recommendation that teachers receive "sensitivity training," three teachers responded that it was the *students* who needed the sensitivity training. As one put it, "They insist there probably should be more sensitivity training, okay. What are you gonna give them in sensitivity, somebody should straighten them [students] out. *They* need to be sensitized." The similarity of the three teachers' responses suggests that they had discussed the subject together, and that the inversion of causality—attributing lack of sensitivity to students rather than to teachers—struck a responsive chord. Some teachers also indicated that the debate and subsequent NYSED investigation had created new problems in that minority students and parents were now more likely to "yell discrimination."

Others, however, felt that the debate and NYSED involvement had, at the very least, provided an impetus for change, encouraging them to reassess their own policies and teachers in general to be more sensitive to the needs and perspectives of the Latino community.

> *Jim Reznick:* It was positive in the effect that someone shook the tree to get the fruit, so to speak. Somebody had to get things rustled up a little bit to get some changes.
>
> *Don Ricardi:* I haven't seen any changes yet. But there's work, that kind of educational work that goes on, sometimes as a result, it's going on. [But] I think it was overblown, exaggerated the problems. They're there and they're real, and things need to be done. . . . It made last year very stressful. And we had our share, there were all these other problems, fiscal problems last year, and it did increase the stress, it was like one more thing to deal with.

Among the small core of teachers who had felt from the beginning of the NYSED investigation that the schools were in need of change, the general feeling was that in the classrooms themselves little substantive change had occurred. As social studies teacher Jim Reznick noted:

> No, nothing has come from the State Ed report. That's the only thing they should be—that's the most important thing that should be at the top of the list, not all this administrative garbage, bureaucratic junk. What's the most important thing is changing attitudes in the classroom. And that's the last thing that will usually be done. . . . American history is tough, because everything is thrown at you, from the European ethnocentric point of view.

Jim had, at his own expense, attended the statewide social studies teachers' conference and was excited about some of the ideas for the classroom that he brought back:

> Yeah, the best resource is other teachers. And at these conferences, you have other teachers, that's all the people are. Very few of them are just people from university level who lecture at you. It's people that are out in the classroom, you know, in the battle. . . . [We're so isolated in the classroom] and that's why I'm looking forward to team teaching [scheduled to be implemented the following year] too. I'm sure I'm gonna pick up things from the other teachers that I'm involved with. And hopefully they'll pick up things from me.

His comments point to some of the mechanisms through which traditional school practices can be modified. Discussions with other teachers and attendance at professional conferences enhance opportunities for greater exposure to current research and to teachers who are actively involved in questioning classroom practices.[3]

Sandy Totten's presence was also beginning to have an influence in the school. She had become a local resource for the remedial reading teacher and another teacher, both of whom were looking for multicultural literature to use in their classrooms. The reading teacher began to routinely incorporate some multicultural literature into her program and reported that her Latino and African-American students "really got into it." She now discussed with her students each author's ethnic background and used the literature as a springboard for student talk and writing. Another English teacher began using Theodore Taylor's *The Cay* (1969), a book brought to her attention by Mrs. Totten, in which the main character experiences prejudice. She reported that as a result of reading the book her students had "really opened up about prejudice in their lives." These discussions had also "opened the eyes" of her white students: "I think we all grew together."

Because Sandy Totten rotated and shared classrooms with other teachers, her approach to teaching was also having an impact. One English teacher was now experimenting with small-group work and collaborative learning techniques after observing Sandy's class. However, Sandy Totten received a layoff notice along with more than thirty other staff members in a cost-cutting move designed to reduce an impending property tax increase.[4]

Mrs. Totten's classroom in many respects represents the kind of environment James Cummins (1986; 1989) argues is most likely to produce success with linguistically and culturally diverse students from dominated groups. Drawing on sociological and anthropological research that suggests status and power relations between groups must be incorporated into any analysis of school failure, his framework for empowering minority students integrates many of the elements discussed in previous chapters:

> The central tenet of the framework is that students from "dominated" groups are "empowered" or "disabled" as a direct result of their interactions with educators in the schools. These interactions are mediated by the implicit or explicit role definitions that educators assume in relation to four institutional characteristics of schools. These characteristics reflect the extent to which (1) minority students' language and culture are incorporated into the school program; (2) minority community participation is encouraged as an integral component of children's education; (3) the pedagogy promotes intrinsic motivation on the part of students to use language actively in order to generate their own knowledge; and (4) professionals involved in assessment become advocates for minority students rather than legitimizing the location of the "problem" in the students. (Cummins 1986:21)

Educators' role definitions can be placed along an "additive-subtractive" dimension and they succeed, Cummins argues, to the extent that they view their function as helping students to add to, rather than subtract from, their own linguistic or cultural repertoires. The classroom environment of Sandy Totten can be characterized as "additive" and the active engagement of her Puerto Rican students as an indication of their sense of being included. Within this context students' cultural identities are positively affirmed, and their "ways with words" used as a resource for expanding their repertoire to include the school's "ways with words." In terms of the analytic framework discussed earlier, through such practices the cultural capital of school is reconfigured so that the symbolic resources of minority students are revalued, rather than devalued.

The findings of other educational researchers working with older low-income minority students support the claims of multicultural education advocates and minority community members that such modifications can be important in the classroom. Many low-income minority students report that they do not feel "at home" in the classroom (cf. Gilmore et al. 1993; Nelson-Barber and Meier 1988; Zanger 1994). Working with a group of Latino students in a Boston high school, Zanger found evidence of their feeling "pushed out," "under them" (other student groups), stigmatized for their Hispanic backgrounds and Spanish language, and "left out." Students indicated that their invisibility in the curriculum was problematic, and that being included might help dispel some of the racist misconceptions of other students and elevate their status by legitimizing their ethnicity. Asked to discuss what factors contributed to the dismal academic records of minority students, the students indicated that it is the social dynamics of the schools, both in their interactions with other student groups and with teachers, that lead to alienation, silencing, and decline in student motivation. "Cultural pride is a strong current running throughout much of the data, and it is a desire to be accepted *for who and what they are* about which students are most adamant. . . . Students' outspoken defense of their culture does not mean that they do not want to learn English or adapt to the dominant culture. Rather, they are adamant that this be done in an educational context that is additive rather than subtractive in nature, one that does not seek to supplant their language and culture with another" (Zanger 1994:178–81). Instead school is framed in a subtractive context. The sentiments these students express are not unique; as Margaret Gibson notes in reviewing domestic and international case studies of minority student performance, minority students in general perform better in school "when they feel strongly anchored in the identities of their families, communities, and peers and when they feel supported in pursuing a strategy of selective or additive acculturation" (1997:446).

Incorporating more multicultural texts into the curriculum as a means of redressing past omissions, though a step in the direction of integrating diverse voices and perspectives, is inadequate in and of itself. Celebrating diversity by itself does little to assist students—or teachers—in confronting the contradictions of living in a nation that espouses democracy and equality but was built on and continues to tolerate vast inequalities among groups (Nasaw 1979), the consequences of which teachers confront daily in their classrooms. The success or failure of moves to "open up" literature classrooms and challenge the school canon cannot be measured solely by counting the numbers of authors of color in new anthologies.

The challenges faced by efforts to rework what goes on in schools are daunting but demand our sustained attention if we want to create more equitable educational outcomes. Educators need opportunities to examine the assumptions behind their own classroom pedagogies, and teacher education programs are one arena in which future teachers can be encouraged to rethink those assumptions. For those already in the field, in-service training, in which practitioners attend a short session on some specific knowledge or technique, with little or no follow-up, offers little opportunity for the kinds of far-reaching changes needed to reframe the schooling experiences of minority children; at best it constitutes poor educational practice. Rather, teachers need sustained opportunities to engage in reflective and critical discussion about the conditions of teaching, about the perspectives all teachers bring to classrooms and texts, what those perspectives include and exclude, and the possible consequences for the increasingly diverse students they teach.

Implementing multicultural reforms, as this book suggests, requires close attention to the conditions of schooling that work *against* change. University researchers and educators need to continue to stay directly connected to schools and classrooms, working as partners with teachers and exploring their concerns, perspectives, and responses to reform initiatives. Similarly, top-down initiatives for change must be accompanied by close attention to local conditions, including teacher perspectives and the constraints teachers face.[5]

The complex nature and significance of school–community relationships in seeking to improve educational outcomes for Puerto Rican youth merit particularly close attention. Fostering among teachers and administrators greater recognition of how class, language, and race mediate encounters between parents, children, and schools, and how to bridge those barriers successfully, is essential. In Arnhem the hiring of bilingual aides was much appreciated by Puerto Rican parents as one step in that direction. District officials can go a step further and recruit bilingual or Puerto Rican teachers. If, indeed, it is as difficult to recruit such teachers as officials claim, they might follow the steps taken by Garden City, Kansas, school officials. There, in response to a rapidly growing population of Mexican origin, the district offered college scholarships to local Chicano youth who promised to return to teach in the district for three years. Officials then went on to further develop their "Grow Your Own" program by promising to reimburse district employees—including teachers, cooks, custodians, and aides—for college courses toward bilingual or ESL certification (Harrison 1998).

Working to lower the barriers that so profoundly segregate sectors of the American community is vital to the country's well-being. Barriers in Arnhem can further be reduced by seeking local solutions such as using school buildings for community events that bring parents to school grounds; meeting parents in the community center in the East End; or involving the sector of the community most resistant to bilingual and multicultural education initiatives, Euro-American seniors, in school-related activities that foster contact with Latino youth.

State actions can also lend official support for educational initiatives that benefit diverse students. Arnhem school officials and teachers collaborated with State Education officials, academics, and community organizations to develop a 300-page document responding to the New York State Education Department concerns. It laid out plans for implementing district goals that evolved from the report recommendations. Important movement did in fact occur: the school now sends out bilingual materials, it hired bilingual aides, the ESL program was revamped (though bilingual education initiatives were sidelined), some curriculum reform was attempted, and a small group of interested teachers and administrators began to seriously examine the issues raised by the NYSED and community activists. The impetus for change, however, slowed considerably in the face of declining revenues that resulted in the elimination of department chairs, cuts in funds for educational workshops, and teacher layoffs.

Political action remains essential. As the 1996 election returns indicate (Ayres 1996), Latinos nationwide are responding to legislation they perceive as anti-Latino or not in their own best interests by becoming more politically involved. The success of a coalition of community members in electing a Puerto Rican to the Arnhem school board points to the potential for organizing across racial groups through appeal to democratic principles.

Toward the Future

The debate over the schools in Arnhem examined in these pages took place within a larger context in which minority leaders at state and national levels have contested their representation in school and university curricula and their unequal access to resources and positions of power (see, for example, Hancock 1990; Henry 1990; Reinhold 1991; Sobol 1989; Whitaker 1991). These larger debates over school knowledge and the unequal distribution of resources and power in American society in turn provided a ready vocabulary for local minority community members and university students to express their own sense of exclusion and disempowerment in schools and society and to demand that the schools better serve their community's needs. It remains an open question, however, what would be the outcome of even the most optimal schooling conditions for Puerto Rican youth, given the larger economic realities of life in a deindustrializing economy and the grim economic realities that confront Puerto Ricans on the island.

One hundred years after Puerto Rico's forced incorporation into the United States, Puerto Ricans have yet to achieve equity with mainstream Americans, and remain among the poorest of all groups of Americans. The prospects for improvement in the near future appear tenuous. The expanding economy, beginning in the 1940s, that made upward mobility possible for white ethnics has changed drastically. The inequalities of income in the United States are now greater than at any time since the 1930s (Lind 1995), de-industrialization continues apace, and federal support for ameliorating the consequences of poverty and inequality has eroded. In the new deindustrializing era many employment opportunities no longer exist for groups, such as the majority of Puerto Rican citizens of this country, who were poorly positioned to take advantage of the postwar economic boom. Approaching the twenty-first century, we may also question the feasibility of implementing significant change in impoverished inner city schools across the nation without government support for eradicating the vast disparities in school funding, and without public support for jobs creation programs that will reach working-class people of color. Without a greater public commitment to a more equitable distribution of employment and educational resources, positive change will be hampered further. Given the competition for the shrinking number of jobs that can provide a living wage, we may anticipate that the current gap between the "haves" and the "have-nots" will continue to grow without a greater public commitment to a more equitable distribution of employment and educational resources (Bonacich 1990).

Research findings support those who argue that what

happens in schools can make a difference in the struggle to achieve more equitable educational outcomes. Changing the schools will not be an easy matter, as events in Arnhem illustrate, but the creation of forums for "discussion and debate about how equity and social justice are best achieved through education" (Kohl 1995) is critical. Educators and community members interested in effecting educational change can start by heeding the voices of Puerto Ricans and those of other educationally and economically disenfranchised groups. The responses of Puerto Rican students in Arnhem, when asked how they felt about Nuyorican author Nicholasa Mohr's books, point to their perceptiveness of the many ways in which U.S schools have traditionally rendered invisible the realities of their lives beyond the school doors. Their responses also underline the urgent need to continue to work toward a more inclusive, equitable, and just society:

> *Miguel Gomez:* I like her stuff, 'cause she talks—you know–she just came out right straight like she didn't care. She came out right straight saying what she felt. She writes about what is going on, you know, more like about prejudice.
>
> *Joey Cintrón:* I thought it was good. Because it was like, more like our times. Like all the other books are like real old and they taught us about like ancient history and stuff like that. This one was like you could relate to it. . . . Like New York City, like with all the people there like, having a hard time and stuff like that, with the money and stuff. . . . 'Cause you know like a lot of people are out—like these times are like that. Like they don't got a lot of money. Like in New York City. They—you could picture it in your mind.
>
> *Carmen Morales:* It [Mohr's book *Felita*] was good. 'Cause it told about prejudism and we learned a lot out of it, like not to pick on people because of their color.

Sonia Cruz: I think it [*Felita*] was *so* good. She talks in Spanish and English. Like in true life.

Arnhem's story may be uniquely its own, shaped by its own local history and actors, but at the same time its story is as national as it is local. "AmeRican," puns Nuyorican poet Tato Laviera (1985), with the emphasis on the first and third syllables, assertively injecting the "Rican" presence and experience into the American framework. Talking "American" is about talking in many voices. The ongoing negotiation of what counts as the American experience as we continue to redefine what it means to be "American," and in the process what all Americans are entitled to, takes place in both national debates and local daily struggles. As Ana Celia Zentella (1997) so forcefully and eloquently reminds us, the American dream is not one dreamed in English only. It never was. Only recently have we begun to approach that understanding, and to explore the implications of the racial, ethnic, and class divisions that constitute the real forces threatening to "disunite" America.[6]

Notes

Introduction

1. Many spokespersons from so-called "minority" groups now advocate replacing the term with "people of color" because in their opinion "minority" has taken on negative connotations and, used to refer collectively to non–European-origin groups, will soon be statistically inaccurate (in some areas of the country and in many schools, it already is inaccurate). See Nieto (1992) for a more detailed examination of appropriate terminology. I use the term because it was still universally applied in Arnhem, and also use the term "people of color." Whereas Latino and African-American spokespersons generally used the term to encompass all "nonwhites," Euro-American senior citizens in the community used it as a shorthand for Latinos and African Americans, but generally not Asian Americans.

2. In Arnhem it is Euro-Americans who routinely refer to local Puerto Ricans, Costa Ricans, Dominicans, and other South Americans as "Hispanics." Minority community leaders also frequently use the term publicly when referring collectively to such peoples. The term has been challenged by Latino spokespersons (e.g., Melville 1988; Nieto 1992) who feel it glosses over important interethnic differences and does not acknowledge the group's African and indigenous roots. I use the term "Latino," which is preferred by many politically active community leaders and younger members of the community, throughout the text. Latinos in Arnhem generally refer to particular individuals by reference to their homeland (as Dominican, Costa Rican, etc.).

3. Sonia Nieto's book *Affirming Diversity: The Sociopolitical Context of Multicultural Education* (1996), which draws from this large body of educational literature, provides an excellent example of how the various strands of research and theory have enriched and influenced each other.

4. See, for example, arguments put forth in Au 1993; Banks 1988; Banks 1991; Cummins 1989; Harris 1992; Levine et al. 1995; New York State Social Studies Review and Development Committee 1991; Nieto 1996; Ramsey, Vold, and Williams 1989; Sleeter 1991.

5. "Diagnostic events," as Moore (1987) notes, can serve as valuable

sources for uncovering how cultural meanings are constructed, affirmed, and resisted.

6. Frankenberg defines "discourses" as "historically constituted bodies of ideas providing conceptual frameworks for individuals, made material in the design and creation of institutions and shaping daily practices, interpersonal interactions, and social relations" (1993:265). I use the term both in this sense and in the local sense of synthesizing what particular groups (e.g., community Seniors or teachers) were putting forward in the community debate and in school discussions (and of course these groups drew on "historically constituted" discourses to derive their own). The sense in which the term is being used can be understood through the context, and I rely more on the phrase "discursive repertoires" for the first meaning.

7. Frankenberg prefers to use the terms "color-evasiveness" and "power evasiveness" to underline that this discursive repertoire contains these elements, and because the term "color-blind" constructs "color" as a disability. I use the term "color-blind" frequently because it was one commonly used by my informants, but also critique the practice in a similar manner.

8. Social theorists and analysts such as W.E.B. DuBois and Carey McWilliams had earlier written from such perspectives, but their work had little resonance at the time and failed to move the national dialogue along such lines.

9. To protect teacher confidentiality I have sometimes changed minor biographical details or avoided the kinds of biographic information (e.g., gender, subject area taught) that if provided might threaten the anonymity of teachers who were particularly concerned about being identified.

Chapter 1

1. *Arnhem Record* is a pseudonym. Full citation information is available from the author.

2. The history of Arnhem is derived from interviews with community members, archival research, and a book on the city's history. Citation information on the book and newspaper articles is available from the author.

3. Many Italian Americans in the community were also active in the soccer league, and such connections (along with other advantages noted later) may have enhanced interethnic relations.

4. The term "(im)migrants" refers to people migrating from other countries, as well as internal migration movements, which include

Puerto Ricans moving from Puerto Rico and other regions of the United States to Arnhem. Despite the fact that Puerto Ricans have been U.S. citizens since 1917, when the U.S. government unilaterally granted them citizenship status, many Euro-American community members routinely refer to them as "immigrants." This reflects the fact that although they are legally migrants, they are culturally immigrants, with a distinct cultural identity and language (Spanish).

5. A recent unpublished doctoral dissertation on "Arnhem" explores this aspect of the Latino experience in more depth. Citation information is available from the author.

6. Many in the community feel that the most recent census seriously undercounted Latinos, whose mobility, possible distrust of government officials, and (in some cases) illegal status make them less likely to be counted accurately by census takers. The school count also cannot be used as an accurate gauge because of the higher dropout rate among Latino students.

7. This reaction to being taken as Puerto Rican could also be a function of Latinos' strong identification with their homelands, but several of my Latino informants felt it had more to do with the negative stereotypes of Puerto Ricans in the community.

8. Given the likelihood that Latinos were undercounted because of their mobility, (in some cases) illegal status, or reluctance to participate, the differences in the statistics on income, education, employment, and home language may be greater than these numbers suggest.

9. Data taken from a local "Latino Community Needs Assessment 1989" report prepared by a Latino community agency in Arnhem (citation information available from the author).

10. Information based on 1990 U.S. Census data.

Chapter 2

1. See, for example, Loewen 1995; Nash 1974; Takaki 1989, 1993; and Zinn 1980 for multicultural perspectives on U.S. history that examine in depth the forces of marginalization and exclusion.

2. It is striking to note that in 1940, 77 percent of African Americans still lived in the South (Smith and Pedersen 1997). Those who moved north–more than five million in the following three decades—migrated to urban areas suffering economic decline, and thus faced both northern prejudice and discrimination (albeit less overt than in the South) and the difficulty of finding meaningful employment in a deindustrializing economy.

3. For more detailed information on the experiences of these groups

in the U.S.A., see, for example, Acuña 1988; de León, 1983; History Task Force 1979; López 1980; McWilliams 1990; Moore and Pachon 1985; Rodríguez 1989; Rodríguez, Sanchéz Korrol, and Alers 1980; Sanchéz Korrol 1983.

4. Endnote as it appears in Hochschild (1995): The phrase is from Rae (1988).

5. One result of those changes has been the surge in immigration from Latin American and Asian countries that in recent years has generated media analyses of the implications of the "browning" of America (e.g., Gray 1991; Henry 1990) and given further impetus to multiculturalist struggles.

6. This is not to deny that biological variability exists, but to say that such variability does not conform to the discrete racial categories Americans "see." As genetic studies have demonstrated individuals from different "racial" groups may be more similar to one another than to those members of their assigned "racial" groups. See Keita and Kittles (1997) for a discussion of the research.

7. As Omi and Winant (1994:180) also note, Phipps's unsuccessful attempt to change her classification and the unconstitutionality of the law resulted in a legislative effort that led to the repeal of the law.

8. Gould later repeated Morton's tests and concluded that Morton had unconsciously finagled to get the results he did, based on his preexisting expectations. See Gould 1981 for an extensive analysis of the era and critique of the tests.

9. Alfred Binet, the originator of the test, did not equate intelligence with the test score, nor did he assume it measured inherited limitations. See Gould 1981.

10. Arguments for multilingualism, part of the multicultural thrust, also have historic precedents. Public and private schools in the Midwest, for instance, taught the children of German immigrants in German, a practice that continued until the anti-German hysteria of the World War I era (Heath 1983b).

11. By 1840, as common school reformers were initiating their crusades, approximately three-quarters of the adult population could read and write. The existing elementary school system produced adequate numbers of educated workers to fill the minority of jobs that required literacy in the workplace (Bowles and Gintis 1976:169).

12. See, for example, Steinberg's (1989) review of the literature attributing Italian American students' lack of educational achievement to their traditional value structure.

13. Postwar government largesse (including low-cost mortgages and bank loans) was not equitably distributed, however. In effect, these

programs constituted "affirmative action programs for white males because they were decidedly not extended to African Americans or to women of any race" (Sacks 1994:90–91). See Sacks (1994:90–92) for a discussion of the literature on how African Americans and women were largely excluded from taking advantage of these programs and the expanding economy. Among other things, African Americans faced renewed racist violence, were often first to be fired, were effectively denied benefits by government agencies, and were excluded from many white institutions of higher education.

14. The growing percentages from each social group entering college after the war are striking: lower middle-class attendance went from 20 percent in 1940 to 38 percent in 1950, to 45 percent in 1960, to 64 percent by 1970; skilled upper working-class attendance rose from 5 percent in 1940 to 12 percent in 1950, to 25 percent in 1960, to 40 percent in 1970 (Davis 1986:192).

Chapter 3

1. "Boricua" is derived from the term "Borinquen," the name given to the island of Puerto Rico by its pre-Hispanic inhabitants.

2. Policy decisions as to whether to teach in English or Spanish and when to introduce English vacillated considerably during the first half of the century (Glazer and Moynihan 1970). Not until 1952, with passage of the Commonwealth Constitution, did teaching in Spanish become law.

3. The parallels to the responses of Arnhem's senior citizens, covered in depth in Chapter 4, are striking.

4. "Nuyorican" (or sometimes "neorican") refers to the second and later generations, whose experiences on the mainland have created a cultural orientation that differentiates them from their island counterparts.

5. The return flow that began in the late 1960s has also been connected to the poor living conditions in inner-city ghettos, including concerns over increasing crime rates and fear of drug addiction in children (see, for example, López 1980).

6. Another anthropologist working in the region speculates that Puerto Rican job applicants may be excluded from better-paying factory jobs in the city in part through the use of required tests that call for mathematical skills and facility with written English unrelated to the actual skills needed on the job. See author for citation information.

7. There are important group exceptions, including Cubans and many South Americans, for whom class advantages and (in the case of Cubans) refugee status (with federal assistance for businesses available) have translated into economic and educational advantages. See, for example, Ford Foundation (1984) or Moore and Pachon (1985).

8. Statistics are based on 1994 data from the U.S. Bureau of the Census. See *American Almanac 1995–1996*.

9. Data were provided by school district officials in June 1990; citation information is available from the author.

10. U.S. Bureau of the Census, *Current Population Reports*, Series P-60, no.188, and P-20, no. 475 (cited in Parrillo 1997:397).

11. Among these trends was a notable shift in wealth toward the upper end. In 1976 the top 1 percent of U.S. families owned 22 percent of the national wealth; in 1992 they owned 42 percent (Wills 1996:36).

12. Jacoby (1994) also points to the potential for the "culture wars" to distract attention from such serious issues that threaten national well-being.

13. Gibson, for example (1993), examines how for Punjabi students the cultural environment of the home promoted school success (despite encounters with racism) through a strategy of "accommodation and acculturation without assimilation." (1993:122).

14. Ogbu and Matute-Bianchi (1986), for instance, suggest that among Mexican-Americans, survival strategies have included passing (as white); establishment of patron-client relations; caste leakage; collective struggle; and deviant behavior.

Chapter 4

1. This is not the case in all Western pluralistic societies. The term "multicultural education," for instance, is suspect in Canada for its "song-and-dance" connotations (Cummins 1997).

2. Latina community organizer Virginia Colón did not publicly identify herself with any segment of the Latino community. She was actually a second-generation Mexican American raised in the Midwest, but many Latinos in Arnhem were unsure of her ethnic roots. As a "Latina" community organizer, this facilitated her being seen as not favoring one group over another. Her story resonated very powerfully with the largely Puerto Rican audience, and it is for this reason that I include it.

3. Citations taken from *Latino Community Needs Assessment 1991* (Arnhem, NY). Publication information does not appear in the bibliography in order to preserve the anonymity of the community.

4. John Marris did not publicly identify with a white ethnic group.

5. The board was composed of nine Euro-Americans and one Costa Rican–American businessman (who rarely spoke at public meetings). Of the nine Euro-American members, seven were senior citizens and fiscal conservatives; six of the seven voted in a bloc so consistently that they were labeled in the local press the "Gang of Six."

6. See Glazer 1997 for one perspective on New York's attempts to address these issues in the curriculum.

7. While most of the people speaking out were Latinos, one of the outspoken proponents for educational change at this meeting and in the ensuing public debate was an African-American woman who struggled to broaden the debate from its focus on the educational needs of Latino children to the educational needs of minority children in general. Shortly after the conflict developed she organized the "Fellowship against Racism" (FAR) with the assistance of local religious leaders, the goal of which was to educate people to recognize and combat racism.

8. Local Asian Americans did not participate in this or any subsequent aspect of the public debate.

9. Several of the speakers were regular local radio talk show callers and members of the "Arnhem Study Group" formed by Marris in 1989 to explore ways to reduce school taxes. This group had been instrumental in organizing the senior citizen population for the most recent school board election and controlled the majority of votes on the board. When two board members later called for Marris's resignation, the board voted seven to three not to remove him.

10. Largely missing from the public discourse were the views of younger Euro-Americans in the community, as well as the sentiments of nonpolitically active minority community members.

11. I want to thank Bonnie Urciuoli for pointing out the similarities.

Chapter 5

1. Data are based on the completed questionnaires of forty-seven teachers.

2. A local television news broadcast at the time reported that three out of four teachers in New York State had been teaching for sixteen or more years and that more than half of all New York public school teachers were between the ages of forty-one and fifty-six.

3. Three younger teachers expressed privately their feelings that a small number of teachers were biased in their dealings with Latino students and pointed to faculty room conversations where teachers made disparaging comments about Latinos as evidence. The biases, they felt, took the form of being more confrontational with Latino students or less willing to give the students the support they needed.

4. Most of the school research was conducted at the secondary level, concentrating on the junior high school. I do not have sufficient data to generalize about the elementary schools.

5. The school district did offer a course in Spanish for teachers, but it folded after one session because of a lack of response.

6. Collier and Thomas's studies, based on extensive research over several years, found that nonnative speakers of English who received no schooling in their first language took seven to ten years or more to achieve the age and grade-level norms of their native English-speaking peers. Those with two to three years of first language instruction before to coming to the United States took at least five to seven years. While nonnative speakers did reasonably well in the first four years of elementary school regardless of whether they received instruction in their first language, they did less and less well as they moved up the grades if they were receiving little or no academic and cognitive development in their native language. See Collier (1995) for an in-depth analysis of their research findings and publications.

7. Ironically, lunchroom policies fostered segregation: students who brought their lunches were allowed to take them out of the cafeteria and sit in the gymnasium bleachers, while those who bought lunches (overwhelmingly students on free or reduced-price lunches) had to remain in the cafeteria. The policy was later changed.

8. This teacher did later implement the ESL teacher's suggestions and reported very positive responses from students.

9. The NYSED report, for the most part, put the blame on the school board and on institutional policies and practices, including an inadequate ESL/bilingual education program, tracking practices, curriculum selections, and the lack of strong school–community relations.

10. The school board at that time had a reputation for favoritism and arbitrary decisions. According to local talk, for instance, a custodian (despite glowing recommendations) was denied appointment to the head custodial position because in the previous year, acting on instructions from his superior to report the presence of any nonstaff members in the school building after hours, he had turned in the name of one of the school board members.

11. In my opinion my status as a former public school teacher helped facilitate my access to classrooms and interviews with teachers, though some teachers requested that I observe only their "better-behaved" classes. Teachers' discomfort with being observed is certainly not unique to Arnhem. I found it to be true in the three schools I had previously worked in, and as a traditionally trained teacher I, too, felt uncomfortable.

12. There were notable exceptions: three untenured teachers with a strong interest in the education of minority students spoke openly about their perceptions and concerns (with the promise of anonymity), pressed for any information I might have on educating minority students, and expressed no concerns about my taping in their classrooms.

13. Although the community debate provided the impetus for evaluating literature selections, there has also been a growing emphasis in both the professional English language arts literature and teacher conferences on reevaluating the literature canon.

14. This was a response more strongly echoed by reading teachers, who worked only with "low readers," who came primarily from lower-class backgrounds.

15. It must be pointed out that such a tidy scheme obscures the complex ways in which such concerns are linked (but it allows us to understand general themes).

16. It consists of (a) an introductory paragraph with a thesis statement; (b) three paragraphs, each making a different point; and (c) a concluding paragraph. Nystrand and Gamoran (1991) posit that the format lacks authenticity because teachers predetermine the type of response (e.g., three main points) expected.

17. "Detracking," in which students are placed in academically heterogenous groups, and "teaming," in which teachers coordinate their lessons and work with teams of students, are elements of middle school philosophy.

18. This was common in many classes I observed, and I do not single out her classroom as the exception.

19. Mrs. Lane considered stories with girls as major characters to be "girls' stories," while stories with males were deemed appropriate for all students. Nicholasa Mohr's stories frequently have female protagonists. The following discussion, which had taken place the previous day as Mrs. Lane prepared the class to think of questions to ask Mohr when she came to visit, may have influenced students' perceptions of the "gendering" of Mohr's works:

Mrs. Lane: Can we ask this question (whether the story reflects the author's own experiences growing up) of her?

Sandra: No! She might start crying.

Robert: Aren't these girls' books?

Mrs. Lane: That was my complaint too.

20. The three newest faculty members indicated that they had taken no such courses.

21. The issue of whether basals and anthologies "deskill" teachers has also been hotly debated (see Apple 1986; Baumann 1992; Shannon 1993).

22. Fine calls this tactic "maintaining silencing through (contrived) democracy" (1987:168).

23. Euro-American students were also excited to have a "real live author" in their midst, and Mohr received an enthusiastic reception from

students both during her presentation and at the reception following, where she signed books.

Chapter 6

1. See Bigler 1994a for a lengthier analysis of these differences.

2. See Collins 1988 for a review of the literature.

3. A detailed historical and interactional analysis of the Standard/vernacular conflict in schooling, explicitly developing the notion of "hegemonic practices," is provided in Collins 1989.

4. I observed an average of two to three times per week over most of the school year. I routinely spoke informally with the teachers following classroom observation.

5. Many teachers were reluctant to participate in such activities even when assured of anonymity, though most did ultimately agree to the taping of interviews. Anecdotal evidence suggests such responses are not uncommon among teachers in general, who fear that such data could lead to their losing their jobs.

6. These differences across tracks are common; see, for example, findings in Oakes 1985; summary in Gehrke, Knapp, and Sirotnik 1992.

7. In this instance I did not have an opportunity to question Mrs. Lane about her decision to move quickly away from Sonia's comment; however, as noted in the previous chapter, when asked why she had ignored a white male student's unsolicited comment "Freed the niggers" (said under his breath but loud enough for some students to hear it), she had indicated that she was unwilling to "create a conflict" in the classroom by drawing attention to it.

8. Excerpts are taken from preliminary drafts and do not reflect any later spelling corrections or changes in sentence structure.

9. Her style actually paralleled more closely the participation structure Pamela McCollum (1989) found in Puerto Rican classrooms. Unlike in North American classrooms, where recitation lessons are common, McCollum found "instructional conversations" to be the norm in the Puerto Rican classes she observed. She posits that the differing classroom participation structures found in most mainland classrooms may contribute to interactive difficulties between mainland teachers and Puerto Rican students.

10. Footnote as it appears in Bloome's text: "The term Standard English is problematic because it suggests a standard by which other varieties of English and other languages are measured and compared. While such measurements may occur, there is nothing inherent in Standard English that makes it a standard."

Chapter 7

1. This was not a representative sample, though it did include long-time residents, 1980s migrants from New York City, and recent arrivals from Puerto Rico. I spoke at length with eighteen Latino parents with children in the schools, including both participants and nonparticipants in the debate. Reasons given by those who did not become publicly involved in the debate (all followed it closely) included not wanting to incur more negative attention from members of the white community, not wanting to get involved politically, and, in several instances, personal dislike of one of the community agency activists.

2. The following year the minister resigned because of ill health. The sole Latino (Puerto Rican) running for a seat on the board, a woman who had been an active participant in the debate, lost the election to a senior citizen who had previously been part of the "Gang of Six."

3. An excellent resource published by teachers and educators interested in issues of equity and social justice in urban schools is the newspaper *Rethinking Schools*. Their address is *Rethinking Schools*, 1001 East Keefe Avenue, Milwaukee, WI 53212. Their web page can be accessed at www.rethinkingschools.org.

4. Mrs. Totten was hired back.

5. For an excellent in-depth examination of how programs for educational reform in urban schools can end up reproducing the status quo and the conditions of teaching, see McQuillan 1998.

6. The phrase "disuniting of America" became popular with historian Arthur Schlesinger's (1991) publication of *The Disuniting of America*.

Bibliography

Acuña, Rodolfo. 1988. *Occupied America: A History of Chicanos (*3rd ed). New York: Harper and Row.
Agar, Michael. 1983. "Political Talk: Thematic Analysis of a Policy Argument." *Policy Studies Review* 2 (4): 601–14.
Aguirre, Adalberto. 1978. *An Experimental Sociolinguistic Study of Chicano Bilingualism.* San Francisco: R & E Research Associates.
Alba, Richard. 1985. *Italian Americans: Into the Twilight of Ethnicity.* Englewood Cliffs, NJ: Prentice Hall.
———. 1988. "The Twilight of Ethnicity among Americans of European Ancestry: The Case of Italians." In *Ethnicity and Race in the U.S.A.,* ed. Richard Alba, 134–58. New York: Routledge.
———. 1990. *Ethnic Identity: The Transformation of White America.* New Haven, CT: Yale University Press.
American Almanac 1995–1996. 1995. Austin, TX: Reference Press.
Anderson, Benedict. 1983. *Imagined Communities: Reflections on the Origin and Spread of Nationalism.* New York: Verso.
Apple, Michael. 1986. *Teachers and Texts.* New York: Routledge.
Applebee, Arthur. 1990. *Literature Instruction in American Schools.* Report No. 1.4. Albany, NY: National Research Center on Literature Teaching and Learning, State University of New York, University at Albany.
———. 1991. *A Study of High School Literature Anthologies.* Report No. 1.5. Albany, NY: National Research Center on Literature Teaching and Learning, State University of New York, University at Albany.
———. 1993. *Beyond the Lesson: Reconstructing Curriculum as a Domain for Culturally Significant Conversations.* Report No. 1.7. Albany, NY: National Research Center on Literature Teaching and Learning, State University of New York, University at Albany.
Attinasi, John. 1994. "Racism, Language Variety, and Urban U.S. Minorities: Issues in Bilingualism and Bidialectalism." In *Race,* ed. Steven Gregory and Roger Sanjek, 319–47. New Brunswick, NJ: Rutgers University Press.
Au, Kathryn. 1993. *Literacy Instruction in Multicultural Settings.* New York: Harcourt Brace College Publishers.
Au, Kathryn, and Cathie Jordan. 1981. "Teaching Reading to Hawaiian

Children: Finding a Culturally Appropriate Solution." In *Culture and the Bilingual Classroom: Studies in Classroom Ethnography,* ed. Henry Trueba, Grace Pung Guthrie, and Kathryn Au, 139–52. Rowley, MA: Newbury House.

Ayres, B. Drummond. 1996. "The Expanding Hispanic Vote Shakes Republican Strongholds." *New York Times,* November 10: 1, 27.

Balibar, Etienne, and Immanuel Wallerstein. 1991. *Race, Nation, Class: Ambiguous Identities.* New York: Verso.

Banks, James. 1988. *Multiethnic Education: Theory and Practice.* Boston: Allyn & Bacon.

———. 1991. "A Curriculum for Empowerment, Action, and Change." In *Empowerment through Multicultural Education,* ed. Christine Sleeter, 125–42. Albany: State University of New York Press.

———. 1997. *Teaching Strategies for Ethnic Studies* (6th ed.). Boston: Allyn & Bacon.

Banks, James, and Cherry McGee Banks, eds. 1997. *Multicultural Education: Issues and Perspectives* (3rd ed.). Needham Heights, MA: Allyn & Bacon.

Barrera, Rosalinda, Olga Liguori, and Loretta Salas. 1992. "Ideas a Literature Can Grow On: Key Insights for Enriching and Expanding Children's Literature about the Mexican-American Experience." In *Teaching Multicultural Literature in Grades K–8,* ed. Violet Harris, 203–42. Norwood, MA: Christopher-Gordon Publishers.

Baumann, James. 1992. "Basal Reading Programs and the Deskilling of Teachers: A Critical Examination of the Arguments." *Reading Research Quarterly* 27 (4): 390–98.

Benmayor, Rina, Ana Juarbe, Celia Alvarez, and Blanca Vazquez Erazo. 1988. "Stories to Live By: Continuity and Change in Three Generations of Puerto Rican Women." *Oral History Review* 16 (2): 1–46.

Bennett, Adrian, and Pedro Pedraza. 1988. "Political Dimensions of Discourse: Consciousness and Literacy in a Puerto Rican Neighborhood in East Harlem." In *Speech and Ways of Speaking in a Bilingual Puerto Rican Community,* ed. Celia Alvarez et al., 193–222. New York: Centro de Estudios Puertorriqueños.

Bereiter, Carl, and Siegfried Engelmann. 1966. *Teaching Disadvantaged Children in Preschool.* New York: Prentice Hall.

Bigler, Ellen. 1994a. *Multiculturalism in Upstate New York: Contested Identities and the Schooling of Puerto Rican Youth in a De-industrializing Economy.* Ph.D. dissertation, Anthropology Department, University at Albany, State University of New York.

———. 1994b. *Talking "American": Dialoguing on Difference in Upstate New York.* Report No. 7.2. Albany, NY: National Research Center on Literature Teaching and Learning, State University of New York, University at Albany.

———. 1996a. *On Exclusion and Inclusion in Classroom Texts and Talk.* Report No. 7.5. Albany, NY: National Research Center on Literature Teaching and Learning, State University of New York, University at Albany.

———. 1996b. "Telling Stories: On Ethnicity, Exclusion, and Education in Upstate New York." *Anthropology & Education Quarterly* 27 (2): 186–203.

———. 1997. "Dangerous Discourses: Language Politics and Classroom Practices in Upstate New York." *CENTRO* IX (9): 26–42. New York: Centro de Estudios Puertorriqueños, Hunter College, City University of New York.

Bigler, Ellen, and James Collins. 1995. *Dangerous Discourses: The Politics of Multicultural Literature in Community and Classroom.* Report No. 7.4. Albany, NY: National Research Center on Literature Teaching and Learning, State University of New York, University at Albany.

Bishop, Rudine Sims. 1992. "Multicultural Literature for Children: Making Informed Choices." In *Teaching Multicultural Literature in Grades K–8,* ed. Violet Harris, 37–54. Norwood, MA: Christopher-Gordon Publishers.

Blauner, Robert. 1972. *Racial Oppression in America.* New York: Harper & Row.

Bloome, David. 1991. "Anthropology and Research on Teaching the English Language Arts." In *Handbook of Research on Teaching the English Language Arts,* ed. James Flood et al., 46–56. New York: Macmillan.

Bonacich, Edna. 1990. "Inequality in America: The Failure of the American System for People of Color." In *U.S. Race Relations in the 1980s and 1990s: Challenges and Alternatives,* ed. Gail Thomas, 187–208. New York: Hemisphere Publishing.

Bonilla, Frank, and Ricardo Campos. 1981. "A Wealth of Poor: Puerto Ricans in the New Economic Order." *Daedalus* 110 (Spring): 133–76.

Bourdieu, Pierre. 1986. "The Forms of Capital." In *Handbook of Theory and Research for the Sociology of Education,* ed. John Richardson, 241–58. New York: Greenwood Press.

Bourdieu, Pierre, and Jean-Claude Passeron. 1977 [1970]. *Reproduction in Education, Society and Culture.* London: Sage.

Bowles, Samuel, and Herbert Gintis. 1976. *Schooling in Capitalist America.* New York: Basic Books.

Britton, James, and Merron Chorny. 1991. "Current Issues and Future Directions." In *Handbook of Research on Teaching the English Language Arts,* ed. James Flood et al., 110–20. New York: Macmillan.

Bruce-Noboa, James. 1987. "A Question of Identity: What's in a Name? Chicanos and Riqueños." In *Images and Identities: The Puerto Rican in Two World Contexts,* ed. Asela Rodríguez de Laguna, 229–35. New Brunswick, NJ: Transaction Books.

Candeloro, Dominic. 1992. "Italian Americans." In *Multiculturalism in the United States: A Comparative Guide to Acculturation and Ethnicity,* ed. John Buenker and Lorman Ratner, 173–92. Westport, CT: Greenwood Press.

Carter, Thomas, and Robert Segura. 1979. *Mexican-Americans in School: A Decade of Change.* New York: CEEB.

Cazden, Courtney, Dell Hymes, and Vera John, eds. 1972. *Functions of Language in the Classroom.* New York: Teachers College Press.

Chock, Phyllis. 1989. "The Landscape of Enchantment: Redaction in a Theory of Ethnicity." *Cultural Anthropology* 4: 163–81.

———. 1995. "Culturalism: Pluralism, Culture, and Race in the *Harvard Encyclopedia of American Ethnic Groups.*" *Ethnicities* 1 (4): 301–23.

Clay, Marie, and Courtney Cazden. 1990. "A Vygotskian Interpretation of Reading Recovery." In *Vygotsky and Education: Instructional Implications and Applications of Socio-historical Psychology,* ed. Luis Moll, 206–22. Cambridge, UK: Cambridge University Press.

Cochran-Smith, Marilyn. 1995. "Color Blindness and Basket Making Are Not the Answers: Confronting the Dilemmas of Race, Culture, and Language Diversity in Teacher Education." *American Educational Research Journal* 32 (3): 493–522.

Cohen, Phil. 1996. "Homing Devices." In *Re-Situating Identities: The Politics of Race, Ethnicity, and Culture,* ed. Vered Amit-Talai and Caroline Knowles, 68–82. Ontario: Broadview Press.

Collier, Virginia. 1995. *Promoting Academic Success for ESL Students: Understanding Second Language Acquisition for School.* Elizabeth, NJ: New Jersey Teachers of English to Speakers of Other Languages–Bilingual Educators.

Collins, James. 1988. "Language and Class in Minority Education." *Anthropology & Education Quarterly* 14 (December): 299–326.

———. 1989. "Hegemonic Practice: Literacy and Standard Language in Public Schooling." *Journal of Education* 171 (2): 9–34.

Connerton, Paul. 1989. *How Societies Remember.* Cambridge, UK: Cambridge University Press.

Cook-Gumperz, Jenny. 1986a. "Literacy and Schooling: An Unchanging Equation?" In *The Social Construction of Literacy,* ed. Jenny Cook-Gumperz, 16–44. Cambridge, UK: Cambridge University Press.

———. ed. 1986b. *The Social Construction of Literacy.* Cambridge, UK: Cambridge University Press.

Cordero Guzmán, Héctor. 1993. "The Structure of Inequality and the Status of Puerto Rican Youth in the U.S." *CENTRO* V (1): 100–115. New York: Centro de Estudios Puertorriqueños, Hunter College, City University of New York.

Cortés, Carlos. 1991. "Empowerment through Media Literacy: A Multicultural Approach." In *Empowerment Through Multicultural Education,* ed. Christine Sleeter, 143–58. Albany, NY: State University of New York Press.

Cortes, Felix, Angel Falcón, and Juan Flores. 1976. "The Cultural Expression of Puerto Ricans in New York: A Theoretical Perspective and Critical Review." *Latin American Perspectives* 3: 117–50.

Costo, Rupert, and Jeanette Henry, eds. 1970. *Textbooks and the American Indian.* San Francisco: Indian Historian Press.

Council on Interracial Books for Children. 1975. "Chicano Culture in Children's Literature: Stereotypes, Distortions, and Omissions." *Interracial Books for Children Bulletin* 5: (7–8) 7–14.

———. 1976. "Asian Americans in Children's Books." *Interracial Books for Children Bulletin* 7 (2–3):1–39.

Covello, Leonard. 1972. *The Social Background of the Italo-American School Child.* Totowa, NJ: Rowman & Littlefield.

Crawford, James. 1992. *Hold Your Tongue: Bilingualism and the Politics of "English Only."* Reading, MA: Addison-Wesley.

———. 1995. *Bilingual Education: History, Politics, Theory, and Practice* (3rd ed.). Los Angeles: Bilingual Educational Services, Inc.

Cross, Harry, et al. 1990. *Employer Hiring Policies: Differential Treatment of Hispanic and Anglo Job Seekers.* Washington, DC: The Urban Institute.

Cuban, Larry. 1984. *How Teachers Taught: Constancy and Change in American Classrooms 1890–1980.* New York: Longman.

Cummins, James. 1986. "Empowering Minority Students: A Framework for Intervention." *Harvard Educational Review* 56 (1): 18–36.

———. 1989. *Empowering Minority Students.* Sacramento: California Association for Bilingual Education.

———. 1997. "Minority Status and Schooling in Canada." In *Anthropology & Education Quarterly* 28 (3): 411–30.

D'Amato, John. 1993. "Resistance and Compliance in Minority Classrooms." In *Minority Education: Anthropological Perspectives,* ed. Evelyn Jacob and Cathie Jordan, 181–207. Norwood, NJ: Ablex.

Davidson, Ann Locke. 1996. *Making and Molding Identity in Schools: Student Narratives on Race, Gender, and Academic Engagement.* Albany: State University of New York Press.

Davis, Mike. 1986. *Prisoners of the American Dream: Politics and Economy in the History of the U.S. Working Class.* London: Verso.

de León Arnoldo. 1983. *They Called Them Greasers: Anglo Attitudes Towards Mexicans in Texas, 1821–1900*. Austin: University of Texas.

Delgado-Gaitan, Concha. 1991. "Involving Parents in the Schools: A Process of Empowerment." *American Journal of Education* 100: 20–46.

Delpit, Lisa. 1986. "Skills and Other Dilemmas of a Progressive Black Educator." *Harvard Educational Review* 56 (4): 379–85.

DeVos, George. 1973. "Japan's Outcastes: The Problem of the Burakumin." In *The Fourth World: Victims of Group Oppression*, ed. Ben Whitaker, 308–27. New York: Shocken Books.

di Leonardo, Micaela. 1992. "White Lies, Black Myths." *Village Voice* 37 (September 22): 29–36.

———. 1994. "White Ethnicities, Identity Politics, and Baby Bear's Chair." *Social Text* 41: 165–91.

Edelsky, Carole. 1991. *With Literacy and Justice for All*. London: Falmer.

———. 1994. "Education for Democracy." *Language Arts* (71): 252–7.

Edwards, John. 1982. "Language Attitudes and Their Implications." In *Attitudes towards Language Variation*, ed. Ellen Ryan and Howard Giles. London: Edward Arnold Ltd.

Erickson, Frederick. 1987. "Transformation and School Success: The Politics and Culture of Educational Achievement." *Anthropology & Education Quarterly* 18 (4): 335–56.

Erickson, Frederick, and Gary Bekker. 1986. "On Anthropology." In *The Contributions of the Social Sciences to Educational Policy and Practice: 1965–1985*. Berkeley, CA: McCutchan.

Esteves, Sandra María. 1974. *Yerba Buena*. Greenfield Center, NY: Greenfield Review Press.

Fanon, Frantz. 1968. *The Wretched of the Earth*. New York: Grove.

Farr, Marcia. 1991. "Dialects, Culture, and Teaching the English Language Arts." In *Handbook of Research on Teaching the English Language Arts*, ed. James Flood et al., 365–71. New York: Macmillan.

Farr, Roger, and Michael Beck. 1991. "Formal Methods of Evaluation." In *Handbook on Teaching the English Language Arts*, ed. James Flood et al., 489–501. New York: Macmillan.

Fasold, Ralph, and Roger Shuy. 1970. Preface to *Teaching Standard English in the Inner City*. Washington, DC: Center for Applied Linguistics.

Fernandez, James. 1986. *Persuasions and Performances: The Play of Tropes in Culture*. Bloomington: Indiana University Press.

Finders, Margaret, and Cynthia Lewis. 1994. "Why Some Parents Don't Come to School." *Educational Leadership* 51 (8): 50–54.

Fine, Michele. 1987. "Silencing in Public Schools." *Language Arts* 64 (2):157–74.

Fine, Michele, Lois Weis, Judi Addelston, and Julia Marusza. 1997.

"White Loss." In *Beyond Black and White: New Faces and Voices in U.S. Schools*, ed. Maxine Seller and Lois Weis. Albany: State University of New York Press.

Flores, Juan. 1985. "'Que Assimilated, Brother, Yo Soy Asimilao': The Structuring of Puerto Rican Identity in the U.S." *Journal of Ethnic Studies* 13 (Fall): 1–16.

———. 1991. "Cortijo's Revenge." *CENTRO* III (2): 8–21. New York: Centro de Estudios Puertorriqueños, Hunter College, City University of New York.

———. 1993. "'Puerto Rican and Proud, Boyee!': Rap, Roots and Amnesia." *CENTRO* V(1): 22–32. New York: Centro de Estudios Puertorriqueños, Hunter College, City University of New York.

———. 1996. "Pan-Latino/Trans-Latino: Puerto Ricans in the 'New Nueva York.'" *CENTRO* VIII (1 & 2): 170–86. New York: Centro de Estudios Puertorriqueños, Hunter College, City University of New York.

Flores, Juan, John Attinasi, and Pedro Pedraza. 1981. "La Carreta Made a U-Turn: Puerto Rican Language and Culture in the United States." *Daedalus* 110 (Spring): 193–217.

Foley, Douglas. 1991. "Reconsidering Anthropological Explanations of Ethnic School Failure." *Anthropology & Education Quarterly* 22 (1): 60–83.

Ford Foundation. 1984. *Hispanics: Challenges and Opportunities*. New York: Self.

Fordham, Signithia, and John Ogbu. 1986. "Black Students' School Success: Coping with the 'Burden of Acting White.'" *Urban Review* 18 (3): 176–206.

Frankenberg, Ruth. 1993. *White Women, Race Matters: The Social Construction of Whiteness*. Minneapolis: University of Minnesota Press.

Freire, Paolo. 1970. *Pedagogy of the Oppressed*. New York: Seabury Press.

———. 1985. *The Politics of Education*. South Hadley, MA: Bergin & Garvey.

Galdámez, Manuel. 1993. Hispanic Parents and School Practitioners. A Study of Home-School Relations in a Multiethnic Hispanic Community. Dissertation. School of Education, State University of New York, University at Albany.

Gans, Herbert. 1979. "Symbolic Ethnicity: The Future of Ethnic Groups and Cultures in America." *Ethnic and Racial Studies* 2 (January): 1–20.

Gardner, Lewis, ed. 1979. *Scope English Program Reading Anthology*. New York: Scholastic.

Gates, Henry Louis. 1995. "Multiculturalism: A Conversation among Different Voices." In *Rethinking Schools: An Agenda for Change*, ed. David Levine, Robert Lowe, Bob Peterson, and Rita Tenorio, 7–8. New York: New Press.

Gehrke, Natalie, Michael Knapp, and Kenneth Sirotnik. 1992. "In Search of the School Curriculum." In *Review of Research in Education*, ed. Gerald Grant, 51–110. Washington, DC: American Educational Research Association.

Gibson, Margaret. 1993. "The School Performance of Immigrant Minorities: A Comparative View." In *Minority Education: Anthropological Perspectives*, eds. Evelyn Jacob and Cathie Jordan, 113–28. Norwood, NJ: Ablex.

———. 1997. "Conclusion: Complicating the Immigrant/Involuntary Minority Typology." *Anthropology & Education Quarterly* 28 (3): 431–54.

Gillborn, David. 1990. *Race, Ethnicity and Education: Teaching and Learning in Multi-ethnic Schools*. London: Unwin Hyman.

Gillmore, Perry, Shelly Goldman, Ray McDermott, and David Smith. 1993. "Failure's Failure." In *Minority Education: Anthropological Perspectives*, ed. Evelyn Jacob and Cathie Jordan, 209–34. Norwood, NJ: Ablex.

Giroux, Henry, and Peter McClaren. 1988. "Critical Theory, Cultural Literacy, and the Closing of the American Mind: A Review of Hirsch and Bloom." *Harvard Educational Review* 58 (2): 172–94.

Glasser, Ruth. 1995. "*En Casa en Connecticut:* Towards a Historiography of Puerto Ricans Outside of New York City." *CENTRO* VII (1): 50–9. New York: Centro de Estudios Puertorriqueños, Hunter College, City University of New York.

Glazer, Nathan. 1993. "Is Assimilation Dead?" *Annals of the American Academy of Political and Social Science* 530 (November): 122–36.

———. 1997. *We Are All Multiculturalists Now*. Cambridge, MA: Harvard University Press.

Glazer, Nathan, and Daniel Moynihan. 1970. *Beyond the Melting Pot*. Cambridge, MA: MIT Press.

Globe Literature (red level). 1990. Englewood Cliffs, NJ: Globe Book Company.

Goffman, Erving. 1959. *The Presentation of Self in Everyday Life*. New York: Doubleday.

Goodlad, John. 1984. *A Place Called School*. New York: McGraw-Hill.

Goodrich, Frances, and Albert Hackett. 1989. *The Diary of Anne Frank* (play). In *Prentice Hall Literature* (silver edition), 303–68. Englewood Cliffs, NJ: Prentice Hall.

Gordon, Avery, and Christopher Newfield. 1996. *Mapping Multiculturalism*. Minneapolis: University of Minnesota Press.

Gordon, Milton. 1991. "Assimilation in America: Theory and Reality." In *Majority and Minority: The Dynamics of Race and Ethnicity in American Life* (5th ed.), ed. Norman R. Yetman, 248–61. Needham Heights, MA: Allyn & Bacon. Originally printed in *Daedalus* 90, no. 2 (spring 1961): 263–85.

Gould, Stephen. 1981. *The Mismeasure of Man*. New York: Norton.

Grant, Carl, ed. 1992. *Research and Multicultural Education: From the Margins to the Mainstream*. London: Falmer Press.

Gray, Paul. 1991. "Whose America?" *Time,* 8 July: 12–17.

Greeley, Andrew. 1991. "The Ethnic Miracle." In *Majority and Minority: The Dynamics of Race and Ethnicity in American Life,* ed. Norman Yetman, 275–85. Boston: Allyn & Bacon.

Greer, Colin. 1972. *The Great School Legend*. New York: Basic Books.

Gregory, Stephen. 1993. "Race, Rubbish, and Resistance: Empowering Difference in Community Politics." *Cultural Anthropology* 8: 24–48.

Grosfoguel, Ramón. 1995. "Caribbean Colonial Immigrants in the Metropoles: A Research Agenda." *CENTRO* VII (1): 82–95. New York: Centro de Estudios Puertorriqueños, Hunter College, City University of New York.

Grosfoguel, Ramón, and Chloé Georas. 1996. "The Racialization of Latino Caribbean Migrants in the New York Metropolitan Area." *CENTRO* VIII (1 & 2): 190–201. New York: Centro de Estudios Puertorriqueños, Hunter College, City University of New York.

Gumperz, John. 1982. *Discourse Strategies*. Cambridge, UK: Cambridge University Press.

Hale, Edward Everett. 1963. "The Man without a Country" (reprint). In *Adventures for Readers,* 358–74. New York: Harcourt, Brace & World.

Hancock, LynNell. 1990. "Whose America Is This, Anyway?" *Voice,* 9 September: 37–9.

Harman, Susan, and Carole Edelsky. 1989. "The Risks of Whole Language Literacy: Alienation and Connection." *Language Arts* 66 (4): 392–408.

Harrington, Michael. 1984. *The New American Poverty*. New York: Holt, Rinehart & Winston.

Harris, Violet, ed. 1992. *Teaching Multicultural Literature in Grades K–8*. Norwood, MA: Christopher-Gordon Publishers.

Harrison, Mary. 1998. "Homegrown Solutions." *Teaching Tolerance* (Spring): 21–5.

Heath, Shirley Brice. 1983a. *Ways with Words*. Cambridge, UK: Cambridge University Press.

———. 1983b. "English in Our Language Heritage." In *Language in the USA,* ed. Charles Ferguson and Shirley Brice Heath, 6–20. Cambridge, UK: Cambridge University Press.

Heller, Celia. 1966. *Mexican-American Youth: Forgotten Youth at the Crossroads*. New York: Random House.

Henry, William. 1990. "Beyond the Melting Pot." *Time,* April 9: 28–31.

Henshel, Richard, and Robert Silverman. 1975. *Perceptions in Criminology*. New York: Columbia University Press.

Herrnstein, Richard, and Charles Murray. 1994. *The Bell Curve: The Reshaping of American Life by Differences in Intelligence.* New York: Free Press.

Hidalgo, Nitza. 1992. "'i saw puerto rico once': A Review of the Literature on Puerto Rican Families and School Achievement in the United States." Report No. 12 (October). Boston: Center on Families, Communities, Schools and Children's Learning.

Higham, John. 1981 [1970]. *Strangers in the Land: Patterns of American Nativism, 1860–1925.* New York: Atheneum.

Hirsch, E. D. 1987. *Cultural Literacy.* Boston: Houghton Mifflin.

History Task Force, Centro de Estudios Puertorriqueños. 1979. *Labor Migration under Capitalism: The Puerto Rican Experience.* New York: Monthly Review Press.

Hochschild, Jennifer. 1995. *Facing up to the American Dream: Race, Class, and the Soul of the Nation.* Princeton, NJ: Princeton University Press.

Hollinger, David. 1995. *Postethnic America: Beyond Multiculturalism.* New York: Basic Books.

Hughes, Robert. 1993. *Culture of Complaint: The Fraying of America.* Oxford: Oxford University Press.

Hymowitz, Kay Sunstein. 1991. "Babar the Racist." *New Republic* (August 19 and 26): 12–14.

Ignatiev, Noel. 1995. *How the Irish Became White.* New York: Routledge.

Irving, Washington. 1963. "The Legend of Sleepy Hollow" (reprint). In *Adventures for Readers,* 375–97. New York: Harcourt, Brace & World.

Jacob, Evelyn, and Cathie Jordan, eds. 1993. *Minority Education: Anthropological Perspectives.* Norwood, NJ: Ablex Publishing.

Jacoby, Russell. 1994. *Dogmatic Wisdom: How the Culture Wars Divert Education and Distract America.* New York: Anchor Books.

Jensen, Arthur. 1969. "How Much Can We Boost I.Q. and Scholastic Achievement?" *Harvard Educational Review* 39, 1–123.

Jimenez Román, Miriam. 1996. "Un hombre (negro) del pueblo: José Celso Barbosa and the Puerto Rican 'Race' toward Whiteness." *CENTRO* VIII (1 & 2): 8–29. New York: Centro de Estudios Puertorriqueños, Hunter College, City University of New York.

Johnston, Peter. 1992. *Constructive Evaluation of Literate Activity.* New York: Longman.

Jones, Malcolm. 1991. "It's a Not So Small World." *Newsweek,* September 9: 64–5.

Jordan, Sarah, and Alan Purves. 1993. *Issues in the Responses of Students to Culturally Diverse Texts: A Preliminary Study.* Report No. 7.3. Albany, NY: National Research Center on Literature Teaching and Learning, State University of New York, University at Albany.

Jordan, Winthrop. 1977. *White over Black: American Attitudes toward the Negro, 1550–1812.* New York: Norton.

Kantowicz, Edward. 1992. "Polish-Americans." In *Multiculturalism in the United States: A Comparative Guide to Acculturation and Ethnicity,* ed. John D. Buenker and Lorman A. Ratner, 131–48. Westport, CT: Greenwood Press.

Keddie, Nell, ed. 1973. *Tinker, Tailor . . . The Myth of Cultural Deprivation.* Harmondsworth, UK: Penguin.

Keita, S.O.Y., and Rick Kittles. 1997. "The Persistence of Racial Thinking and the Myth of Racial Divergence." *American Anthropologist* 99 (3): 534–44.

Kenyatta, Mary, and Robert Tai. 1997. "Symposium: Ethnicity and Education." *Harvard Educational Review* 67 (2): vii–ix.

Klor de Alva, J. Jorge. 1988. "Telling Hispanics Apart: Latino Sociocultural Diversity." In *The Hispanic Experience in the United States: Contemporary Issues and Perspectives,* ed. Edna Acosta-Belén and Barbara Sjostrom, 107–36. New York: Praeger.

———. 1989. "Aztlan, Borinquen and Hispanic Nationalism in the United States." In *Aztlan: Essays on the Chicano Homeland,* ed. Rudolfo Anaya and Francisco Lomeli. Albuquerque: Academia/El Norte Publications.

Kohl, Herbert. 1994. *"I Won't Learn from You" and Other Thoughts on Creative Maladjustment.* New York: New Press.

———. 1995. Foreword. In *Rethinking Schools: An Agenda for Change,* ed. David Levine, Robert Lowe, Bob Peterson, and Rita Tenorio, xi–xiii. New York: New Press.

Kozol, Jonathan. 1991. *Savage Inequalities: Children in America's Schools.* New York: Crown.

———. 1994. "Giant Steps Backward: Romance of the Ghetto School." *The Nation* 258 (20): 703–8.

Labov, William. 1972. "The Logic of Nonstandard English." In *Language and Social Context,* ed. Pier Paolo Giglioli, 179–215. London: Penguin.

Ladson-Billings, Gloria. 1995. "Toward a Theory of Culturally Relevant Pedagogy." *American Educational Research Journal* 32 (3): 465–92.

Lamont, Michele, and Annette Lareau. 1988. "Cultural Capital: Allusions, Gaps and Glissandos in Recent Theoretical Developments." *Sociological Theory* 6 (Fall): 153–68.

Langer, Judith, and Arthur Applebee. 1986. "Reading and Writing Instruction: Toward a Theory of Teaching and Learning." In *Review of Research in Education,* ed. Ernst Rothkopf, 171–94. Washington, DC: American Educational Research Association.

Lareau, Annette. 1989. *Home Advantage: Social Class and Parental Intervention in Elementary Education.* New York: Falmer Press.

Larkin, Joseph, and Christine Sleeter. 1995. Introduction. In *Developing Multicultural Teacher Education Curricula,* ed. Joseph Larkin and Christine Sleeter, vii–xi. Albany, NY: State University of New York Press.

Larrick, Nancy. 1965. "The All-White World of Children's Books." *Saturday Review,* September 11: 63–5, 84–5.

Laviera, Tato. 1985. *AmerRican.* Houston: Arte Publico.

Leacock, Eleanor, eds. 1971. *The Culture of Poverty: A Critique.* New York: Simon & Shuster.

Leap, William. 1981. "American Indian Languages." In *Language in the USA,* ed. Charles Ferguson and Shirley Brice Heath, 116–44. Cambridge, UK: Cambridge University Press.

Lee, Enid. 1995. "Taking Multicultural, Anti-racist Education Seriously: An Interview with Enid Lee." In *Rethinking Schools: An Agenda for Change,* ed. David Levine, Robert Lowe, Bob Peterson, and Rita Tenorio, 9–16. New York: New Press.

Levine, David, Robert Lowe, Bob Peterson, and Rita Tenorio, eds. 1995. *Rethinking Schools: An Agenda for Change.* New York: New Press.

Lieberman, M. 1972. "'Some Day My Prince Will Come': Female Acculturation through the Fairy Tale." *College English* 34 (3): 383–93.

Lieberson, Stanley. 1985. "Stereotypes: Their Consequences for Race and Ethnic Interaction." In *Research in Race and Ethnic Relations: A Research Annual,* ed. C. Marrett and C. Leggon, 113–37. Greenwich, CT: JAI Press.

Lieberson, Stanley, and Mary Waters. 1988. *From Many Strands: Ethnic and Racial Groups in Contemporary America.* New York: Russell Sage Foundation.

Lind, Michael. 1995. "To Have and Have Not: Notes on the Progress of the American Class War." *Harper's* (June): 35–47.

Lindfors, Judith. 1987. *Children's Language and Learning* (2nd ed.). Englewood Cliffs, NJ: Prentice-Hall.

Lindgren, Merri, ed. 1991. *The Multicolored Mirror: Cultural Substance in Literature for Children and Young Adults.* Fort Atkinson, WI: Highsmith Press.

Loewen, James W. 1995. *Lies My Teacher Told Me: Everything Your American History Textbook Got Wrong.* New York: New Press.

London, Jack. 1931. *The Call of the Wild.* New York: Macmillan.

López, Adalberto. 1980. "The Puerto Rican Diaspora: A Survey." In *The Puerto Ricans: Their History, Culture, and Society,* ed. Adalberto López, 313–44. Rochester, VT: Schenkman.

Macedo, Donaldo. 1993. "Literacy for Stupidification: The Pedagogy of Big Lies." *Harvard Educational Review,* 63 (2): 183–206.

Macias, José, ed. 1996. "Racial and Ethnic Exclusion: A Problem for Anthropology and Education." *Anthropology & Education Quarterly* 27 (2): 141–50.

MacLeod, Jay. 1995. *Ain't No Makin' It: Aspirations and Attainment in a Low-Income Neighborhood* (2nd ed.). Boulder, CO: Westview Press.

Maldonado, Rita. 1976. "Why Puerto Ricans Migrated to the United States in 1947–73." *Monthly Labor Review* 99 (Summer): 7–18.

Marlos, Litsa, and Ana Celia Zentella. 1978. "A Quantified Analysis of Code Switching by Four Philadelphia Puerto Rican Adolescents." *Pennsylvania Review of Linguistics* 3: 46–57.

Marshall, James, Mary Beth Klages, and Richard Fehlman. 1990. *Discussions of Literature in Lower-Track Classrooms*. Report No. 2.10. Albany, NY: Center for the Learning and Teaching of Literature, University at Albany, State University of New York.

Martinez, Cristina. 1988. *Phenomenology of Ethnic Identity and Migration among Puerto Rican Migrants*. PhD. dissertation, Boston University.

Massey, Douglas, and Nancy Denton. 1993. *American Apartheid: Segregation and the Making of the Underclass*. Cambridge, MA: Harvard University Press.

McCollum, Pamela. 1989. "Turn-Allocation in Lessons with North American and Puerto Rican Students: A Comparative Study." *Anthropology & Education Quarterly* 20 (2): 133–56.

McCormick, John, and Aric Press. 1997. "Pomp and Promises." *Newsweek* (June 16): 44–6.

McKenney, Nampeo, Michael Levin, and Alfred Tella. 1985. "A Sociodemographic Profile of Italian Americans." In *The Italian Americans: New Perspectives in Italian Immigration and Ethnicity*, ed. Lydio Tomasi, 3–31. Staten Island, NY: Center for Migration Studies of New York.

McQuillan, Patrick James. 1998. *Educational Opportunity in an Urban American High School*. Albany, NY: State University of New York Press.

McWilliams, Carey. 1990. *North from Mexico: The Spanish Speaking People of the United States*. New York: Praeger.

Mehan, Hugh. 1979. *Learning Lessons*. Cambridge, MA: Harvard University Press.

Mehan, Hugh, Lea Hubbard, and Irene Villanueva. 1994. "Forming Academic Identities: Accommodation without Assimilation among Involuntary Minorities." *Anthropology & Education Quarterly* 25 (2): 91–117.

Meier, Deborah. 1992. "Get the Story Straight: Myth, Lies and Public Schools." *The Nation* 255 (8): 271–2.

———. 1995. *The Power of Their Ideas: Lessons for America from a Small School in Harlem*. Boston: Beacon Press.

Melville, Margarita. 1988. "Hispanics: Race, Class or Ethnicity?" *Journal of Ethnic Studies* 16 (1): 67–83.

Menchaca, Martha, and Richard Valencia. 1990. "Anglo-Saxon Ideologies in the 1920s–1930s: Their Impact on the Segregation of Mexican Students in California." *Anthropology & Education Quarterly* 21 (3): 222–49.

Mercado, Carmen, and Luis Moll. 1997. "The Study of Funds of Knowledge: Collaborative Research in Latino Homes." *CENTRO* IX (9): 26–42. New York: Centro de Estudios Puertorriqueños, Hunter College, City University of New York.

Messerli, Jonathan. 1972. *Horace Mann*. New York: Knopf.

Miller, Suzanne. 1992. *Creating Change: Toward a Dialogic Pedagogy*. Report No. 1.8. Albany, NY: The National Research Center on Literature Teaching and Learning, University at Albany, State University of New York.

Miner, Barbara. 1991. "New Paint on an Old Jalopy." *Rethinking Schools* 5 (4): 5.

Miranda, Leticia. 1991. *Latino Child Poverty in the United States*. Washington, DC: Children's Defense Fund.

Mohatt, Gerald, and Frederick Erickson. 1981. "Cultural Differences in Teaching Styles in an Odawa School: A Sociolinguistic Approach." In *Culture and the Bilingual Classroom,* ed. Henry Trueba, Grace Guthrie, and Kathryn Au, 105–19. Rowley, MA: Newbury House.

Mohawk, John. 1992. "Looking for Columbus: Thoughts on the Past, Present and Future of Humanity." In *The State of Native America: Genocide, Colonization, and Resistance,* ed. M. Annette Jaimes, 439–44. Boston: South End Press.

Mohr, Eugene. 1982. *The Nuyorican Experience*. Westport, CT: Greenwood Press.

Mohr, Nicholasa. 1973. *Nilda*. New York: Harper & Row.

———. 1979. *Felita*. New York: Dial.

———. 1986a. *El Bronx Remembered*. Houston: Arte Público Press.

———. 1986b. *Going Home*. New York: Dial.

Moll, Luis, and Rosa Díaz. 1987. "Teaching Writing as Communication: The Use of Ethnographic Findings in Classroom Practice." In *Literacy and Schooling,* ed. David Bloome, 193–221. Norwood, NJ: Ablex.

Moore, Joan, and Harry Pachon. 1985. *Hispanics in the United States*. Englewood Cliffs, NJ: Prentice Hall.

Moore, Sally Falk. 1987. "Explaining the Present: Theoretical Dilemmas in Processual Ethnography." *American Ethnologist* 14 (4): 727–36.

Morales, Julio. 1986. *Puerto Rican Poverty and Migration: We Just Had to Try Elsewhere*. New York: Praeger.

Morris, Nancy. 1995. *Puerto Rico: Culture, Politics, and Identity*. Westport, CT: Praeger.

Mosier, Richard. 1947. *Making the American Mind*. New York: King's College Press.

Murphy, Robert. 1970. *The Dialectics of Social Life*. New York: Basic Books.

Nasaw, David. 1979. *Schooled to Order: A Social History of Public Schooling in the United States*. New York: Oxford University Press.

Nash, Gary. 1974. *Red, White, and Black*. Englewood Cliffs, NJ: Prentice Hall.

Navarro, Mireya. 1997. "A New Barbie in Puerto Rico Divides Island and Mainland." *New York Times*, December 27 (NE): A1, A9.

Negrón de Montilla, Aida. 1970. *Americanization in Puerto Rico and the Public School System, 1900–1930*. Rio Piedras, Puerto Rico: Editorial Edil.

———. 1975. *Americanization in Puerto Rico and the Public School Syetem, 1900–1930* (2nd ed.). Rio Picodras, Puerto Rico: Editorial Edil.

Nelson, Candace, and Marta Tienda. 1988. "The Structuring of Hispanic Ethnicity: Historical and Contemporary Perspectives." In *Ethnicity and Race in the U.S.A.*, ed. Richard Alba, 49–74. London: Routledge.

Nelson-Barber, Sharon, and Terry Meier. 1988. "Multicultural Context a Key Factor in Teaching." *Academic Connections* (Spring): 1–11. New York: Office of Academic Affairs, The College Board.

Newfield, Christopher, and Avery Gordon. 1996. "Multiculturalism's Unfinished Business." In *Mapping Multiculturalism*, ed. Avery Gordon and Christopher Newfield, 76–115. Minneapolis: University of Minnesota Press.

Newman, Katherine. 1993. *Declining Fortunes: The Withering of the American Dream*. New York: Basic Books.

New York State Social Studies Review and Development Committee. 1991. *One Nation, Many Peoples: A Declaration of Cultural Interdependence*. Albany, NY: State Education Department.

Nieto, Sonia. 1992. *Affirming Diversity: The Sociopolitical Context of Multicultural Education* White Plains, NY: Longman.

———. 1996. *Affirming Diversity: The Sociopolitical Context of Multicultural Education* (2nd ed.). White Plains, NY: Longman.

Novak, Michael. 1971. *The Rise of the Unmeltable Ethnics: Politics and Culture in the Seventies*. New York: Macmillan.

Nystrand, Martin, and Adam Gamoran. 1991. "Instructional Discourse, Student Engagement, and Literature Achievement." *Research in the Teaching of English* 25 (3): 261–89.

Oakes, Jeannie. 1985. *Keeping Track: How Schools Structure Inequality*. New Haven, CT: Yale University Press.

Oboler, Suzanne. 1995. *Ethnic Labels, Latino Lives: Identity and the Politics of*

(Re)presentation in the United States. Minneapolis: University of Minnesota Press.

Ogbu, John. 1978. *Minority Education and Caste: The American System in Cross-Cultural Perspective*. New York: Academic Press.

———. 1987. "Variability in Minority School Performance: A Problem in Search of an Explanation." *Anthropology & Education Quarterly* 18 (4): 312–34.

———. 1988. "Class Stratification, Racial Stratification and Schooling." In *Class, Race, and Gender in American Education*, ed. Lois Weis, 163–82. Albany, NY: State University of New York Press.

Ogbu, John, and Maria Matute-Bianchi. 1986. "Understanding Sociocultural Factors: Knowledge, Identity, and School Adjustment." In *Beyond Language: Social and Cultural Factors in Schooling Language Minority Students*, 73–142. Los Angeles: Center for the Evaluation, Dissemination and Assessment Center at California State University.

Ogbu, John, and Herbert Simons. 1998. "Voluntary and Involuntary Minorities: A Cultural-Ecological Theory of School Performance with Some Implications for Education." *Anthropology & Education Quarterly* 29 (2):155–88.

Omi, Michael, and Howard Winant. 1986. *Racial Formation in the United States: From the 1960s to the 1980s*. New York: Routledge and Kegan Paul.

———. 1994. *Racial Formation in the United States: From the 1960s to the 1990s* (2nd ed.). New York: Routledge.

Ortner, Sherry. 1991. "Reading America: Preliminary Notes on Class and Culture." In *Recapturing Anthropology*, ed. Richard G. Fox, 163–89. Santa Fe: School of American Research Press.

Paley, Vivian. 1979. *White Teacher*. Cambridge, MA: Harvard University Press.

Park, Robert. 1950. *Race and Culture*. Glencoe, IL: Free Press.

Parrillo, Vincent. 1997. *Strangers to These Shores: Race and Ethnic Relations in the United States* (5th ed.) . Boston: Allyn & Bacon.

Pedraza, Pedro. 1997. "Puerto Ricans and the Politics of School Reform." *CENTRO* IX (9) (Winter 1996–97): 74–85. New York: Centro de Estudios Puertorriqueños, Hunter College, City University of New York.

Phelan, Patricia, and Ann Locke Davidson, eds. 1993. *Renegotiating Cultural Diversity in American Schools*. New York: Teachers College Press.

Philips, Susan. 1972. "Participant Structures and Communicative Competence: Warm Springs Children in Community and Classroom." In *Functions of Language in the Classroom*, ed. Courtney Cazden, Vera John, and Dell Hymes, 370–94. New York: Teachers College Press.

———. 1983. *The Invisible Culture: Communication in Classroom and Community on the Warm Springs Indian Reservation*. New York: Longman.

Piestrup, Ann. 1973. *Black Dialect Interference and Accommodation of Reading Instruction in First Grade*. Monograph of the Language Behavior Research Laboratory, University of California, Berkeley.

Poplack, Shana. 1978. *Syntactic Structure and Social Function of Code-Switching*. Working Paper #2. New York: Centro de Estudios Puertorriqueños, Hunter College, City University of New York.

Portes, Alejandro, and Ruben Rumbaut.1990. *Immigrant America: A Portrait*. Berkeley: University of California Press.

Prentice-Hall Literature. 1989. Silver Edition. Englewood Cliffs, NJ: Prentice Hall.

Purves, Alan, and Oliver Niles. 1984. "The Challenge to Education to Produce Literate Citizens: Becoming Readers in a Complex Society." In *Eighty-third Yearbook of the National Society for the Study of Education,* ed. Alan Purves and Oliver Niles, 1–15. Chicago: University of Chicago Press.

———. 1991. *The Ideology of Canons and Cultural Concerns in the Literature Curriculum*. Report No. 6.4. Albany, NY: National Research Center on Literature Teaching and Learning. State University of New York, University at Albany.

Rae, Douglas. 1988. "Knowing Power." In *Power, Inequality, and Democratic Politics,* ed. Ian Shapiro and Grant Reeher, 17–49. Boulder, CO: Westview Press.

Ramirez, Arnulfo. 1981. "Language Attitudes and the Speech of Spanish-English Bilingual Pupils." In *Latino Language and Communicative Behavior,* ed. Robert Duran, 217–32. Norwood, NJ: Ablex Publishing.

Ramsey, Patricia, Edwina Vold, and Leslie Williams. 1989. *Multicultural Education: A Sourcebook*. New York: Garland Publishing.

Ravitch, Diane. 1990. "E Pluribus Plures." *American Scholar* 59 (3): 337–54.

Reinhold, Robert. 1991. "Class Struggle." *New York Times Magazine,* September 29: 26–9, 46–7, 52.

Resnick, Daniel. 1982. "History of Educational Testing." In *Ability Testing: Uses, Consequences and Controversies. Part II: Documentation Section,* eds. Alexandra Wigdor and Wendell Garner, 173–94. Washington, DC: National Academy Press.

Rich, Adrienne. 1986. "Invisibility in Academe." In *Blood, Bread, and Poetry: Selected Prose 1979–1985,* 198–201. New York: Norton.

Rodríguez, Clara. 1989. *Puerto Ricans: Born in the U.S.A.* Boston: Unwin Hyman.

———. 1994. "Challenging Racial Hegemony: Puerto Ricans in the United States. In *Race,* ed. Steven Gregory and Roger Sanjek, 131–45. New Brunswick, NJ: Rutgers University Press.

Rodríquez, Clara, Virginia Sánchez Korrol, and José Oscar Alars, eds.

1980. *The Puerto Rican Struggle: Essays on Survival in the United States.* New York: Puerto Rican Migration Consortium.

Rodríguez-Morazzani, Roberto. 1996. "Beyond the Rainbow: Mapping the Discourse on Puerto Ricans and 'Race'" *CENTRO* VIII (1 & 2):151–69. New York: Centro de Estudios Puertorriqueños, Hunter College, City University of New York.

———. 1997. "Puerto Ricans and Education Reform in the U.S.: A Preliminary Exploration." CENTRO IX (9): 58–73. New York: Centro de Estudios Puertorriqueños, Hunter College, City University of New York.

Roediger, David. 1991. *The Wages of Whiteness: Race and the Making of the American Working Class.* New York: Verso.

Rosaldo, Renato. 1989. *Culture and Truth: The Remaking of Social Analysis.* Boston: Beacon Press.

Rosenblum, Karen, and Toni-Michele Travis. 1996. *The Meaning of Difference: American Constructions of Race, Sex and Gender, Social Class, and Sexual Orientation.* New York: McGraw-Hill.

Rubin, Lillian. 1992 [1976]. *Worlds of Pain: Life in the Working-Class Family.* New York: Basic Books.

———. 1994. *Families on the Fault Line.* New York: HarperCollins Publishers.

Sacks, Karen Brodkin. 1994. "How Did Jews Become White Folks?" In *Race,* ed. Steven Gregory and Roger Sanjek, 78–102. New Brunswick, NJ: Rutgers University Press.

Sanchéz Korrol, Virginia. 1983. *From Colonia to Community: History of Puerto Ricans in New York City, 1917–1948.* Westport, CT: Greenwood Press.

Sanjek, Roger. 1994. "Intermarriage and the Future of Races." In *Race,* ed. Steven Gregory and Roger Sanjek, 103–30. New Brunswick, NJ: Rutgers University Press.

Schlesinger, Arthur Jr. 1991. *The Disuniting of America: Reflections on a Multicultural Society.* New York: Norton.

Scollon, Ronald, and Suzanne Scollon. 1981. *Narrative, Literacy and Face in Interethnic Communication.* Norwood, NJ: Ablex.

Seda Bonilla, Eduardo. 1977. "Who Is a Puerto Rican: Problems of Sociocultural Identity in Puerto Rico." *Caribbean Studies* 17 (April-July): 105–21.

———. 1983. "Race as a Folk Taxonomy." In *Social Research in Puerto Rico: Science, Humanism and Society,* ed. Ronald Duncan et al. San Juan: InterAmerican University Press.

Seligman, C. R., G. R. Tucker, and W. E. Lambert. 1972. "The Effects of Speech Styles and Other Attributes on Teachers' Attitudes." *Language in Society* 1: 31–142.

Sengupta, Somini. 1997. "Teaching is a Hot Career Prospect." *New York Times Education Life* Section 4A (August 3): 46.

Shanker, Albert. 1971. "Where We Stand: The Big Lie about Public Schools." *New York Times*, 19 May.

Shannon, P. 1993. "Critique of False Generosity: A Response to Baumann." *Reading Research Quarterly* 28 (1): 8–14.

Shor, Ira. 1986. "Equality Is Excellence: Transforming Teacher Education and the Learning Process." *Harvard Educational Review* 56 (4): 406–26.

Shujaa, Mwalimu. 1991. "Teachers' Responses to the Implementation of an African/African American Curriculum Content Infusion Policy." Final Report. Submitted to New York African American Institute, State University of New York, State University Plaza, Albany NY.

Simmons, John. 1991. "The Junior High School Years." In *Handbook of Research on Teaching the English Language Arts*, ed. James Flood, Julie Jensen, Diane Lapp, and James Squire, 320–30. New York: Macmillan.

Sleeter, Christine, ed. 1991. *Empowerment through Multicultural Education*. Albany, NY: State University of New York Press.

———. 1995. "Teaching Whites about Racism." In *Practicing What We Teach: Confronting Diversity in Teacher Education*, ed. Renee Martin, 117–30. Albany, NY: State University of New York Press.

Sleeter, Christine, and Carl Grant. 1988. *Making Choices for Multicultural Education: Five Approaches to Race, Class and Gender*. Columbus, OH: Merrill Publishing.

———. 1991. "Race, Class, Gender, and Disability in Current Textbooks." In *The Politics of the Textbook*, ed. Michael Apple and Linda Christian-Smith, 78–110. New York: Routledge.

Smedley, Agnes. 1993. *Race in North America: Origin and Evolution of a Worldview*. Boulder, CO: Westview Press.

Smith, Thomas, Beth Aronstamm Young, Yupin Bae, Susan Choy, and Nabeel Alsalam. 1997. *The Condition of Education 1997* (NCES 97–388). U.S. Department of Education, National Center for Education Statistics. Washington, DC: U.S. Government Printing Office.

Smith, Vern, and Daniel Pedersen. 1997. "South Toward Home." *Newsweek*, July 14: 36–8.

Sobol, Thomas. 1989. *A Curriculum of Inclusion: Report of the Commissioner's Task Force on Minorities: Equity and Excellence*. Albany, NY: State Education Department.

Sollors, Werner. 1986. *Beyond Ethnicity: Consent and Descent in American Culture*. New York: Oxford University Press.

Soto, Lourdes Diaz. 1997. *Language, Culture, and Power: Bilingual Families and the Struggle for Quality Education*. Albany: State University of New York Press.

Sowell, Thomas. 1977. "New Light on Black I.Q." *New York Times Magazine*, 27 March.

Springfield, Massachusetts, School Committee, 1854. Annual Report.

Stains, Laurence. 1994. "The Latinization of Allentown, Pa." *New York Times Magazine,* 15 May: 56–62.

Steinbeck, John. 1973. *The Red Pony*. New York: Bantam Books.

Steinberg, Stephen. 1989. *The Ethnic Myth: Race, Ethnicity, and Class in America* (2nd ed.). Boston: Beacon Press.

Suarez-Orozco, Marcelo. 1987. "Becoming Somebody: Central American Immigrants in U.S. Inner-City Schools." *Anthropology & Education Quarterly* 18 (December): 287–99.

Sue, Stanley, and Amado Padilla. 1986. "Ethnic Minority Issues in the United States: Challenges for the Educational System." In *Beyond Language: Social and Cultural Factors in Schooling Language Minority Students,* 35–72. Los Angeles: Evaluation, Dissemination and Assessment Center at California State University.

Swartz, Ellen. 1992. "Multicultural Education: From a Compensatory to a Scholarly Foundation." In *Research and Multicultural Education: From the Margins to the Mainstream,* ed. Carl Grant, 32–43. Washington, DC: Falmer Press.

Takaki, Ronald. 1989. *Strangers from a Different Shore*. New York: Penguin.

———. 1993. *A Different Mirror*. Boston: Little Brown.

———. 1997. Panelist, "Ethnicity and Education Forum: What Difference Does Difference Make?" (December 12, 1996). In *Harvard Educational Review* 67 (2): 169–87.

Taylor, Theodore. 1969. *The Cay*. New York: Avon Books.

Tharp, Roland, and Ronald Gallimore. 1989. *Rousing Minds to Life: Teaching, Learning, and Schooling in Social Context*. Cambridge, UK: Cambridge University Press.

Thomas, Piri. 1967. *Down These Mean Streets*. New York: Knopf.

Thurow, Lester. 1995. "Companies Merge; Families Break Up." *New York Times,* September 3: E1.

Torres, Andrés. 1995. *Between Melting Pot and Mosaic: African Americans and Puerto Ricans in the New York Political Economy*. Philadelphia: Temple University Press.

Trueba, Henry. 1988. *Raising Silent Voices: Educating the Linguistic Minorities for the 21st Century*. New York: Newbury House Publishers/Harper & Row.

Urciuoli, Bonnie. 1993. "Representing Class: Who Decides?" *Anthropological Quarterly* 66 (4): 203–10.

———.1996. *Exposing Prejudice: Puerto Rican Experiences of Language, Race, and Class*. Boulder, CO: Westview Press.

Vaźquez, Jesse. 1989. "Puerto Rican Studies in the 1990s: Taking the Next Turn in the Road." *CENTRO* II (6): 8–19. New York: Centro de

Estudios Puertorriqueños, Hunter College, City University of New York.

Vega, Bernardo. 1984. *Memoirs of Bernardo Vega: A Contribution to the History of the Puerto Rican Community in New York,* ed. César Andreu Iglesias. New York: Monthly Review Press.

Vogt, Lynn, Cathie Jordan, and Roland Tharp. 1993. "Explaining School Failure, Producing School Success: Two Cases." In *Minority Education: Anthropological Perspectives,* ed. Evelyn Jacob and Cathie Jordan, 53–66. Norwood, NJ: Ablex.

Walsh, Catherine. 1987. "Language, Meaning, and Voice: Puerto Rican Students' Struggle for a Speaking Consciousness." *Language Arts* 64 (2): 195–206.

———. 1991. *Pedagogy and the Struggle for Voice: Issues of Language, Power, and Schooling for Puerto Ricans.* South Hadley, MA: Bergin & Garvey.

Waters, Mary C. 1990. *Ethnic Options: Choosing Identities in America.* Berkeley: University of California Press.

Weis, Lois, ed. 1988. *Class, Race, & Gender in American Education.* Albany, NY: State University of New York Press.

———. 1990. *Working Class without Work: High-School Students in a Deindustrializing Economy.* New York: Routledge, Chapman & Hall.

Wetherell, Margaret, and Jonathan Potter. 1992. *Mapping the Language of Racism: Discourse and the Legitimation of Exploitation.* New York: Columbia University Press.

Whitaker, Mark. 1991. "A Crisis of Shattered Dreams." *Newsweek,* 6 May: 28–31.

Williams, Brackette. 1989. "A Class Act: Anthropology and the Race to Nation across Ethnic Terrain." *Annual Review of Anthropology* 18: 401–44.

Wills, Gary. 1996. "It's His Party." *New York Times Magazine,* August 11: 32–7, 52–9.

Woolard, Kathryn. 1989. "Sentences in the Language Prison: The Rhetorical Structuring of an American Language Policy Debate." *American Ethnologist* May (16): 268–78.

Young Lords Party. 1971. *Palante: Young Lords Party.* New York: McGraw-Hill.

Zanger, Virginia Vogel. 1994. "'Not Joined In': The Social Context of English Literacy Development for Hispanic Youth." In *Literacy across Languages and Cultures,* ed. Bernardo Ferdman, Rose-Marie Weber, and Arnulfo Ramírez, 171–98. Albany, NY: State University of New York Press.

Zangwill, Israel. 1909. *The Melting-Pot: Drama in Four Acts.* New York: Macmillan.

Zenón Cruz, Isabelo. 1975. *Narcisco Descubre Su Trasero*. Humacao, Puerto Rico: Editorial Furidi.

Zentella, Ana Celia. 1981. "Language Variety among Puerto Ricans." In *Language in the USA*, ed. Charles Ferguson and Shirley Brice Heath, 218–38. Cambridge, UK: Cambridge University Press.

———. 1985. "The Fate of Spanish in the United States: The Puerto Rican Experience." In *The Language of Inequality*, ed. Nessa Wolfson and Joan Manes, 41–59. New York: Mouton Publishers.

———. 1988. "Language Politics in the U.S.A.: The English-Only Movement." In *Literature, Language, and Politics*, ed. Betty Jean Craige, 39–53. Athens: University of Georgia Press.

———. 1997. *Growing Up Bilingual: Puerto Rican Children in New York*. Malden, MA: Blackwell Publishers.

Zinn, Howard. 1980. *A People's History of the United States*. New York: Harper and Row.

Index